Gang Entry and Exit in Cape Town

Gang Entry and Exit in Cape Town: Getting Beyond the Streets in Africa's Deadliest City

BY

DARIUSZ DZIEWANSKI

University of Cape Town's Faculty of Law, South Africa

emerald
PUBLISHING

United Kingdom – North America – Japan – India – Malaysia – China

Emerald Publishing Limited
Howard House, Wagon Lane, Bingley BD16 1WA, UK

First edition 2021

Reprints and permissions service
Contact: permissions@emeraldinsight.com

British Library Cataloguing in Publication Data
A catalogue record for this book is available from the British Library

ISBN: 978-1-83909-731-7 (Print)
ISBN: 978-1-83909-730-0 (Online)
ISBN: 978-1-83909-732-4 (Epub)
ISBN: 978-1-83909-733-1 (Paperback)

ISOQAR certified
Management System,
awarded to Emerald
for adherence to
Environmental
standard
ISO 14001:2004.

ISOQAR
REGISTERED
Certificate Number 1985
ISO 14001

INVESTOR IN PEOPLE

Table of Contents

Map of Cape Town   *vii*

Preface   *ix*

Acknowledgements   *xvii*

Chapter 1   Blood In, Blood Out?   *1*

Chapter 2   The Landscape of African Gangs   *19*

Chapter 3   A City Still Segregated   *39*

Chapter 4   Leaving the Streets   *77*

Chapter 5   Walking the Righteous Path   *107*

Chapter 6   Gavin   *125*

Chapter 7   Beyond the Street   *147*

References   *157*

Index   *177*

Map of Cape Town

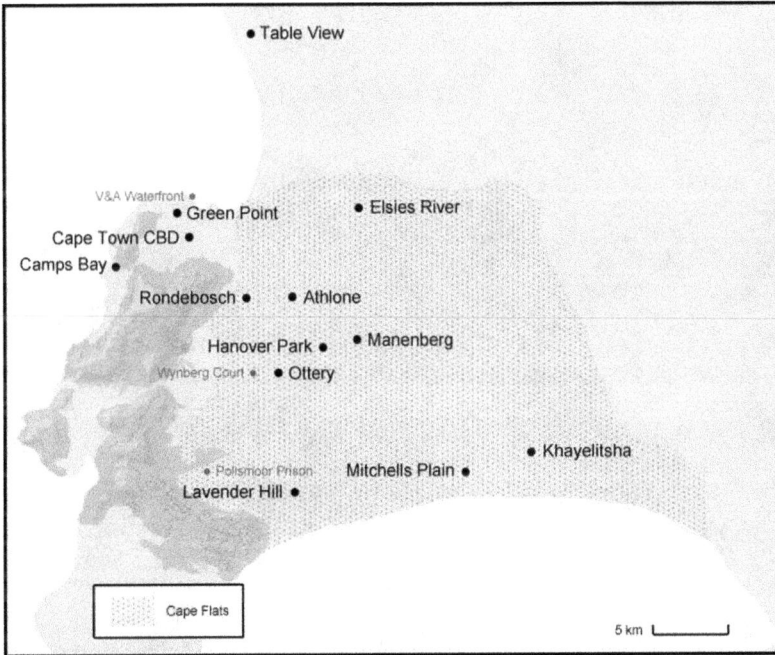

Preface

At the heart of it, ethnography is about stories. The ethnographic research this book is based on is a collection of personal histories from young people attempting to leave gangs and rebuild their lives in Cape Town, South Africa – one of the most segregated and deadliest cities in the world. Their stories connect to a more profound narrative about a country that itself is still attempting to recover after losing generations to the tyranny of racial persecution under apartheid. Anybody insisting that characters, setting, plot and conflict must necessarily find a satisfying resolution at the end of a story might find the following pages vexing. They are full of frustrated intentions and unresolved endings. Each person in this publication has left gangs, sure. But each is to this day in his or her own way wrestling with a familiar list of personal and social issues; the joblessness, racism, isolation and hopelessness that drove them into gangs in the first place, still to a large extent continue to define their lives as ex-members. That such difficulties persist even after exit makes their narratives no less compelling. One could argue persuasively, actually, that it is all the more necessary for this reason to give voice to stories like these. They serve as a lamentable reminder of the tragedy and bravery that define the existence of the majority of young men and women in Cape Town – both inside and outside of 'the streets'.

Let us recognise one person, in particular, whose story is central to this book. Gavin (Ottery male, 30 years)[1] had spent over half of his life in gangs when I met him. He was still, at that point, a prominent member of both the Mongrels street gang and the 28s prison gang. Our introduction came at a halfway house Gavin was released to after serving a 10-year murder sentence in the notorious Pollsmoor Prison, a maximum security penal facility that holds some of South Africa's most dangerous criminals. That was in 2013, shortly after I landed in Cape Town to begin this project. Our paths would proceed to intertwine over the next years in the labyrinth of sheet metal, distressed wood and dust that make up the patchwork of squatter camps – or *kampies*[2] – hidden in and around the Capetonian suburb of Ottery. The predominately poor and working-class neighbourhood is situated some 20 minutes by car southeast of downtown, and is the place where Gavin's gang, the Mongrels, have their headquarters. The Mongrels are one of

---

[1] All names have been changed.

[2] *Kampie* refers broadly to an informal settlement. But Gavin often uses the term in reference to the small Ottery settlement that he lives in.

the city's biggest and oldest gangs, tracing their origins back to Cape Town's historical District Six neighbourhood. Today, their 'MG' insignia claims walls, buildings and bodies in their stronghold of Ottery, just as the names of gangs like the Americans, Sexy Boys, Hard Livings, Junky Funky Kids, Laughing Boys and the Ghetto Kids dominate communities such as Hanover Park, Manenberg, Mitchells Plain and Delft. I would come to know many of these areas well, spending hundreds of hours talking to and hanging out with the men and women who live there. Our shared interactions offered a vivid view of the physical contexts and felt experiences of Cape Town's township communities, helping to dispel some of the preconceptions that inevitably arise when outsiders like me attempt to break into, comprehend and depict an unfamiliar moral universe.

One of my first entries into a township was with Gavin, in fact. I accompanied him on a trip to a *kampie* near Ottery, where he was controlling sales of *tik*, *unga*, *dagga* and buttons[3] for the Mongrels. It is a part of Cape Town where my white face was undoubtedly as unusual to the residents there as their community was to me. Gavin offered some words in preparation as we entered the settlement. 'Don't be scared [when we arrive]. You must be a motherfucker. You must just be like: I don't give a fuck; like, gangster bro', he declared with a laugh. 'You musn't show people you [have] fear... or they will take you for *poes*'.[4] I dismissed his advice as good-natured teasing, and did not give it much thought, preoccupied as I was with maintaining my footing as we snaked through the *kampie's* dim and uneven passages. I would later come to appreciate that Gavin was conveying to me a very important lesson: there are places in Cape Town where your security cannot be taken for granted, where you have to nonstop stand up for yourself or you risk being labelled vulnerable and being made into a victim. I do not mean to sensationalise our trip that night. It passed without trouble. Yet, it was also undeniably saturated with a series of small, spirited provocations. Most were projected through the haze of smoke, voices, bodies and beats of a *shebeen*,[5] where Gavin's gang brothers intermittently goaded me into fictitious quarrels and confrontations, trying to see if I would take up their theatrical displays of aggression. It was also in the *shebeen* where a group of women demanded that I show them 'how the white man dances', their insistence punctuated by laughter and suggestive gyrations. Another group of tipsy middle-aged men kept insisting that my foreignness – and presumed affluence – obligated that I buy them 'a bottle'. Underlying their jocularity seemed to be a hope that I would relent as the joke wore on. I almost did.

Others pushed and prodded in their own ways. Occasionally Gavin would interject protectively. Sometimes he would leave me to fend for myself, or would physically and verbally urge me towards the tumult, to the great delight of

---

[3]Colloquial terms for methamphetamine, heroin, marijuana and Mandrax, respectively; the last is a popular sedative medication also sold under international brand names Quaalude and Sopor.

[4]Literally a derogatory term denoting female genitalia; but also used against a person who is considered weak and disrespected.

[5]An illicit bar or club where excisable alcoholic beverages are sold without a licence.

onlookers. As the night progressed I started to suspect that what I was being pulled into was a type of trial, to ascertain if I could establish myself as 'a motherfucker' according to the logic Gavin outlined beforehand. This suspicion was confirmed when he later confessed at one point intentionally leaving me alone, when going to tend to some business matters in another part of the settlement. 'Yeah, I left [you], just to see how you handle it – see if you could be a motherfucker', he revealed with a smirk.

I offer this anecdote to contextualise this book, and to give readers a tangible example of the types of interpersonal exchanges that brought plotlines like Gavin's to life. It should come across already that research was participatory in nature, often involving significant interaction and time spent with subjects and settings. Embedded study of this sort tries to find and give voice through immersion, rather than trying to disguise its intentions 'behind the role of an invisible and omniscient third-person narrator' (Scheper-Hughes, 1993, p. 25). In enquiring into hidden topics like gangs, especially, one must necessarily go beyond sterile researcher–subject relationships, stepping into people's personal lives and, at times, walking the line that separates the author and the participant. It is only like this that one can hope to get any sense of how society functions in peripheral places like Cape Town's township areas, where people strain against one another, as each struggles in his or her own way against the structuring and socialising forces shaping informal living. The hope is that anthropological study, through its participant–observation methods and culturally relative awareness, 'can play an important role in fostering a public debate over the human cost of poverty and racism, as well as nefarious forms of violence that reproduce inequality' (Bourgois, 2011b, p. 307).

The staging of that first night I passed in the *kampie* with Gavin had a mischievous-but-comical tone to it, produced by the type of attention afforded the foreign friend of a well-known gangster. The average community resident would not be allowed equal leeway. For them, tests would be part of a very real competition to demarcate a place among their neighbours in a life characterised by stifling scarcity. I would later discover similar dynamics at play in other communities. I witnessed time and again how commonplace exchanges quickly escalated into hostile arguments between residents. As an outsider, I was an oddity and an object of benign interest, rather than a threat to be confronted, and was largely insulated from such dangers. I was not, however, shielded from an undercurrent of social friction created by people gesticulating, demanding, shouting, jostling, grabbing and relentlessly exerting pressure on one another in the way I described above. The subsequent township visits I made during my years of research frequently left me drained, my energy sapped by the need to rebuff the steady incursions into my personal space. This, of course, is not to misrepresent such neighbourhoods as unsympathetic or crass. Far from it. I cannot begin to describe the abundance of thoughtful, witty, sensitive, gracious and intimate interactions I had there. But there is no escaping the fact that township life has a certain unavoidable severity. It is easy to imagine how the long-term effects of this environment could produce in some a gruff and callused demeanour, providing the proverbial thick skin needed to live there.

While central Cape Town epitomises the well-contented urban centre, millions living on the city's outskirts compete for dignity and opportunity because they are denied livelihoods, housing, policing, sanitation, water and other necessities. As a visitor to the *kampie*, I can leave when I want to, retreating into comfort and calm. Equivalent options are not available to Gavin, his family, neighbours, Mongrel brothers or most of the people I write about. For them, being 'a motherfucker' is neither playful nor theatrical. It is a matter of survival:

> You need to be hard like this place to survive here. So that [others] can't make a carpet of you. So that they can't walk over you. If somebody raises their voice, you also will know how to raise your voice. You won't cry. You won't show emotions. You'll kill if you have to. Even if you are not a gangster, or somebody that goes through this life – you are just an ordinary person that stays in Ottery – but still you need to keep you hard... That's how they will understand you here. That is how they will respect you.

With my first-hand experiential connection to Gavin's life I better understand the overbearing weight of his words. He is a living testament to how someone can be rubbed raw over time by the systemic imbalances, racism and insecurity that envelop a community. What I am describing is a symptom of South African social hierarchies hundreds of years in the making, institutionally engrained over decades lost to apartheid and left unresolved in its aftermath. In 1948, the white supremacist National Party began a policy of 'separateness' that institutionalised racial division in South Africa, splitting by race who South Africans could marry, where they could reside, what work they could do and where they could go to school. They gave the white minority preferential treatment over other races in all social, economic and political areas. Apartheid officially came to an end in 1994, but racialised poverty, inequality, segregation and unrest remain abjectly ingrained in South African cities like Cape Town to date.

This book does not – and cannot – excuse the pernicious effects gangs have in Cape Town. What it does is acknowledge that gangs have a past, as well as contemporary causes and consequences that cannot be separated from a persistently unequal social system, which skews by race and by class who wins and loses among the city's inhabitants. By taking such a vantage point, we can more clearly see the perspective of young people like Gavin, and better appreciate what days and nights are like spent amid the circumstances in which they are socialised:

> You can see how the little kids grow up in the ghetto here, you know. Their parents grew up with the pain [of apartheid]. Now they take that kid – only 3–4 years old – going hard on that little kid... There's always swear words, there's always pain coming out. He don't understand the pain. But his mother or his father just pass the pain to him. Now when he gets thirteen or fourteen, now he releases the pain. But now his mother also wants to sit back and check: wow why's my son so dangerous? Why is he a killer?

> Because she did pass the pain on to him when he was young. He grew up with that mentality of: I only understand pain, I only understand this way of talking and acting – rough, rude, bad. This is the way my mother spoke to me. That is printed on my mentality.

Language and action are structured over the course of days, years and generations to harden youngsters, honing them into a repertoire of survival practices that offers the best chance at withstanding the pains they endure. Gangs are one such survival mechanism. One does not necessarily need to join a gang for protection. A tiny fraction of Capetonians become gangsters, about 100,000 (Civilian Secretariat for Police, 2016) in a city of roughly four million people. But the gang member is unquestionably the foremost embodiment of defensiveness, toughness and truculence in the townships. It should not therefore be surprising that innumerable young men and women might be drawn to gangs for the social utility they offer.

Gangsterism's protective power became gravely evident as I witnessed Gavin's attempts to leave the Mongrels. He was shot at and almost killed three times, beaten and hospitalised twice, and stabbed once during his disengagement. Without the brotherhood to look out for him, Gavin was left alone and unguarded. Others seemed to sense it. His closest friends, not themselves gang members, persistently pestered him for being victimised as he was, suggesting that he deserved what he got because he did not fight back viciously and pitilessly enough. They were now labelling him as the exact same thing Gavin himself had previously warned me to avoid becoming – a *poes*. Despite Gavin's efforts to remain indifferent to the heckling and laughter, it became too much at times. On various occasions he would be pulled into fights with his friends – even stabbing two of them. He tried to walk away before one such altercation, but the man baiting him would not cease, causing Gavin to lash out. 'I had this little knife that I carry now, and I stabbed him... I snapped, you know. I just saw him taking me for a bitch bro. I couldn't let it go on', said Gavin. His targeted rage belied a less discriminate fury that was projected not at one individual, but at anybody who might try to hurt him in the future; stabbing somebody was a way of carving out a safe haven for himself within an environment he was trying to, but could not, escape from.

I would later watch Gavin and the man he stabbed struggle towards an uneasy rapprochement. Associations in small spaces inevitably overlap, squeezing people together in spite of themselves. They were forced into an edgy dialogue one day, following a few hours spent soaking up beer and sun on a grimy summer afternoon. The two men were hemmed in, stuck in the uncertainty of the moment, as the rest of us held our breath to see how it all would play out. As they talked, others chimed in. The conversation became brusque, charged and then antagonistic. Luckily, it settled again, and we finally managed to pull Gavin away. At various times I had observed tensions arising like this, unexpectedly, between friends, family and neighbours, coming to crescendo in an instance that might just as well lead to blows, as to reflection, reconciliation or further revelry. The day I just described finished up only in more merriment. For an instant, though, it teetered on a knife-edge. A single move the wrong way and it all could have ended terribly.

Insecurity is the reality for millions of people in the city; crime statistics will tell you that much. However, numbers cannot convey the palpable instability that well-off Capetonians are mostly isolated from. The vignettes described above offer some insight into the ways that society and culture are built up in township communities. They also glimpse behind the curtain of the fieldwork process connected to this book, to peer outside of the physical and symbolic borders that define the social landscape I surveyed and wrote about.

Notes from 'The Field'

Gavin's life history is just one of 24 collected for this book.[6] Each narrative is that of a former gang member who had successfully disengaged for at least one year – many were out for much longer. While the majority of the formal interviews with this group were carried out in the early stages of 2018, some in this sample were among the first people I met when I touched down in Cape Town in 2016. From that time, I had the opportunity to witness the lives of many interviewees outside of the confines of the interview process, in informal conversations and observations that were unencumbered by lists of questions, note-taking or recording devices. My exchanges with the main sample of 24 intermingled with numerous interviews and informal conversations with other gang members, as well as with discussions I had with parents, teachers, health professionals, social workers, civil society representatives, community campaigners, politicians and fellow researchers. It takes qualitative work of some breadth and depth to access the hidden or illegal aspects of our societies, by digging and scratching at the paradoxes and intricacies underneath relations in peripheral spaces. Even if the outputs of the broader study were not always penned directly into the pages of this book, it would be fair to say that its text is the cumulative product of research and writing on gangs in Cape Town for six-plus years.

The end result is a collage of snapshots from layered life histories, created around a biographical timeline that grew in relation to every interviewee's movements into and out of gangs. As Godfrey and Richardson rightly indicate, methodologies of this type provide 'a significant, theoretically dense, and diverse sub-set of historical and social-scientific enquiry' (2004, p. 144). Framing research as life history chooses awareness, elaboration and understanding, countering current trends in the criminological field to standardise and reduce the lives of gang members into sterile social categories to be broken down and mastered (Fraser, 2015). Allowing research subjects to situate themselves in their own narratives mitigates the stigma of savagery that is so often levelled at members of Cape Town's gangs. Their personal accounts also have the power to convey complicated ideas and difficult topics with humility and humanity, bringing the

---

[6]My initial engagement as a gang researcher in Cape Town relied heavily on gatekeepers from local civil society organisations. These first connections later snowballed into additional contacts within and between communities across the city, all of which were important in sourcing participants for this study.

study from the purely scientific into the realm of the personal, more amply representing lived realities. Much can be unearthed when mining the idiosyncrasies of a single life. In discussing him- or herself, individuals invariably make a narrative connection to the social, cultural, economic and political forces that influence people like them (Ojermark, 2007). Moreover, theory and data are represented below through a journalistic style of writing that seeks to animate interviewees' biographies. The intention is to provide access to the situational meaning of participants' statements, weaving context and dialogue into the fabric of their lives, in a way that humanises their experiences with street culture.

From all of the life histories considered below, Gavin's alone is presented as something resembling a biography, while aspects of other life histories are touched on sporadically in self-contained snippets throughout this publication, as they fit the topics presented. From our short introduction to Gavin's life we can already see the uncertain course members tread when leaving gangs. His uneasy transition embodies a conclusion without clarity, which is true of every character arc in this book. Its pages describe protagonists taking tentative steps forwards and backwards, moving away from gangs to indefinite endings, rather than by clear leaps towards better futures. It is fair to say that gang disengagement takes a 'zigzag path' (Laub & Sampson, 2001, p. 54)[7] that is ambiguous, irregular and unpredictable, trekked by social actors using available strategies, resources and opportunities to escape the deadly hold of the streets. Most people in this study organised their gang exits around generalisable behavioural schemas defined by some version of: family, work and religion. Of course, every transition had its own character and bearing, but domestic repertoires, workplace repertoires and religious repertoires provided ex-gangsters access to the type of non-gang social networks and cultural capital that gave them the best chance of getting out of gang life into normal life. The characters presented below might remain, for the most part, trapped in insecure lives and unstable livelihoods. Still, they offer incontestable examples that disengagement is possible, their journeys yielding insights that can inform efforts to attenuate gang violence – whether in Cape Town, or in other unequal and insecure cities around the world.

---

[7]Something also found in studies of exit from delinquency (Bushway et al., 2001), terrorism (Horgan, 2009), piracy and right-wing hate groups (Bjorgo, 2008) and drug trafficking (Campbell & Hansen, 2012).

Acknowledgements

Sincere appreciation goes out to all who directly and indirectly participated in and supported this project. To begin with, thank you to Rotary International for so generously funding part of this study. I also cannot but express endless gratitude to my family, without whose love I would not have pressed on. Each of you, in your unique way, was a source of strength, comfort and motivation. This success is yours, as much as it is mine. But, above all, I would like to acknowledge those people who were selflessly and unabashedly willing to give voice to the tragedy and bravery that define life for many young Capetonians. The stories you shared stay with me as a testament to the beauty of the human spirit. I hope that I did those narratives justice, and in retelling them am able to – in some small way – contribute to our common aspiration of making a secure and fulfilling life a right enjoyed by each and every person living in Cape Town.

Chapter 1

Blood In, Blood Out?

To the casual observer, Cape Town looks glossy and serene. With its picturesque panoramas of Table Mountain and its fashionable shops and restaurants, the city earned the distinction of World Design Capital in 2014, and is regularly ranked among the world's top tourist destinations. But it also consistently makes it to the global list of deadliest cities. In 2019, it had the highest murder rate in Africa, and the eighth highest worldwide (CCSPJP, 2020). No more than 20 minutes away from Cape Town's central 'City Bowl', fierce gun battles raged between competing gangs on the 'Cape Flats', the expansive, sandy outskirts where the city's townships are located. This is the other side of the so-called 'Mother City'[1], the part not presented on postcards or travel websites, where the vast majority of its shooting is concentrated (ISS, 2019). Murder rates in Cape Town have been rising since the turn of the decade, and are now much higher than in South Africa's other major urban centres (SACN, 2019). Police statistics indicate an average of more than two gangland murders every day in the Western Cape Province whose capital is Cape Town, about one-third of all killings there (SAPS, 2018).

Some estimates purport that there are around 130 gangs,[2] with up to 100,000 members, operating in Cape Town and its surrounds (Civilian Secretariat for Police, 2016). Among these are a number of street gangs[3] of considerable size and permanence. There are also three prison gangs – known collectively as 'the number' – that have a long and arcane history of ritualised violence that has permeated the four corners of South Africa's correctional system (Steinberg, 2004a). While prison and street gangs have historically stayed separate, versions of the number gangs – the 26s, 27s and 28s – can now be found throughout Cape Town too. Towards the

---

[1]What is probably the most popular explanation for this nickname refers to the fact that Cape Town is the original site of colonial settlement in Africa.

[2]This estimate has been in circulation since at least the mid-2000s. But Standing comments that 'This number is not to be relied on, however, as the way in which gangs are counted is not methodologically rigorous; SAPS experts admit that the figure is a rough estimate' (2006, p. 103).

[3]Participants in this study belonged to some of the city's most feared gangs: Americans, Hard Livings, Mongrels, Ghetto Kids and Laughing Boys. Other prominent street gangs are: Terrible Josters, Junky Funky Kids, Jesters and Junior Cisko Yakkies. The 28s prison gang, and to a lesser extent the 27s and 26s, also continue to establish themselves independently on the streets.

Gang Entry and Exit in Cape Town, 1–18
Copyright © 2021 Dariusz Dziewanski
Published under exclusive licence by Emerald Publishing Limited
doi:10.1108/978-1-83909-730-020210001

bottom end of the underworld pecking order is a latticework of smaller, turf-based proto-gangs that usually ally with more established street gangs (Pinnock, 2016). It is mainly in Cape Coloured townships that one finds institutionalised organised street groupings (Hagedorn, 2008), whereas gangs in Black townships are usually relatively small cliques and crews (Sefali, 2014). It is also Coloured street gangs that dominate news headlines, and are the gang category that will be this book's primary focus. They often span several communities, and can be made up of hundreds and thousands of members (Roloff, 2014). Because of the size of street gangs, their members do not operate together in a unified manner, but sustain the gang's unity via a combination of shared cultural practices like specific tattoos, dress codes and slang, as well as through a mutual animosity to outsiders and collective memories of the gang's past (Standing, 2003). The biggest of Cape Town's gangs – like the Americans and Hard Livings – have evolved into street syndicates, or super-gangs, which are highly organised and are franchised across the city (Goga, 2014b).

The Americans are reputed to be the largest gang, and one of the most violent. The 'American nation' is made up of many thousands of members who are organised around the red, white and blue of the United States flag, a symbol that they have imported from across the Atlantic and emblazoned onto clothes, graffiti and tattoos across Cape Town. The Americans are affiliated with smaller groups that might also fight under the US banner,[4] while retaining their own gang identities. Gangs like the Hard Livings, Mongrels, Laughing Boys and Ghetto Kids by contrast affiliate under the British flag, standing together as a measure against the dominance of their larger Amerophile adversaries. Of course, the frenzied nature of Capetonian gangsterism means that alliances are in flux all the time, shifting and splintering as gangs are born, grow and die off in the battle to control the city's illegal economies. The grasp of gangsters touches every aspect of life, reaching into pockets of crooked cops, corrupt politicians and frightened business owners (Shaw, 2017), and even into the core of the city. Throngs of foreign travellers stumbling through the lively din of Long Street's club scene remain largely oblivious to the fact that security and drugs along the strip are also swayed by gangs (Dolley, 2019).

Still, it is the Coloured communities of the Cape Flats that are the heartland of gangsterism in Cape Town. Gangs there run violent drug businesses and control protection, taxis and prostitution rackets. It is down the barrel of a firearm or with a knife's blade that they carve up Coloured communities, taking anything from a building, street or block, to large parts of entire townships. When gang leaders want to expand their empires, they send street soldiers out to shoot at competing gang members. Teenagers – or younger – frequently open fire on their enemies from down a residential street or across a school field, sending civilians ducking for cover and rival gangsters running to get their own hardware in retaliation.

---

[4]Groups like the Dollar Kids, Derwent Kids, Dixie Boys and Spoilt Brats might typically be aligned with the Americans. But alliances are localised and shifting. For instance, at the time of writing this the Spoilt Brats were fighting under the British flag in Hanover Park, but were aligned with the Americans in places like Tafelsig in Mitchells Plain.

Other gang-related violence is more targeted. The assassination of an adversary might be planned for days, weeks or months before.

Violence is central to the existence and functioning of gangs everywhere. International research has shown that gang participation generally amplifies rates of violent offending (Sweeten, Pyrooz, & Piquero, 2013), as well as violent victimisation (Peterson, Taylor, & Esbensen, 2004). Most importantly, it underpins the drug economy (Plüddemann, Parry, Louw, & Burton, 2002). Gangs are a real estate business. More turf equals more drug sales, which buys more weaponry to capture yet more ground. Violent acts may also be incorporated into gang admission ceremonies. The head of a prominent Cape Flats gang prevention initiative stated that the act of 'taking blood' in initiation is a driver of gang-related violence; other key sources of conflict include: disputes over territory, fights over drugs, personal altercations, exit ceremonies and disagreements over females. Once in the gang, loyalty is proved through atrocity, putting an exclamation point on a process that separates recruits from community and family, bonding them to the gang through blood (Pinnock, 1997). Violence is also used punitively against anybody stepping outside the rules or alliances of a gang. Only the worst transgressions end in murder, however. Warm bodies are more useful, after all, than are cold ones. 'The Hard Livings will break your legs and pay for the hospital bill', a Manenberg-based community activist told me, when discussing how the gang punishes members who step out of line. Bruises and broken bones are inscribed upon the body of the transgressor, teaching hard lessons to all members about what is and is not acceptable behaviour. Gang punishments and disputes can also be directed at outsiders, usually opposing gangs, in violence aimed equally at expressing catharsis and domination. 'Sometimes me and my brothers we have an argument and we both fetch a gun and want to shoot each other... Then we go [shoot the enemy], because we don't want to shoot each other', said a member of the Laughing Boys.

If the shooting starts, it can be difficult to stop. Gang life is ruled by the notion of 'blood for blood', stipulating that when one person gets killed, another must soon die as payback. Every salvo of bullets is treated as an alibi for the next. Wars start with a single incident and spin out into cycles of revenge, as retaliatory assaults, stabbings and shootings swallow up entire communities for months at a time. One death cascades into another, and then another and another. Dozens may eventually die from a single gang war. In addition to the many lives senselessly lost, the price of violence can include: disrupted access to education and other services, restricted mobility, lost livelihoods and diverted public investments. There are tens of millions of rands spent yearly on efforts to quell gang-related violence in the city by different levels of government (Nyathi, 2018) – treating gunshot wounds alone costs up to about 25,000 rands per patient (Lindwa, 2019).[5]

---

[5]Around the time of writing one US dollar was worth almost 15 South African rands, and one British pound was valued at about 20 rands.

Like this, gangsterism is continually being woven into the very fabric of social life in Cape Town, giving the aberrant the veneer of the normal, as people try to carry on with family, work and friendships as best they can. In spite of the carnage, many Cape Flats residents are fascinated by gangs, succumbing to a structurally induced version of Stockholm syndrome that compels them to idolise their tormentors in an unconscious and desperate bid for self-preservation. Even those residents who oppose gangs have no option but to live with them. Workers commuting to and from jobs pass by open-air drug markets, while children entertain themselves under mosaics of drying clothes strung between apartment blocks that double as gang hideouts. All too frequently, such scenes are disrupted by gun blasts. After the last shot is spent, police and residents congregate to assess the damage done. Though daily life typically quickly resumes, each violent act lives on as residents discuss gang battles and their resultant arrests, injuries and killings. These spirited discussions can move seamlessly from the spectacular and macabre to more prosaic topics like who has a new job, a new relationship or a new haircut.

As violence disperses imperceptibly into the normal course of things, it becomes 'routinized' in an established 'part of a larger context of wholly expectable, indeed even anticipated, behavior' (Scheper-Hughes, 1993, pp. 229 and 272). Taking stock of who was injured and killed during any given week became normal procedure throughout this study. Many young people I met had their lives cut tragically short as a result of gang-related murders. Eighteen-year-old Charlie was slayed after successfully making it out of the Dollar Kids gang, shot execution-style for his past affiliations while working on a road construction project. Dillon – just 16 – also made it out, only to be dispatched by the Americans because his father was still a gang leader. Kyle was killed by fellow Laughing Boys member to settle a drug debt, leaving behind a wife and child after struggling to get away from the gang and out of a drug addiction. There were many more who I knew personally, as well as those who I did not, whose premature deaths were brought on senselessly by the pernicious and persistent menace of gang violence.

Stories like these give the impression that gang membership is inevitably 'blood in and blood out'. This well-known Cape Flats adage is an ominous reference to the death warrant ostensibly signed for anybody trying to flee the streets. But to what extent are such dire depictions accurate? On some level, public fascination with sensational news stories leads to a disproportionate amount of attention being placed on the most extreme aspects of gang activity. After all, the media is governed by its own axioms, favouring reports that adhere to the saying: 'if it bleeds, it leads'. American gang researchers Decker and Lauritsen observed that gang members also have a stake in highlighting the bloodiest aspects of gangsterism, since 'the viability of their gang depends on the ability of active gang members to maintain the perception that quitting the gang is nearly impossible' (2002, p. 61). In the Capetonian context, Standing (2006) noted that the ubiquity of stories about gang members being murdered upon denouncing the gang leaves many afraid to attempt the same, although they might like to try. In our own way too, gang scholars focus on the most morbid features of gang life. Most international criminological literature concentrates on participation in gang activities, with comparatively little being written about if, how and why people leave gangs. This also compounds the belief that the sole way out is in a body bag.

That is not to imply that no literature on exit exists. Research dating back to Fredric Thrasher's (1927) pioneering study of Chicago gangs almost a century ago found that members leave as they mature, get married and find employment. Subsequent studies also indicated that people are able to 'mature out' of gangs (Hagedorn, 1994; Hagedorn & Macon 1988; New York City Youth Board, 1960; Pyrooz, 2014; Suttles, 1968; Thornberry, Huizinga, & Loeber, 2004). However, current disengagement literature is largely based in high-income settings like the United States (see: Decker & Lauritsen, 2002; Sweeten et al., 2013; Thornberry, Krohn, Lizotte, Smith, & Tobin, 2003), so it remains unclear to what extent its lessons are transferable to lower-income contexts. It is reasonable to assume gang leaving might be affected by the relatively more severe levels of deprivation and insecurity found in South African townships.

To be sure, I have seen men and women depart gangs in Cape Town. As well, other local researchers have provided anecdotal evidence, usually as an adjunct to scholarship that concentrates on other gang topics. For instance, after revisiting the Heideveld township that had been the site of his ethnographic work on a small gang called the Homeboys, Jensen stated:

> It was with the greatest relief that I returned three years later to find that the Homeboys had ceased to exist as a group. Several had married and moved away. Two had become police officers! The rest either worked or studied. (Jensen, n.d. in Standing, 2006, p. 133)

Rodgers and Jensen (2015) also presented case studies of out-of-gang transitions in Cape Town, demonstrating that members can disengage via romantic relationships and religion. Other scholars, on the contrary, have expressed more pessimistic sentiments regarding members' potential to depart Cape gangs. Lindegaard (2017), for one, found that people's gang personas are largely durable across time, while Standing stated that: 'wandering into the gang and remaining an entrenched member can be seen as an unavoidable consequence of the social and economic contradictions of life on the [Cape] Flats' (2006, p. 135). In *The Number,* Steinberg also wrote forcefully about the struggles of a poor Coloured man scrambling to find the straight and narrow path, only to be repeatedly redirected into criminality, gangs and prison.

The numerous aborted attempts at disengagement I have personally witnessed further corroborate how difficult this is to do. Important obstacles to exit are: threats of violence, criminalisation by police, diminished social options and stigma that can follow gang membership (Feavel & Pyrooz, 2014). Another obvious impediment is that criminal records all but sink possibilities of staying financially afloat in an economy where the tide of unemployment is already so high (Standing, 2005). Hustling might be the solitary recourse an ex-gangster feels he or she has to make ends meet (Hagedorn, 1994). Somebody without the right social connections will find it especially difficult to land formal work

(Brotherton & Barrios, 2011). By contrast, gangs are looking to hire 24/7, and are the one place where being an ex-prisoner actually increases his or her chances of employment. As a result, many youngsters on the Cape Flats grow up thinking that becoming a gangster is the surest way to attain financial freedom, and that prison is a rite of passage that is required to enhance one's street credibility and move up the ranks of the gang (Samara, 2011).

The City Bowl offers preferable alternatives. Living there follows a line of thinking developed by French sociologist Pierre Bourdieu (1977, 1986), who believed that the well-to-do and well-connected have access to prestigious schools and elite networks that can be a big boost to their professional prospects. Not every job opportunity is posted on an employment site. Knowing the right person can help uncover these. Then knowing how to sell yourself properly can help you land the job. Growing up with a silver spoon, going to a top school and joining a swanky club teach one how to handle hoity-toity customs and conventions, which are advantageous to ascending the corporate ladder. Such 'cultural capital' (Bourdieu, 1986, pp. 243–248) is slippery and elusive, and difficult to grasp for outsiders to high society. This makes it exclusive and valuable. Knowing the 'proper' way to enunciate a word, the latest fashion trend, when to laugh at a joke or even what people are laughing about conveys an intimate familiarity with upper-class circles, which in turn verifies one's belonging there. In fact, every social space has idiosyncrasies that draw a distinction between insiders and interlopers. Townships operate according to their own bits of cultural code, just like the city centre does. Think back to the lessons Gavin offered me in the preface as I entered the commotion of the *kampie*. That setting was as indiscernible to me as the stuffy ambiance of Cape Town's colonial Mount Nelson Hotel might have been to him. Whereas bluster and bellicosity would certainly get you booted from the Mount Nelson, being a wild, unshrinking and angry 'motherfucker' is important 'street capital' (Sandberg, 2008, p. 156) – a street cultural competence and recognisably legitimate form of authority in informal settings – for a gangster trying to preside over the drug market in a slum community.

Gang researchers writing on 'street culture' (Bourgois, 2002; Fraser, 2015; Ilan, 2015; Sandberg & Pedersen, 2011) have built on Bourdieu's theories and concepts – cultural capital, along with 'social field' (1993, pp. 30–31) and 'habitus' (1988, p. 782) – to show how young people everywhere in the world who are born into the pressure cooker of urban vulnerability might turn to gangs as a rational response to irrational social circumstances. Rather than accepting trifling wages, inhumane working conditions and racial prejudice, youngsters instead celebrate their marginality as a badge of honour, drawing pride and power in what the privileged classes would find shocking and shameful. What is broadly referred to as street culture in academic literature is popularly called 'gangsterism' (Standing, 2005, p. 12) in Capetonian street vernacular; it is an observable set of social practices – drug use, profligacy, hedonism, risk-taking, hypersensitivity, intimidation and aggression – that pitches loyalty to gangs against commitment to polite society. For its adherents, gangsterism promises protection (Jensen, 2006), dignity (Jensen, 2008) and income (Pinnock, 2016), in a context where equal economic opportunity (Crankshaw, 2012), active and responsive policing (O'Regan & Pikoli,

2014) and accessible criminal justice (Gould, 2014) are generally unavailable. The 'structural power' (Wolf, 1990, p. 587) of economic inequality, community deprivation and racial division hits Coloured communities in Cape Town hard, putting the balance of probabilities against the people who live there. So people make do, out of a desire to catalyse something from nothing. Gangs are made up of tough, poorly educated young men and women who have nowhere to go, and whose greatest resource is their indomitable will to live and die on their own terms. What might otherwise be judged by some as the moral failing of somebody simply opting to behave badly or criminally, is anything but.

Make no mistake, though, street culture is a self-defeating strategy in the long run. It is the already-excluded clashing with each other in order to not be the one who is left depressed, destitute, disfigured or dead, in an attempt to rise above their circumstances by pulling down those around them. Too much time spent cheating, stealing and fighting sooner or later attaches itself to them as a socialising and organising principle of how life ought to be lived – in competition, in confrontation and in constant conflict. Violence becomes culturally internalised in ways that compound the conditions that originally caused it. Whereas a preparatory school, a top university and an office job lead to mainstream cultural participation, a long-term commitment to street culture imprints gang tattoos, street slang, puffed-up personas and erratic demeanours onto hitmen, drug merchants, thieves, pimps and the other usual suspects found in lawless localities around the world (Shammas, 2018). The consequence is a 'locking-in effect' (Shammas & Sandberg, 2016, p. 209) into a sociological straightjacket that holds captive whole neighbourhoods to volatility and violence, with what seems like no way out.

There is great analytical value – and moral power – in demonstrating how crime and violence are reproduced in relation to structural oppression and lack of opportunity, especially in refuting criminological arguments depicting gang members as sociopaths (Yablonsky, 1959, 1970). But over-representing the potency of street culture's socially reproductive power presents its own problems. Reading street cultural literature can leave one feeling hopeless sometimes, giving off the impression that getting out of the grip of gangs and escaping the streets is unimaginable. In this regard, street culturalists tend to mirror the shortcomings of the Bourdieusian social theory their work is based on. Bourdieu was criticised for his partiality towards the structuring aspects of society, leaving little space for the ways that personal agency can change culture or the ways that societal relations might be restructured (Evens, 1999; Giroux, 2001). For their part, Bourdieusian criminologists emphasise the rigid reproductive effects of crime, gangs and violence, while taking not enough notice of how street culture can be shaken up, or how gang members and other criminal actors might be able to shake free from the streets.

This book focuses on personal transformation as a counterweight to the prominence of social reproduction in street cultural writings. It brings Bourdieusian criminology into conversation with international literature on gang disengagement and publications on gangs in Cape Town, showing that gang members there can break from street culture when exiting gangs. The disengagement narratives of Gavin and 23 other ex-gangsters are used to illuminate available pathways out of gangs, sparking a light at the end of the tunnel for anybody wanting to follow in their footsteps. Family life, work life and religious life serve as beacons for the rehabilitated, as they reorient themselves in a new world. For any cynics left wondering if the 'ex' is all an act – and sceptics are many – domesticity, professionalism and faith provided evidence that their redemption narrative is for real. Taken together, these are the three quintessential elements that encapsulate what many interviewees referred to as the 'normal life'. That everybody in this book managed to find some semblance of normal and legitimate living proves that gang members can start anew. Their experiences should be a source of inspiration to gang members also wishing to disengage, as well as a valuable source of information for anybody looking to offer a hand to help them do so.

1.1 A History of Violence

But before forging ahead into personal stories of gang disengagement, it is important to first situate these in the historical and social context that they take place in. To start, one cannot speak at length about Coloured street gangs in the city without first commenting on the history, place and identity of South Africa's Coloured population. Whereas the term 'Coloured' may be considered antiquated and offensive in places like the United States and United Kingdom, in South Africa many people self-identify with this racial and cultural category. This is not to imply that the label does not carry considerable historical baggage. It is a social classification associated with violent European coercion into a single racial categorisation phenotypically varied communities of highly diverse geographical and cultural origins (Adhikari, 1992). Apartheid codified Coloured people as one of South Africa's official racial categories.[6] The country's Coloured population was given a 'higher status' than the Black population, but a lower one than whites. Their middleness has meant that Coloured people have always occupied an ambiguous social position. They have a relatively smaller population and lower political representation than Blacks, and less economic power than whites. The following quote from Marike de Klerk, former First Lady of South Africa, is indicative of the limbo Coloureds find themselves living in. She described Coloured people as 'a negative group... a no-person. They are the leftovers. They are the people that were left after the nations were sorted out. They are the rest' (Adhikari, 2005, p. 13). Lacking a distinct identity, Coloured people had to find ways to generate meaningful participation in society. Joining gangs is one attempt at achieving this. 'If you want to know why we coloureds have gangs', one commentator told gang researcher Andre Standing, 'the problem is that we coloureds wish we were white... we don't know who we are or where we came from'. (2005, p. 14)

---

[6]South Africa's official ethnic categories are: Black African, Coloured, Indian/Asian and white.

The pernicious social engineering of the apartheid project contributed to modern-day gang formation in Cape Town in other important ways as well. After the National Party was elected in 1948 on policies of racial 'separateness' – apartheid's literal translation from Afrikaans – the 1950 Group Areas Act further segregated the country into race categories, including bans on racially mixed neighbourhoods (Mabin, 1992). In Cape Town, apartheid city planners attacked communities like District Six, a former inner-city residential area once celebrated for its racial diversity, generational depth and social cohesion (Cassidy, 2012). When District Six was declared a whites-only area in 1966, more than 60,000 people were violently uprooted from midtown and scattered across the Capetonian hinterland, their homes razed or hawked to white owners (Jaki, 2016). The scars left on the city's southern slopes are a reminder of the damage done to their neighbourhood. Although District Six evictees did include South Africans of Black, Indian, Chinese, Malay decent, along with a small number of whites, Western contends that the overwhelming majority of the removees were Cape Coloureds:

> I would assert that the trauma of the mass removal for them is proportionately greater because their space at the foot of the mountain of Cape Town was one true source of pride in themselves as a distinguishable ethnic entity. Thus, for them the obliteration of District Six is a humiliation that leaves an aching lacuna in self-concept and self-esteem and a profound and bitter resentment. (1997, pp. 152–153)

Households and friendships were torn apart, resulting in material strains, psychological stresses and upset marital relationships, as well as dispersed kinship networks that were previously used to mitigate social duress (Pinnock, 2016). District Six remains for many Coloured people a painful reminder of the agonies and losses of apartheid.[7]

The dislocation of the Coloured community harrowed the ground for the gangs that sprang up afterwards. Links between the removals and gang formation might be more complicated than this,[8] but in his compressive analysis of organised crime on the Cape Flats Standing noted that 'almost without exception, all people interviewed for this study explain that the policy of forced removals is the root cause of gangs in the Coloured community now' (2006,

---

[7]The realities of District Six were probably less hospitable than the romanticised place the neighbourhood retains in public memory. For one, the area had its own gangs. Groups like the Globe preceded those that can be found on the Cape Flats today (Pinnock, n.d.). But they were mostly contained through the community's close-knit camaraderie and collective controls (Samara, 2011).

[8]According to Glaser (2000), gang affiliations are likely to be uprooted and destroyed during social disorganisation, and gangs might only reappear once neighbourhoods have redeveloped personal and territorial familiarity. Standing (2006) also notes that social disorganisation theories downplay the presence of non-whites who had already settled in communities on the Cape Flats at the time of the removals.

p. 13). Gangsterism gives individuals and groups an alternative for meeting needs that social institutions in disordered and weakened communities cannot fulfil (Shaw & McKay, 1942). Lambrechts (2012) argues that disorganisation in Cape Town shredded the social fabric of extended Coloured families, encouraging the formation of bands of bored adolescents that provided a sense of belonging and empowerment, as well as a way to pass the time for youth who were otherwise socially and financially adrift.

Cape Coloured gangs were able to take advantage of the havoc created by apartheid in other ways as well. In speaking about the Cape Flats during the anti-apartheid uprisings and the resultant state of emergency that shook South Africa in the 1980s, Steinberg indicates that

> ...there was plenty to excite the imagination of the budding gangster, not just the activist. The activity on the street was not nearly as orderly and disciplined as sometimes maintained. Much of it was unguided, youthful euphoria. (2004, p. 146)

It was even suggested that gangs actively collaborated with the apartheid government as part of its counterrevolutionary war (Khoisan, 2001). Gangsters are opportunists. As they were aiding and abetting the state, Coloured gangs were also playing the other side of 'the struggle', providing a form of protection against security forces (Rodgers & Jensen, 2008). Ultimately, the role of Coloured gangs in the fight against apartheid was ambiguous, unlike South Africa's Black gangs, which were for the most part subsumed in the revolutionary struggle (Kynoch, 1998).

The eventual fall of the apartheid regime in 1994 brought big changes to South Africa. Nelson Mandela was leading the African National Congress to a resounding win in the country's first non-racial elections, Archbishop Desmond Tutu was chairing the country's Truth and Reconciliation Commission and a new inclusive constitution enshrined human rights and affirmed the democratic values of human equality, dignity and freedom. South Africa was also opening its borders after trade and investment sanctions had imposed years of international isolation. The air was electrified with optimism, as South Africans took in their blossoming prospects. Gangsters also sensed the possibilities on offer in the global underworld. A softening of border restrictions brought transnational organised crime into the country, as up-and-coming corner boys and home-grown hustlers formed part-nerships with Italian-American *Cosa Nostra*, Chinese Triads, Russia mafia, Nigerian drug pushers and varied other criminal operators that came surging in (Shaw, 1998). Cocaine and heroin sales began piling up alongside those from existing drug markets for marijuana and Mandrax[9] (Standing, 2006). As drug and

---

[9]Mandrax is a brand of the popular sedative methaqualone, also sold under the brand name Quaalude. It was intended to be used as a sleeping pill, but became popular as a recreational drug in South Africa in the 1970s (Standing, 2006).

criminal networks spread, so too did the power, profits and professionalistion of Coloured gangs in Cape Town. No longer were they just clusters of teenagers hanging around 'defending' their neighbourhoods from intruding hooligans, the city's gangs ascended the criminal ladder to become sophisticated drug and crime empires in their own right (Kinnes, 2000). The end result is that gang culture in Coloured communities on the Cape Flats is more prevalent than elsewhere in contemporary South Africa, despite what was a comparatively late start (Kynoch, 2008).

1.2 Apartheid All Over Again

Cape Town is now widely known as a global capital of violence, and the Cape Flats is regarded as its most dangerous area. It is a place where multi-millionaire druglords terrorise their communities and evade prosecution by intimidating witnesses and buying off police. When that does not work, they resort to even more bold-faced tactics. Most brazenly, a senior member of the Western Cape's Anti-Gang Unit was shot to death in 2020 outside his own house by an assassin with links to the Terrible West Siders gang (Nombembe, 2020). Although it is the powerful and wealthy godfathers at the top of Cape gang's organisational charts that garner the most media attention, 'the majority of those who operate in the criminal economy are simultaneously socially excluded and criminally exploited' (Standing, 2003, p. 8). Crime bosses have houses in comfortable neighbourhoods, profitable businesses to feed their bank accounts and the right connections to keep themselves out of jail. The situation of the average street gangster is considerably worse. He or she is usually squashed into a small geographic area, collects a small and uncertain income and is generally supported entirely by family while in prison. There is an indisputable dissonance between popular imagery of the criminal elite and the criminalised masses under them. It might be because the media shines its spotlight onto the trials of gang leaders and their associates to feed the public's fascination with the gory and extravagant details that surround their lives, making them the face of Cape Town's struggle with gangs. Community-based violence typically gets matter-of-fact reporting of the circumstances of death – not real attention – certainly not in narratives as penetrating and rich as the lives they represent. A failure to properly account for the pain of others co-signs concomitant failures in imagination and empathy, which conceals a great desperation found amid the everyday mess of drugs, criminality, addiction and violence.

Perpetration and victimisation on the Cape Flats are so tightly bound together, there is no picking them apart. 'Violence can never be understood solely in terms of its physicality – force, assault, or the infliction of pain – alone', write Scheper-Hughes and Bourgois (2011, p. 1). According to them, gang-related killings and assaults are not discrete acts, but rather points along a 'continuum of violence ... that also includes assaults on the personhood, dignity, sense of worth or value of the victim'. Viewing violence along a continuum sees it as a series of interrelated forces – ranging from murder, to racism, to dispossession – that conspire together as common forms of coercion and abuse to limit the lives, status, movement and potential of its victims. Gangs are unquestionably violent, but so is the hunger and poverty they are so often a response to. Joblessness is also pitiless and unsparing; inequality, racism and segregation are too – all in ways that are interwoven and inseparable.

When placed along the continuum of violence, Cape Town's so-called 'gang problem' is in fact part of a bigger problem associated with the failures of post-apartheid urban renewal, continued racial stratification and persistent economic deprivation that still ravages people's lives through 'neo-apartheid'[10] (Pieterse, 2009, p. 13). Haferburg states that, despite the political reforms of the 1990s, Cape Town's 'coloured working classes remain trapped in places of extreme poverty located at a considerable distance from middle-class (mostly white) centres of commerce, tourism, and consumption' (2003, p. 95). The result is one of the most unequal cities in the world (Mammon, 2016). Apathy is the new apartheid, and gangs are a non-state alternative through which some vulnerable men and women respond to the hydra of social issues attacking them in an urban setting largely stratified by race and class.

Segregation makes a big city seem small, because Cape Town's almost-four-million-person population is actually an assortment of largely sequestered neighbourhoods. Since communities are mostly single-race zones, poverty is highly racialised. Poverty rates are more than six and four times higher for Black and Coloured households, respectively, than for white ones (City of Cape Town, 2018). Each and every day township dwellers are subject to the unrelenting assault of 'structural violence' (Farmer, Bruce, Stulac, & Keshavjee, 2006, p. e449), which kills human beings over time via the social arrangements that produce alienation, exclusion and deprivation. It starves people slowly; not simply of food, but of pride and the fullness of the human experience. Gangs are a defensive response to the violence of privation and humiliation. Just look at a mapping murder in the city. It is contoured more or less along the same lines that are income brackets and racial groupings, corroborating the unambiguous disparities between what it is like to live – and die – in Cape Town. In 2019, just seven murders were reported to the Cape Town Central Police Station that covers the city's high-priced real estate, fancy restaurants and funky shops (ISS, 2019).[11] Meanwhile, deadly gang battles rage just on the other side of the mountain. Precincts serving the Cape Flats communities where this research project was situated had exponentially more; for that same year, 86 murders were reported to police in Philippi, 57 in Manenberg, 148 in Mitchells Plain and 247 in Delft.

---

[10]'Neo-apartheid' refers to the racialised class marginalisation in contemporary South Africa. This use is distinct from the neo-apartheid of the 1980s that accepted Black urbanisation and economic integration in the attempt to maintain white rule (Kuperus, 1999).

[11]The aggregated number of murders for the same year for police stations serving central communities like Sea Point, Woodstock, Camps Bay and Rondebosch was 14.

Those that are most disenfranchised are the main victims of violence, as well as its main perpetrators. Of course, no single group has cornered the market on violence in Cape Town, or elsewhere, regardless of class, race, gender or geography. I have for myself witnessed brawls between white middle-class Capetonians around town and in its proximal suburban 'safe havens'. Nor is violence tolerated by the vast majority living in township communities. Many thousands of people in gang-affected areas have – over and over – marched and demonstrated against gangs, calling for government action that allays the daily danger and dread they endure. In 2018, activist groups shut down highways and closed roads to make politicians pay attention to gangs, crime and poor living conditions on the Cape Flats. By 2019, little had changed, and they were marching again. 'The mortuaries are filled to capacity and our hospitals are practising battle-field medicine as if we are in a combat zone', event organiser Nadia Mayman De Grass told the *Cape Times* (2019), venting her frustration at the government's predilection for treating gang violence with the institutionalised violence of the military and police. 'Crime is not only a policing issue. We are also talking about socioeconomic issues that need to be addressed if we want to get rid of crime'. The following year activists like Nadia were back marching once more. They are unlikely to stop anytime soon, at least not until political officials start repairing Cape Town's uneven socioeconomic cityscape and reckoning with the broader economic, social and cultural fissures that gangs are a manifestation of. Unfortunately, there is a tendency for the South African state to pathologise gangs, situating them outside of an otherwise healthy society, to be removed or eradicated as one would a tumour – ignoring all the while the maladies in the rest of the social body that caused them.

1.3 Problems with 'The Gang Problem'

The main instrument by which government operations against gangs in South Africa are conducted is the *South African Prevention of Organised Crime Act (POCA)*. Passed in 1998, the law defines gangs as organised crime entities,[12] and tries to tackle them as such – through an offensive meant to wipe out their structures and membership. It is a legislative strategy imported from the United States, where the *Racketeer Influenced and Corrupt Organizations (RICO) Act* was used as part of that country's efforts against the Mafia in the 1970s (Goga, 2014a). But critics of *POCA* call attention to the reality that America's experiences with the mob might not be suitable as a way of orienting gang legislation in South Africa.[13] To begin with, Goredema (2014) suggests that Southern African

---

[12]*POCA* defines gangs as on-going organisations or groups of at least three people that participate in criminal offences, can be identified by a name, sign or symbol and whose members engage in or have engaged in a pattern of criminal activity (Republic of South Africa, 1998).

[13]A comparison of gangs and organised crime in the United States indicates that the characteristics of the latter may not apply well to the former, as even American gangs tend to be more disorganised than criminal syndicates (Decker, 2012).

criminal networks are generally more flexible and fluid than those in the United States. Gastrow (1998) also argues that South African gangs tend to be younger, more territorial and less sophisticated than international organised crime syndicates. As stated by Kinnes (2000) in his study of the evolution of Cape gangs, standardised exogenous definitions of gangs discount indigenous variations in the factors that bring them about: their age composition, their contextualised nature and activities and their level of organisational sophistication.[14]

POCA is part of a global push to smooth over the many irregularities in how gangs are defined in jurisdictions across the world. The idea is that coming to some conclusion on a globalised definition of gangs will streamline strategies to address them. Easier said than done. Researchers themselves have not been able to come to an agreement on the point at which a group begins to be a gang (Ball & Curry, 1995). Take Thrasher's (1927) analysis of gangs in Chicago in the early part of the twentieth century, for example. The categories he established then – diffuse, solidified, conventionalised, criminal and secret societies – were influential in future attempts to understand gangs; the research he did at that time yielded the following definition, which is still widely cited:

> A gang is an interstitial group, originally formed spontaneously, and then integrated through conflict. It is characterized by the following types of behavior: meeting face to face, milling, movement through space as a unit, conflict, and planning. The result of this collective behavior is the development of tradition, unreflective internal structure, esprit de corps, solidarity, morale, group awareness, and attachment to a local territory. (Thrasher 1927, 57)

But Klein and Maxson (2006) point out that many of the groups labelled as gangs by Thrasher would not meet the criteria of what constitutes a street gang today.

Standardising a dynamic and localised concept like gangs is highly problematic. To start with, global definitions are infused with an implied objectivity, although they are, as anything, social constructions of diverse local phenomena. In Cape Town alone there are super-gangs, street gangs, prison gangs, cliques and crews (Roloff, 2014). On top of that, change is one of the few constants in the world of gangs. Cape Coloured gangs, for instance, have evolved from community protection rackets into sophisticated drug smuggling enterprises. Long gone are days when the Globe and the Born Frees 'protected' *shebeens* and gambling dens, and fought each other in District Six with knives and fists (Pinnock, 2016). That past is so distant that it is almost unthinkable to see it as a potential starting point for the semi-automatic gun battles that take place today over multi-million rand narcotics markets. Prison gangs are changing too, with the mythology of the number

---

[14]Even international uses of the term 'gang' range from local schoolyard connections and corner boy collectives to neighbourhood street gangs, criminal syndicates and narco-cartels (Harding & Palasinski, 2016).

morphing and moving outside of jails. Street gangs used to rule the outside world, while prison gangs governed behind bars through the number. That all changed in the late 1990s, when Capetonian drug millionaires like Jackie Lonte, Colin Stansfield and Ernie Lastig were able to purchase prison gang ranks, becoming kingpins inside without having to get any blood on their hands, bypassing the grisly rites of passage required of other initiates (Pinnock, 2016). They were rich and powerful enough to promise prison gangsters money and status in the real world in return for favours at the time (Steinberg, 2004a). This upset an order of things, which had hitherto painstakingly relied on ritualised violence as the sole means of promotion up the prison gang hierarchy, and allowed the number to seep into the free world (Steinberg, 2004b). It is not uncommon to now see 26s, 27s and 28s spray-painted on turf seized by these gangs around Cape Town.

Although gangs in the city have changed drastically over the years, attempts to explain and address them are still very much mired in the past. The authorities cling to *POCA* in the belief that it is a strong legal tool for prosecuting and deterring gang-related crimes. Through it, they have institutionalised an American-style 'war on gangs' that aims to pummel and destroy gang structures through crime-fighting measures and 'hard policing' (Samara, 2011, pp. 124–137). It follows a general international shift to a conservative social philosophy bent on enhancing the ability of law enforcement to suppress gangs and incarcerate their members (Klein & Maxson, 2006). If more money can just be invested into more personnel, more assault rifles, more Kevlar vests and more ammo, maybe South Africa can police its way out of its gang problem. Such thinking follows the logic of mainstream American gang policy that has now become a global gang orthodoxy, side-lining critical perspectives more attuned to the nuances of local understandings, community contexts and historical changes (Fraser, 2015).

In the 1990s and 2000s, South African politicians and police operationalised these so-called 'international best practices' into several heavily resourced and highly publicised special policing operations aimed at combating gangs (Jensen, 2010). For evidence of how this approach has endured we need look no further than the two most prominent anti-gang initiatives implemented by the government in the last years. In late 2018, national police authorities established an Anti-Gang Unit to surveil and arrest 'high-flying gangsters' (Pitt, 2018). South Africa's police minister Bheki Cele and senior police officials have regularly sung the praises of the Anti-Gang Unit, touting their arrest records and the seizures of large quantities of illegal goods, especially firearms (Lamb, 2020). But complete information on successful convictions has been scarce. In the absence of evidence to corroborate the claims of the Cape Town Anti-Gang Unit's efficacy, it is difficult to evaluate its operations. Without more evaluatory research, international gang scholars warn against taking the police minister's words at face value because of the types of mishaps that tend to befall specialised gang units. According to Pranis and Greene (2007, p. 71) they are prone to operational isolation, inadequate training, little oversight, lack of community input and political pressure, which make them an ineffectual strategy for addressing gangs.

The authors concluded by saying that:

> ...the isolation of gang units from host agencies and their tendency to form tight-knit subcultures – not entirely unlike those of gangs – also contributes to a disturbingly high incidence of corruption and other misconduct. (2007, p. 71)

The year after the Anti-Gang Unit was formed, government officials doubled down on law enforcement as the centrepiece of its anti-gang efforts. In 2019, South African National Defence Forces (SANDF) rolled into the Cape Flats as part of Operation Lockdown, running patrols in armoured convoys, helping police to shake down suspects on the street and to kick down doors in search of drugs, guns and gangsters in Cape Town's most violence-affected neighbourhoods (Dzie-wanski, 2019). The belief was that vigorous patrol, arrest and imprisonment would put a substantial dent in criminal operations. Again, the Minister of Police heralded the operation a 'success' (Eyewitness News, 2020), with little proof to support such an upbeat assertion. Actually, there is strong anecdotal evidence that his assessments are wrong. Gangs are just as much of a problem today in Cape Town as they were before the deployments and since the Anti-Gang Unit was formed. This is not the first time paramilitary policing has been tried as an anti-gang strategy in Cape Town either. The army was deployed in 2015 'to crack down on rampant gang violence in the area as part of Operation Fiela' (Legg, 2015b). That they had to be sent in again a few years later signals the futility of prior missions, attesting to the undeniable fact that waging war on gangs may make for good politics, but it makes for bad public policy.

Still, the government continues throwing good money after bad, sending its police – and sometimes its army – to search for gangsters to snatch off the streets, notwithstanding how confusing it can be to tell the 'real' gangster apart from the wannabe. Baggy pants, earrings, sweatshirts with American and British flags and prison slang are pretty commonplace on the Cape Flats, making it a near to impossible task. Young men and women who may be considered gangsters might only associate with gangs to access drugs and social standing, or simply be posing as gangbangers to stay safe (Standing, 2006). Over-policing plays into social anxieties that reify stereotypes of poor Coloured youth, especially men, who are perceived by law enforcement to perpetually be in the incipient stages of acting out criminally. The menacing Cape Flats gangster of today is reminiscent of the kind of racialised scaremongering found in South Africa's past, in the imagery of the *swart gevaar*[15] (Durrheim, 2005) and of Coloured criminality once embodied by the *skollie*[16] (Jensen, 2008). That this type of scaremongering is reductionist and racist is bad enough, but it might be impairing gang prevention efforts as well. Perse-cuting somebody just pretending to be one of the gang can actually cement non-criminal gang connections among individuals who may have had nothing more

---

[15]Black peril.

[16]A colloquial term meaning petty criminal or hoodlum. The word likely comes from the old Dutch *shoelje*, which means scoundrel or scavenger (Pinnock, 2016).

than associative or superficial linkages to them (Katz, 1997). 'Prison is the great networking centre of criminal South Africa', Steinberg (2004b, p. 71) writes. 'Spend four or five years of your life in the 26s, and wherever you go after you will always find a brother with whom to do business'. The odds are that the South African prison will do more to spread gangsterism than to deter it, making it much more likely that non-gang youth will be forced to join a gang, and making those who are already members into better – more hardened – criminals.

The human and economic toll of gang violence is steep; there is no disputing this. However, as Klein and Maxson warn, there are costs to concentrating exclusively on the violent nature of gangs. 'Focusing on the most feared of the behavioural patterns has set a pattern against which almost all future behavioural gang research has had to do battle', they say (Klein & Maxson, 2006, p. 169). It is part of the reason that gang members are commonly presented as cold, calculating killers by media and politicians, a storyline that many in the general public are apt to believe and parrot as well. People are desperately searching for answers. So it is hard to blame frustrated community residents for cheering and waving as armoured vehicles rolled into their violence-affected communities with the army deployment in 2019. But militarised policing has failed to stop the violence, and getting caught up in the most shocking aspects of what gangs are ignores that they are actually diverse, complicated and shifting organisations whose members participate variably in criminality (Thornberry et al., 2003). Although violence, drinking, drug use and drug trafficking are standard, for the most part, gang members 'hang out' and are involved in normal teenage social activities (OJJDP, 1998). As an aside, it should also be mentioned that gangs might also be presented alongside social groupings – such as fraternities – that may have most of the same features as gangs, including a tendency towards violence, but escape the deviant label (Sanday, 2007).

The lack of agreement about how to define the gang creates a type of collectivity for which there is consensus on how to categorise or confront that collectivity – in spite of the great efforts to do so. Some definitively argue against differentiating gangs from other types of groups altogether (Sherif & Sherif, 1964). That is probably a step too far. Given the amplifying effects that violent street culture has in the context of gangs, and the outsized role they have in setting the tone of community norms and practices, probably means that gangs are qualitatively unique from other deviant associations. The energy put into considering, characterising and trying to constrain gangs is therefore reasonable. However, in searching for a solution to the so-called 'gang problem' in Cape Town, some restraint and reflection are necessary to slow the hasty rush towards adopting an aggressively positivist position when conceptualising gangs and contending with their effects. Effectively addressing gangs demands a more thorough diagnostic of the machinations that underpin gang violence and its relationship to society, economy, state, etc., looking primarily at 'why' gangs are, instead of being so preoccupied with 'what' they are. A shift in outlook should more aptly reflect the historical and environmental conditions influencing the forms and activities of gangs found in any given neighbourhood. Only then can researchers and policy-makers hope to decrease gang participation, assisting somebody in a gang to get out, and maybe preventing some from getting in in the first place.

1.4 Re-problematising Gangs

This introduction presented and problematised the notion of 'the gang' in the Capetonian context. It will serve as a jumping-off point for a more encompassing discussion in the next chapter about armed groups in Africa. Other countries on the continent have their own mix of material, political, spatial, racial and cultural forces that have created conditions where gangs and gang-like groupings can thrive. As in Cape Town, gangs in other African cities are the by-products of economic disenfranchisement and social disorganisation, which are attacked and demonised by politicians and police who recurrently put the blame on an underclass of people that they try to root out through hard policing. Still, like moths to a flame, young and vulnerable Africans everywhere are lured to gangs in the hope of achieving status, fortune and some semblance of safety. They will risk the worst for a long shot at street fame. Almost nobody attains this, save for a few criminal elites who keep the gangster dream alive. The majority will remain embroiled in a nightmarish quagmire of deprivation, incarceration and estrangement, infusing gang life with a fatalism that can appear absolute.

As this book progresses, however, we will see that predisposition is not predestination. Gang members do escape, re-imagining themselves in lives outside of the streets. That being said, we will also learn that exiting gang culture is not a straightforward process and can be marked by false starts and unfinished transitions. What is more, poverty, insecurity and ostracism threaten even those men and women who have managed to disengage. Nevertheless, paying heed to stories of gang leaving brings international research on gang disengagement into the Capetonian context. It also offers us an opening to integrate empirical experiences with disengagement in Cape Town to account for ways that street practices can be resisted, and potentially transformed. Adding this new theoretical perspective can hopefully also add meaningful contributions to research, policy and practice aimed at gang prevention in township areas, while informing interventions in similarly disadvantaged and violent urban spaces elsewhere in Africa – and the world.

Chapter 2

The Landscape of African Gangs

Africa's more than 1.2 billion inhabitants are spread across a landmass that is bigger than China, India, the contiguous United States and most of Europe – combined. Sprawling savannahs, lapping shores, rolling valleys and tangled rainforests stand out as perhaps the most prominent features of the continent's celebrated natural beauty. But in the last half-century, an expanding urban topography has been displacing bygone depictions of 'natural Africa', as skyscrapers, suburbs and slums spring up throughout the region. Criminologists have long understood gangs as ubiquitous features of urban life. Up until now, however, they have had relatively little to say about those found in the continent's cities. Most gang studies originate in the United States, Europe, Latin America and the Caribbean. Research on gangs that exist in Africa overwhelmingly concentrates on the same Cape Coloured gangs this book is looking at.

But there are gangs in other African geographies as well. One does not need to go far to find them. Petrus (2015, 2017), for instance, has studied and written about Coloured gangs in the northern areas of Port Elizabeth, a city of about one million that is located about 700 km east of Cape Town. Gangs have flourished in this popular seaside holiday spot, taking advantage of weak authority structures, rampant corruption, unemployment, poverty, insecurity and people's distrust in the state's ability to provide for and protect its citizens. Gang violence in Port Elizabeth, which is also known as Nelson Mandela Bay, contributes to a homicide rate that regularly places it among the 50 most murderous municipalities in the world.[1] Petrus and Kinnes (2019) observe that gangs there provide a sense of identity, some self-protection and access to income, using armed violence to pursue their aims, just like their counterparts in Cape Town do. But Petrus and Kinnes also draw attention to crucial differences between these two South African gang hotspots; gangs on the Cape Flats have grown into criminal enterprises that are much more cohesive, organised and inter-connected than are those in Port Elizabeth.

Gangsterism also has a long lineage in South Africa's biggest city – Johannesburg. As part of his historical analysis of criminal fraternities that operate there, Glaser (2000) identified a range of 'small-time' crews and 'big-time' gangs that made 'Joburg' their home. In particular, he explored the subcultural style of

---

[1] Between 2013 and 2019 it has been among the top 50 cities in the world with the highest murder rates. In 2019, it was ranked 24th in the world (CCSPJP, 2020).

Gang Entry and Exit in Cape Town, 19–37

Copyright © 2021 Dariusz Dziewanski

Published under exclusive licence by Emerald Publishing Limited

doi:10.1108/978-1-83909-730-020210002

tsotsis,[2] Black youth gangs from the township of Soweto, famous for the student-led revolts that started there in 1976 in what is widely viewed as the beginning of the end of apartheid. Unlike Cape-based Coloured gangs, whose identities and organisations were largely maintained throughout the anti-apartheid struggle, Black Sowetan gangsters were engulfed and absorbed by it. Before they became revolutionaries though, marginalised township youth held fast to fighting, bravery, criminality and street style as their main modes of operation, the same 'cultural repertoire' (Hannerz, 1969, p. 191) of gang practices that were displayed by urban subcultures found in other places. Although *tsotsis* share many of the same street cultural traits as their cousins on the southernmost tip of South Africa, Sowetan gangs did not grow and professionalise in the same ways that gangs like the Hard Livings or Americans did. The Black gangs of Soweto continued to display a diverse variety of sizes, identities, motivations and inclinations towards crime. This led Glaser to conclude that 'Gangs are a particular kind of youth association that may be more or less criminal according to circumstances... Crime and gang formation, while often coinciding, follow separate trajectories' (2000, p. 10). Even in the same city one might encounter many permutations of gangs.

Indeed, this is the case in Cape Town, where there are Black gangs as well. They are typically referred to as 'crews' or 'cliques' (Roloff, 2014), and tend to be smaller and less organised than Coloured street gangs. Black Capetonian gangs like the *Vatos* and *Vuras* are more known for fighting with fists, knives and *pangas*[3] than with pistols. 'Unlike coloured gangs, who usually battle with guns over drug turf, the *Vuras* and *Vatos* appear to be influenced by traditional stick fighting in the rural areas from where they, or their parents, often originate', writes Pharie Sefali (2014, p. 2), one of few researchers to investigate these gangs. Her study concludes that gun-related violence is less common among Cape Town's Black gangs because, firstly, hand-to-hand combat is considered more 'manly' to these groups and, secondly, they have less access to firearms than do Coloured gangs. For all that, Black areas are not totally unfamiliar with the crackle of gunfire. Anybody that lives in neighbourhoods like Khayelitsha or Gugulethu knows that gangsters there are prone to their own thuggery. For instance, shortly before this book was published there was a mass shooting in 'Gugs' – as the latter community is known to locals – in which suspects linked to the so-called Boko Haram gang killed seven people and injured two more. The incident confirms that the Black warrior gangs of Khayelitsha and Gugulethu can be quick on the trigger when a situation calls for it, even if they are smaller, less organised and more likely to rely on hand-to-hand combat than the Coloured street gangs of Hanover Park, Manenberg and Mitchells Plain. Cliques and crews in each area in their own ways display many of the same street sensibilities, organising around combativeness and conflict as a way of gaining respect and showing strength. Despite having organisational and cultural differences, they are bound together through common proclivities towards violent street culture. Many

---

[2]A slang word denoting a person who is considered to be a criminal.
[3]A large-bladed knife, like a machete.

Black youngsters in Cape Town look to gangs and gang violence in rebuke to the same exclusion and discrimination faced by Coloured youth (Pinnock, 2016). That this is so indicates that gangs – whether street gangs, cliques or crews – are most likely to sprout roots in the neglected parts of the city, where community development, state control and social order have not satisfactorily taken hold. They flourish where little else survives, spreading like the spiny shrubs and squat grasses that dot the dunes of the Cape Flats, offering succour to those who hold out little hope for blooming in mainstream society.

2.1 Gangs in Africa

Gangs and gang-like groups in the rest of Africa resemble those in South Africa in key ways. All over the continent armed actors are engaged in oppositional street culture, operating in unsustained and ungoverned surroundings where the state has ceded its responsibility to its people. Young Africans adapt by banding together for strength and for clout, endeavouring to get ahead by squeezing opportunities out of informal spaces and illegal markets. Although there is ample evidence that gangs are a continent-wide phenomenon (see: de Benitez, 2007; LeBas, 2013; Matusitz & Repass, 2009; Utas, 2014; Van Damme, 2018), little has been done thus far to relate to each other the hundreds – or thousands – of criminal cadres that exist in cities like Lagos, Nairobi, Kinshasa and Harare. Most studies on gangs in Africa are national in scope, focusing on one to two groups in a single context, giving little in the way of a continental perspective on the subject. There are some exceptions to this rule. Case in point, a chapter on Africa, Asia and Australia by Higginson and Benier (2015) compared gangs in South Africa and Nigeria, illustrating the various ways each gravitate towards violence and criminality in response to discrimination, displacement and acute social and economic inequality. Also, Fraser (2017) scrutinised various African gangs, playing these off of those found in Latin America, Asia and Oceania. He determined that gangs emerge and endure by taking to street culture in unequal urban – or urbanising – communities, but they do so along patterns of subsequent evolution that often diverge, depending on the particular socio-historical circumstances of individual countries, cities and communities. Lastly, an edited volume by Hazen and Rodgers (2014) set out case studies of gangs from South Africa, Kenya and Sierra Leone alongside those from an assortment of continents. They found that there is a push and pull between commonality and difference in gang forms, modalities and typologies, which makes them difficult to singularly define and conceptualise. The quick cross section of South African gangs delivered paragraphs earlier already illustrated the assorted outlaw collectives – cliques, crews and street gangs in different cities – that might reside in any one country. This is to say nothing about the great many more that might be found over the expanse of an entire region or continent. The remainder of this section examines gangs in sub-Saharan Africa, sketching their connections to, and contrasting their differences with, Coloured gangs in Cape Town.

Themes of discrimination, alienation and extreme social and economic disadvantage are central to continental gang studies. All are ingredients in a recipe that combines to make gangs standard fare throughout Africa. Governments get most of the blame for the state of affairs that brings African gangs to be. Corruption, elite capture and embezzlement help funnel public and private resources into the bank accounts of the few well-connected individuals, leaving the majority of Africans empty-handed. In the process, security forces have been co-opted to maintain this status quo, intimidating and at times terrorising local populations without respect for due process of law, clamping down on dissent to further consolidate political power and economic benefits among the upper crust of African society. While this is not true everywhere, there is certainly plenty of condemnation to go around, and considerable consternation among Africans themselves about what is going on with their governance systems. Just half consider their countries as functioning democracies, while a mere 43% are satisfied with how well those democracies are working for them (Mattes, 2019). Present-day governments must be better held to account, in an effort to build greater political integrity in Africa by cleaning up corruption until kickbacks, nepotism, vote-buying and palm-greasing are wiped out. This is a must. Unless political power is consistently exercised in the public interest, rather than to simply sustain power-holders' own wealth or position, it will be difficult to achieve governance that is open, participatory and widely beneficial to all Africans.

While it is just – and necessary – to admonish the state of modern politics in many African countries, one cannot do so without also tying such immediate political problems back to the continent's colonial past. The history of colonialism is one of war and violence. Historical wounds inflicted by colonisers still have not totally healed to this day. They remain raw, chafing and exposed, as economic, social and political injuries that continue to give rise to the distress and disadvantage that lead to the emergence of gangs on all sides of the continent. European imperialists were the original gangsters, invading, occupying, dividing and brutalising during their 'scramble for Africa' in the late nineteenth and early twentieth century. Solely Ethiopia can truly claim to have never have been colonised.[4] The remaining countries had to struggle towards independence through protest, conflict and calamity, in costly decolonisation processes that – generations later – they are still paying for. The partition of the continent by colonial powers arrested the development of African nations, paving the way for graft, stagnation and disparities found there still. Even contemporary corruption is the entrenched extension of the systematic use of material inducements by colonisers to compel traditional, political and bureaucratic elites to collaborate in the colonial project in return for rents and favours (Mulinge & Lesetedi, 1998). The colonial era may have ended in the 1960s, yet colonialism is still very much

---

[4]Ethiopia was briefly occupied by Italy between 1936 and 1941. Also, though Liberia was never conquered by Europeans, it was occupied by freed American slaves who established a de facto colony there in the early 1800s.

present, not only in corruption but also in the continued contestation of borders, cultures, markets and politics that destabilises progress across Africa even today.

It is not just doom and gloom though. Let us not discount that Africa is also a site of significant positive changes and hope. There were 32 peaceful changes of power in between 2015 and 2020. Nineteen times an incumbent head of state stood aside. The steady if uneven rise across the continent of independent judges, vibrant civil society, feisty press and strengthened parliamentary institutions have all made it harder for dodgy leaders to cling to power. So there are persuasive reasons to be bullish on Africa. A little more than a decade after the *The Economist* declared the region 'hopeless' (2000) at the turn of the millennium, the same publication was heralding 'Africa's hopeful economies' (*The Economist*, 2011). The African sun has recently been shining brightly on some of the hottest economies in the world. In 2019, the International Monetary Fund reported that the top five fastest-growing economies were in Africa, with more of the same expected in the years to come. Many countries are taking advantage of the large quantities of natural resources found within their borders, including the largest deposits of cobalt, diamonds, platinum and uranium found anywhere in the world, as well as sizeable supplies of: petroleum, gold, silver, iron, copper, bauxite, timber, cocoa and other resources. The region is rich in other ways too. South Africa is a middle-income nation known for industry and tourism, Kenya's 'Silicon Savannah' is an innovation hub in information technology and the Nigerian film industry – 'Nollywood' – produces the second-most films per year in the world after India.

These are all examples of Africa's progress and potential. They are also the sharp contrast by which the continent's disparities are judged. Despite high aggregate economic growth, sub-Saharan Africa remains highly unequal. Most recent available World Bank data indicate that six countries from the region are among the 10 most unequal in the world. The gap between the prosperity and poverty divides what are in reality two continents. One side is basking in the warm glow of robust economic progress, while the other remains stuck in the dark amid low salaries, high living costs and inadequate social benefits. Many Africans that cannot locate work, housing, food and comfort through legitimate means are forced to source these illegally.

The following pages are a brief, but deliberate, trip through sub-Saharan Africa's criminal netherworld. Our primary point of interest is the continent's gangs. But we stop also to look at looser networks of cliques and crews that traffic in petty transgressions and delinquency, militias and vigilantes that blur the line between protection, predation and politics, as well as gang-adjacent sodalities that take on distinctive forms still. A compendium like this makes no claims to be an exhaustive *tour d'horizon*. It does not visit every country or explore every type of gang-like collective found on the continent. It purposefully and selectively works with available writings to play off of each other variant types of continental criminality. Morselli reasons that there is significant value in being 'able to observe gang members in interaction, but within a wider criminal setting, one that allows us to study the structure of criminal activities and assess gang presence therein' (2008, p. 148). Thus, this chapter casts its comparative net wide and far, in a review of criminological literature throughout sub-Saharan Africa. It goes first to South Africa's regional Southern African neighbours to profile and map the key typologies operating in this area. Later, the chapter stops in East Africa, Central Africa and West Africa to dig into the organisational and behavioural traits of armed groups in those regions, drawing out any lessons learned to bring up-to-date our study of Capetonian gangs.

2.1.1 Southern Africa

Much of Southern African gang writing is seen through the lens of organised crime. Numerous criminal organisations have taken advantage of weak enforcement capabilities, underpaid officials and porous national borders to traffic in sundry illegal goods in the region. Capetonian gangs play an integral role in many of these illicit value chains, especially in relation to drugs and weapons smuggling networks that find an endpoint in Cape Town. For instance, the United Nations International Narcotics Control Board reports that methaqualone, an elemental ingredient in Mandrax, has been shipped through neighbouring Mozambique, Eswatini and Zimbabwe into South Africa (INCB, 2008), where it is eventually sold on the Cape Flats under the street name 'buttons' (INCB, 2014). When it comes to the distribution of marijuana, producers and wholesalers across the region – particularly in Lesotho and Eswatini – sell to middlemen in every corner of South Africa, including to gangs delivering *'dagga'* to the Flats (Paterson, 2009).

But while Capetonian street gangs are an important player in regional criminality, they are just one of many types of groups trading illicit goods in Southern Africa. Looking at the *dagga* coming in from Eswatini shows that it is clusters of Nigerian nationals – about four or five persons – that have become the principal players running cannabis south (Gastrow, Mosse, & Bagenda, 2003). They are much more like small criminal associations than gangs, lacking sufficient size and formalisation to be classified as the latter. Elsewhere in the region, transporters of marijuana vary between large wholesalers and smaller independent merchants (Goga, 2014b). These smugglers are involved in international drug networks that also include gangs. But that does not necessarily make them gangsters. As pointed out by Decker and Pyrooz, 'It is important not to confuse an association of criminals with a criminal association' (2015, p. 295). There are essential organisational and behavioural distinctions that separate gangs from other criminal associations like smuggling rings; gangs tend not to stick to individual illegal specialisations like organised crime groups do, and gangs' penchant for expressing dominance, marking territory and seeking confrontation gives them a level of visibility that others avoid. However, the distinction between gangs and other types of criminal organisations is seldom clear-cut. Decker and Pyrooz themselves grant that 'there are many organizational similarities between gangs and other organized criminal entities, enough to consider them criminal associations as opposed to associations of criminals' (2015, p. 305). Morselli (2008), for instance, indicates that within the gang category there are some factions – Cape Town's super-gangs come to mind – that are closer to organised syndicates than they are to street gangs. Gang researchers cannot dodge the fact of the matter that polymorphism is an inborn feature of their subject of study. Indeed, Standing (2006) argues that even within the same group, crime can be ordered variously at various levels of the organisation; clan-like loyalties prove far more relevant in the localised drug dealing that dominates street-level gang activities, whereas the top tiers of their organograms have the earmarks of organised criminal networks.

All over Southern Africa – as in Africa writ large – criminal categories are far from unambiguous. In the larger pool of regional criminality, there are delinquent posses that exude gang-like qualities, but which might fail to fit most official definitions of what a gang is. To consider one example in detail, street children in the Zimbabwean capital of Harare often live and work together, support each other and fight fiercely to protect their 'base' from outsiders, as gangsters do. For this reason, they might be called gangs, as de Benitez does here:

> Street gang hierarchies both protect and inflict violence. Intimidation
> is the order of the day. Younger children are at the mercy of violent
> behaviour, risking losing earnings and possessions to older, bigger
> boys. As they grow, they in turn socialize new children into street
> based hierarchies and rules enforced by violence. (2007, p. 38)

Others have also pointed out that the street kids of Harare take part in theft, prostitution and the distribution and consumption of drugs (Mugove, 2017), as well as fights with outsiders and each other (Bourdillon, 1994). This does sound a lot like gangs. Indeed, youth in Harare go to the streets for many of the same reasons that juveniles take up with gangs in other localities, flocking together to ameliorate vulnerability and loneliness (Marima, Jordan, & Cormie, 1995; Rurevo & Bourdillon, 2003).

Still, Harare's street kids differ from the street gangs in important ways. Conversations had by researchers with the street children themselves reveal that the violent activities they engage in are usually only of an 'ordinary schoolboy variety' (Marima, Jordan, & Cormie, 1995, p. 22), and not near as savage as those of gangsters. Street gangs are also typically more hierarchical and permanent, while street youth in Zimbabwe might live in temporary arrangements under the patronage of '*monya*', older adolescents who at once look after and exploit those under them (Wright, 2014). Fraser (2017) draws a line through a key distinction in the literature on gangs in Africa: *street children*[5] who are less organised and less violent, versus *street-based youth* like those found in gangs. Taking such distinctions into account, accurately appreciating the peculiarities of the young people we meet on African streets requires that we judiciously regard their varied backgrounds, their distinguishable organisational forms, the social and cultural conditions they face, as well as how they each choose to react to these. Like this

---

[5]The most commonly used definition of 'street children' distinguishes between two categories: children who live in the streets and children who have a home but work for their families in the streets (Aptekar & Stoecklin, 2013).

we can better see youth not as bandits and roughnecks, but as living in the streets as their chosen places, where 'many are appreciated as young people using their initiative to improve their situation' (Bourdillon, 2016, p. 53). As with the street-based youth who join gangs, street children have found a small niche in the world in the physical and cultural milieu of the streets, where they try to make something from nothing, building autonomy and empowerment in what ways they can in an effort to better their lives.

Unfortunately, street children in Harare have historically received considerable adverse publicity in the national press, helping underpin official strategies favouring their harassment and forced relocation (Bourdillon, 1991). In 2005, police laid to waste thousands of 'illegal structures', leaving 700,000 people homeless, following these actions up with a 'crime-fighting measure' codenamed Operation Round Up, as a way of arresting and detaining over 10,000 'vagrants, street kids, touts and other disorderly elements' (Blair, 2006). Being bullied by the cops continues to be a key concern among Harare's street children presently because Zimbabwe's government persists in its intrusive and adversarial policing practices (Mugove & Lincoln, 2015). But roughing up street urchins, and rounding them up for institutionalisation, does nothing to extenuate the unsatisfactory conditions they are mired in. It causes additional physical and psychological damage (Dube, 1997), twinning personal disorder with social disorder by denouncing and dumping on an already at-risk subclass of society.

Such strategies are but a prelude to the way that ostracised collectivities are dealt with around Africa. States all over the continent equally lean on criminal justice approaches that institutionalise, criminalise and further subjugate citizenry that they classify as deviant and delinquent. Whether it is Harare, Cape Town or in cities further afield in Central, West and East Africa, governments are engaged in an on-going game of whack-a-mole. They attempt to pummel street children, street-based youth and other stigmatised groups into submission – usually with little effect. A sceptic could interpret this as a convenient excuse for a political class that has failed to deliver on their duties to young people as citizens and rights-holders. It is easy to attack groups like gangs, pointing to them as dangerously deviant forms of social organisation. What is much more difficult is to pursue a complex and costly agenda of socioeconomic reform – creating jobs, building houses, training police, expanding water access, repairing roads, etc. – to genuinely address the underlying causes of social disorganisation. This is why governments – not just in Africa, but everywhere – insist on the path of least resistance, falling back to disciplinary action as their go-to anti-gang programme, no matter how many times this has failed.

2.1.2 East Africa

The connections of Cape gangs are far-flung, extending well outside of the Southern African region. To start, ties to East African drug markets have played a pivotal role in developing the South African heroin trade, with Tanzanian smugglers making wholesale deliveries to gangs in Cape Town (Haysom, 2019).

Tanzania's 'beachboys' – a subculture of young men known for smuggling by stowing away on container ships – play an important role in the drug supply there (Christie, 2016). Beachboys act as mules and pushers, catering to the city's growing '*unga*' addiction. Military operations in Tanzania's slums have also caused more hardened drug dealers to flee and seek refuge in cities like Cape Town, where they now operate alongside home-grown Cape gangs (Haysom, Gastrow, & Shaw, 2018); Tanzanians have come to control distribution in a few areas (Haysom, 2020). Some have even been initiated into the number while serving time in South African prisons. On the whole, however, Tanzanian criminal groups are still largely subordinate to Capetonian gangsters, who forbid them from carrying firearms, make them pay for protection and disallow them from assembling their own gangs (Haysom, 2020).

There are also those East African criminal groups that do not have direct linkages to Cape Town. Looking at these too tells us something about the motivations and activities of gangs in Africa. Take the *Mungiki*, for example. Called 'Kenya's most notorious criminal gang' (LeBas, 2013, p. 248), they have a membership that might number in the millions. Members of the group have been implicated in extortion schemes, armed robberies, carjackings and bloody battles over taxi routes (Kagwanja, 2006). But the *Mungiki* were not at first criminally inclined. They started off in the 1980s as a religious revolutionary movement that championed cultural rights for Kenya's largest ethnic group – the *Kikuyu* (Wamue, 2001). Their original intent was to advocate for a return to traditional *Kikuyu* customs and values, finding momentum for their movement in feelings of ethnic marginalisation that featured prominently in the group's early self-descriptions (LeBas, 2013). As time passed, the *Mungiki* lost their reformist bearings, morphing into an armed militia that became implicated in butcherous ethno-political clashes, including those that took place after Kenya's 2007 disputed presidential election when 1,500 people were killed as a result of political tribalism (Elfversson & Höglund, 2019). Electoral violence eventually gave way to run-of-the-mill criminality, as the *Mungiki* shifted into the increasingly well-organised and well-resourced organisation it is today.

As they have advanced from rebellion and religion to ballots and bullets they have become a national phobia, a bunch of 'criminal subversives' and 'dreadlocked gangsters' playing a 'barbaric' (Kanneworff, 2008, pp. 115–116) game. The Kenyan government has predictably beat the drums of war against the typecast *Mungiki*, besieging them with a specialised police unit – essentially a death squad that executed 500 suspected members over a period of months in 2007 (KNCHR, 2008). Repressive state measures like these are eerily familiar to most gang researchers. Governments all around the world are waging a 'war on gangs' (Geneva Declaration Secretariat, 2008). So the Kenyan state is not alone in this regard. Be that as it may, it went on the offensive, rather than taking responsibility for its own role in the formation and growth of the *Mungiki*, a pseudo-statal organisation that flourishes amid the failures of governance and development that are endemic to the slums of Nairobi where it currently keeps its home base (Rasmussen, 2014). The social malaise that bolsters up the *Mungiki* is not unlike the circumstances that give life to drug merchants and gang leaders in

Cape Town, who 'should be viewed as both cause *and* [emphasis in original] effect of inadequate state authority and an inability by the state to provide a monopoly of force and basic social and economic security' (Standing, 2006, pp. 232–233). Violent organisations like these are able to assert some form of legitimacy only based on the inability of governments to serve and protect their own constituents.

Where states fail, gangs step in. The *Mungiki* are certainly trying to achieve some form of localised power over communities and markets, which makes them comparable to gangs. But despite being frequently branded as gangsters, *Mungiki* members themselves reject the label, drawing instead on a collective identity woven together from: ideological connections to revolutionary social movements, the struggle for cultural emancipation and an opposition to injustices inflicted by a brutish Kenyan state (Rasmussen, 2014). Indeed, being '*Mungiki*' can mean a multiplicity of things depending on who is speaking about it, and when. It might point to a religio-cultural movement, a local manifestation of anti-globalisation forces, a political organisation, a criminal gang, a vigilante group or some combination of these (Ruteere, 2008). Ebbing and flowing between revolution and criminality – at times fighting the state, and at times fighting for it – the *Mungiki* are a representative case for the dynamism and subjectivity that is characteristic of armed organisations in Africa. There is a general lack of conceptual clarity when it comes to criminal collectives in Kenya too. The term 'gang', for instance, is as a container for all non-state actors involved in violent activities, whether it be historical revolutionary organisations or modern-day urban groups that resemble American gangs (Rasmussen, 2020). The challenges that authorities and researchers have had in particularising what is and what is not a gang in Kenya foreshadows more wide-ranging dilemmas in comparing, categorising and universalising typologies for a social entity that appears mercurial and highly context-specific.

What we can say about gangs and analogous groups is that they emerge in similar situations, as a subcultural community where the disenchanted organise around their frustrations. The *Mungiki's* message rings true among the Kenyan capital's urban poor (Kagwanja, 2003); they purport in various ways to confront the same socioeconomic challenges that youth in all African countries face in their own fight for citizenship. But as armed groups so often do, the *Mungiki* have ended up fighting amid themselves and violating the rights of oppressed citizens, damaging their communities through unlawful and destructive activities (Kilonzo, 2012). The most superlative accounts of their history cannot brush aside the fact that crime and violence related to the *Mungiki* have only worsened social disorder, undermining the interests of the very people they claim to be fighting for. Yet, despite their undeniable corruptness, the *Mungiki* are also a motley, polysemic and ambiguous grouping, whose identity is difficult to encompass in a simple moralistic appraisal, or any singular analytical concept. The amorphous nature of the *Mungiki* is credible evidence of the growing realisation among gang scholars of an urgent need for dynamic and adaptable research techniques:

> New sociological accounts of gangs must therefore attend to issues
> of continuity and change, similarity and difference, structure and

agency in ways that are attentive to the global and local contexts of
the contemporary gang landscape. (Fraser, 2015, p. 29)

Favouring techniques that are flexible, contextual and personal might better
capture both the apparent longevity and changing character of armed organisations in Africa. The result would be more accurate gang research products, less
dramatised anti-gang policies and a better-balanced reflection on the everyday
scramble many Africans engage in to counter the often treacherous social conditions that are too bare, too cramped and too starved to adequately nurse needs
into ambitions in their respective lands.

2.1.3 Central Africa

Central Africans are also no strangers to turmoil and insecurity. Most notably,
from the 1990s, thousands fled economic uncertainty, political instability and
violence in the Democratic Republic of Congo (DRC), in what was the deadliest
conflict seen anywhere since World War II. Some settled down in South Africa.
Most that did so were middle-class and educated (Steinberg, 2005), but among
them were also transnational criminal entrepreneurs that snuck through South
Africa's porous borders (Standing, 2006). Organised crime groups from the DRC
have reportedly been involved in the trafficking of drugs and in the illegal trade of
gold and diverse natural resources into South Africa (Hübschle, 2010) via
smuggling routes from Zimbabwe, Zambia and the Congos (Pinnock, 2016).
More recently, Congolese refugees have also been indirectly linked to illegal
activities in Cape Town's club scene, though their participation is usually limited
to providing muscle as legally employed bouncers (Shaw, 2016).

On-going fighting over DRC's vast amounts of oil, diamonds and gold continues to create instability back in sub-Saharan Africa's biggest nation, nourishing
the delinquent groups, militias and gangs that roam its jungles and streets. One of
DRC's most fearsome armed groups is the *kuluna*, a type of gang infamous
throughout the capital Kinshasa. Going by names like *Armée Rouge*, *Câble Noir*,
Pas d'Entrée, *Etats-Unis* and *Cinquantenaire*,[6] *kuluna* factions are typically made
up of collectives of 10–20 indigent and poorly educated young males, who
organise around strength, daring and indomitability (Human Rights Watch,
2014). Self-described as 'socially dead' (IDRC, 2016), they lack legal means of
overcoming existential concerns in their derelict, dicey and badly planned
neighbourhoods. So they turn instead to theft, prostitution, rape and gangsterism.
The *kuluna* also attach importance to territoriality, seeing turf as part of a
communal identity that is expressed in fights to control neighbourhoods, which
they violently defended against all comers (De Boeck & Baloji, 2016; Van Damme,
2018).

The work of anthropologist Filip De Boeck (2012), who has written about the
group at length, shows that *kuluna* tend to attack authority figures as a way of

---

[6]Meaning red army, black cable, no entry, United States and fiftieth anniversary, respectively.

seizing parts of Kinshasa. Once in power, they take on the traits of a pseudo-state, favouring a type of street cultural jurisprudence that imposes influence through identity-based militarised law and order. Urban authorities have responded by trying to '"sanitise" and recolonise' (De Boeck, 2011, p. 151) the capital. This included the scandalous Operation *Likofi*. Meaning 'punch' in the local language *Lingala*, the 2013 measure was censured by human rights observers for abuses committed by police officers, which included 51 executions and 33 disappearances. Here is yet another illustration of how the law works to the detriment and demise of marginal people in Africa. An investigative report compiled by Human Rights Watch on the operation makes for gruesome reading. 'When the police executed a suspect, they sometimes called people to come look at the body. In many cases, they left the body in the street, perhaps to frighten others' (2014, pp. 2–3), the report found. There is also mounting evidence that Operation *Likofi* is merely a hypocritical ploy concocted by politicians who join forces with the *kuluna* when they need some dirty work done. Many of the same authorities crusading against them are recruiting members to attack political opponents or infiltrate anti-government campaigns (De Boeck, 2018), and have been doing so for years (Human Rights Watch, 2014; Wolters, 2011).[7] Such is the duplicitous game played by the government, surreptitiously pandering to the *kuluna* when it suits their interests, and then turning around to lay into them in public as misfits and scoundrels when that is more expedient.

But the *kuluna* are not the only peripheral group that Congolese officials treat like this. They also have their sights locked on fraternities of homeless youth called *bashege* (or *shege*), who share the streets with the *kuluna*. Like the *kuluna*, the *bashege* also try to make meaning and significance in the remotest corners of Kinshasa (Geenen, 2009), using conflict to protect their domain and the revenues they make from petty theft, drugs and prostitution (Numbi, 2013). So the two groups are quite similar – species of the same genus, both set in a communal urban environment, with shared origins as social outcasts. But they are not exactly alike. A key difference is that the *bashege* eschew the extreme violence practiced by the *kuluna* (Van Damme, 2018). 'The *bashege* [emphasis added] are the pigs in the farmhouse, and the *kuluna* [emphasis added] are the wild boars in the forest. But they are both pigs' (Hendriks, Ponsaers, & Shomba Kinyamba, 2013, p. 91), explained one member of the latter group.

---

[7]Human Rights Watch in The DRC reports that 'The *kuluna* phenomenon began around the time of Congo's national elections in 2006. Joseph Kabila, [Congo's president 2001–2019], came to power in 2001 following the assassination of his father, Laurent Kabila, and claimed victory during the 2006 and 2011 elections. In both elections, Kabila's majority alliance and members of the political opposition used the *kuluna* to provide physical protection to candidates, disrupt demonstrations of competing parties, or target supporters of political opposition. Politicians have also paid the *kuluna* to participate in political demonstrations and inflate the number of their supporters. Politicians on both sides reportedly distributed money, machetes, motorcycles, and other materials to *kuluna* to gain their support' (2014, pp. 12–13).

Even though the *kuluna* are more violent, the Congolese state often lumps the two groups together as a singular threat, using the catch-all heavy-handed measures to try to 'sanitise' Kinshasa of what they consider to be social refuse (De Boeck, 2011). Police destroy *bashege* shacks and otherwise obliterate their territories in an attempt to manage street youth presence in public spaces, sometimes forcibly removing and dumping them in remote spots of the city (Geenen, 2009). That *bashege* and *kuluna* are more and more being referred to interchangeably perhaps reflects the aggressive criminalisation of street children and the ensuing increased use of violence by *bashege* as a defense mechanism (Kahola-Tabu, 2014). It should not be an unexpected convergence. Repression tactics press street children like the *bashege* into taking confrontational postures more readily attached to street-based youth like the *kuluna*. The result is an overall escalation of the types of violent street cultural strategies the state is purportedly fighting, drawing into the fracas street children who are otherwise simply trying to survive on society's sidelines.

2.1.4 West Africa

West African criminal syndicates, and in particular those from Nigeria, also have linkages to Cape Town. As civil war, state collapse and economic decline created the conditions for West African organised crime, locally based criminality extended from its nooks in Nigeria to the more sizeable opportunities offered by the Southern African region, and especially in comparatively affluent South Africa (Shaw, 2002). Only a few years after South Africa's first democratic elections in 1994, Nigerian networks based in Cape Town were already supplying gangs on the Cape Flats with drugs such as *unga* and *tik* (Pinnock, 2016).[8] There are crucial domains of difference between these Nigerian and South African groups though. While gangs are organised around violence, West African criminal organisations are highly fluid webs of close-knit ethnic and clan alliances, whose overriding profit motive makes them anxious not to attract attention by openly engaging in violent acts (Shaw, 2001); internal disputes are customarily resolved by simply shunning and excluding non-cooperating actors from money-making arrangements. When violence is needed it is 'contracted-out' to local hoodlums who are all too willing – and able – to take it on.

Nevertheless, it is armed groups still in Nigeria that actually have the most in common with gangs in Cape Town; for gangs and other groups across the country, urban violence serves as a symbolic demand for the transformation of socioeconomic relations with the Nigerian state (Kwaghga, 2014). Nigeria has the continent's most prosperous economy and its most populated country, accounting

---

[8]Trafficking of narcotics is a significant activity. But they also engage in varied criminal activities like: advanced fee fraud, cheque and credit card fraud, dealing in stolen goods, human trafficking, armed robbery, kidnapping and the use of the Internet for criminal purposes (Shaw, 2001).

for almost one-quarter of all African output and one-in-every-six people. But it also has a history of instability. Precipitous population growth and unplanned urbanisation, especially, are drivers of armed organisation in Nigeria.[9] Akinwale and Aderinto argue that the convergence of these two trends has brought the Nigerian state into crisis:

> The major fallout of the Nigerian crisis of governance is the proliferation of urban violence of various dimensions such as ethno-religious violence, electoral violence, youth militancy and civil unrest. (2011, p. 50)

The frailty of the Nigerian state seeds the poverty, unemployment, corruption and injustice that become the recruitment grounds for gangs, militants, militias and many other classes of combatants; these include terrorist cells, such as the ill-famed Boko Haram[10] that operates in the country's north, as well as the Movement for the Emancipation of the Niger Delta (MEND)[11] in the country's oil-rich southern delta (Okolo & Ejime, 2018). Curry indicates that terrorist groups like Boko Haram and MEND and street gangs have mutual motivations, with each using violence as a form of 'self-help' (2011, pp. 99–100). But he also outlines a number of differences between terrorism and gangsterism: gangs are more likely to be localised, profit-driven and engaged in a miscellany of crimes, whereas terrorists are ordinarily driven by ideology, have cross-national networks and are more criminally specialised. The presence of other types of Nigerian 'self-help' security forces – like the Bakassi Boys – is also in large part explained as an adaptation to the failure of the government and its security institutions (Ibrahim, 2006). Whereas Nigerian vigilante squads may not appear to exactly fit the criteria for a gang either, their attempts to accrue authority by controlling and defending urban areas are very suggestive of what gangs do. When they first started, the Bakassi Boys strove to gain legitimacy from local ethnicities by protecting them against crime in the absence of effective public safety services. As the Bakassi Boys came of age, however, organisational slippage has made them

---

[9]Nigeria experienced massive urbanisation and population growth during the twentieth century. According to World Bank statistics, the population of the country has grown from about 45 million in 1960 to almost 200 million in 2018, and more than half of all Nigerians now live in cities; in 1960, only about 15% of Nigeria's population was urban.

[10]Boko Haram is best known for its fundamentalist ideology. But they are also an offshoot of extreme poverty prevalent in northern Nigeria, and the belief that the political economy of the country has historically been skewed to the benefit of the south (Olaniyan & Asuelime, 2014).

[11]Many of MEND's grievances have also anchored their resistance on exclusion from the benefits of the oil industry, and the resultant lack of social development, inadequate governance, widespread poverty and high levels of unemployment that are still the norm in the Niger Delta region in spite of more than half a century of oil production (Courson, 2009).

increasingly inclined to self-interested violent crime. 'The irony of the Bakassi Boys', writes Smith, is that:

> ...they were eventually discredited precisely because they came to be seen as co-opted by politicians... [Their] vigilantism served to deflect or to obscure the role of politicians and the state in perpetuating the conditions that produce crime, insecurity, and inequality. (2007, p. 129)

So we can see that these Nigerian militias have some gang-like characteristics, even if they cannot be clearly defined as such.

Another interesting parallel between the Bakassi Boys and violent groups in Cape Town is to People Against Gangsterism and Drugs (PAGAD), a Capetonian vigilante organisation that gained prominence in the mid-1990s for ambushing gangsters and firebombing their houses. PAGAD famously shot and immolated Rashaad Staggie outside his home in Salt River, killing the leader of the Hard Livings gang and leaving his twin brother Rashied in charge. Pratten (2008) suggests that vigilantes found in South Africa, in Nigeria and elsewhere in Africa all spring from deficiencies in state authority, poor governance and inadequate production of social and political order. However, vigilantism is an ineffective form of opposition because it does not transform or transcend the inefficient state. Protection groups instead become weapons used for survival and short-term gain, only serving to weaken the state to an even greater degree (Kwaghga, 2014). Further, there appears to be a fine line between self-help and self-interest, as many collectives formed for the purposes of protest and protection slide into predation. For instance, the 'jungle justice' of the Bakassi Boys eventually spread into attacks on politicians and members of other ethnicities (Harnischfeger, 2003). In Cape Town, PAGAD's anti-gang *raison d'être* gave way to acts of urban terrorism against South African police, as well as to onslaughts on religious, business and civilian targets that were deemed to contradict their fundamentalist Islamic belief system (Dixon & Johns, 2001). In other words, the self-defence group devolved to resemble the very gangsters it pitted itself against originally.

In Nigeria, research on gangs is focused on a pair of cities: Lagos and Kano. These are the nation's two biggest urban centres and places that have increased manifold since the mid-twentieth century. Lagos, the bigger of the two, is now a mega city where inadequate infrastructure, unequal provision of services, housing shortages, high crime rates and street violence are pronounced (Aliyu & Amadu, 2017). Its crowded, cracking streets might be the setting where shortfalls of governance are most apparent in Nigeria. The main arbiters of criminality and violence in Lagos are known as 'area boys': loosely organised gangs of small-time criminals usually made up of street children and jobless minors languishing around the city, who band together to try to stay alive by dealing out various delinquencies (Heap, 2009). Their lives are circumscribed spatially and socioeconomically, revolving around the localities they live in (Gore & Pratten, 2003). So some factions of area boys inevitably gravitate towards criminal activity as an alternative for empowerment, by running protection rackets, selling drugs, robbing and stealing, and embarking on turf wars with contending crews (Salaam & Brown, 2012). 'Area boys also engaged in gang warfare on the streets to nourish macho images. Rival outfits engage each other in brutal fighting to demonstrate superiority', writes Adisa (1994, p. 162). They are like the majority of street-inclined youth, crammed together by restrictive opportunity structures. With poor choices on all sides, they turn against others like them to win whatever small advantages are available, never mind if they might get hurt in the process.

Public discourse around area boys fixates on the more obscene dimensions of what they do and who they are. As such, it tends to be dictated more by fear than by fact. Since colonial times the 'juvenile delinquent' has been a distinct social concern in Lagos, cooked up from collective anxieties and wild conjectures that oftentimes conflated an urban way of life – working and playing in the street – with real offences, criminalising young people by lumping street traders in with organised street gangs (Fourchard, 2006). Crude speculation precipitated uncritical policy-making. Young men and women in Nigeria are subject to what Kirschner calls 'epistemic terrorisation' (2009, p. 369) whereby they are treated as a problem to be objectified, organised, controlled and disciplined. By denouncing youth as 'delinquents', the Nigerian government has enacted an administrative machinery that does nothing but turn a large portion of young urban populations into criminals (Fourchard, 2010).

A more humanistic analysis of Lagos street children yields a much different version of facts. For instance, Heap disputes the lurid stories detailed in Nigerian newspapers of organised area boy gangs lawlessly plundering and pillaging from respectable citizens; on the contrary, he portrays them as lost youngsters banding together to better look after themselves. 'For those single youths living on the streets, joining others in similar predicaments offered them group protection and solace against the destitution of their situations' (2009, pp. 50–51), he wrote. According to Heap, boys drifted into comradeship, but not necessarily into criminal organisation. They begged, pickpocketed, stole and touted. Not with coordinated intent, but in a relatively spontaneous way because it satisfied crucial material and physical needs through opportunities offered outside of mainstream city life. Lagos is not the only spot Nigerian youth live like this. Some version of street children or street-based youth can be found in cities throughout; young men and women all over the country are turning to subcultural collectivities as an alternative to the failed state apparatus (Ajibade, 2006). Intense unemployment, lack of economic growth and an ongoing governance crisis are prompting young Nigerians to redefine their present realities by creating meaning in new social worlds through innovative forms of street-based association (Kakwagh & Ikwuba, 2010).

It is in Nigeria's second city, Kano, where we find what might be its most frightening gang – the *yandaba* (or *yan daba*). They have been described as 'gangs of unemployed youth who reject the poor conditions to which their social back-ground has relegated them by taking refuge in criminal and violent activities' (Ya'u, 2000, p. 162). Youngsters from lower socioeconomic backgrounds make up the greater part of their constituency, partaking in a number of familiar street practices: extensive drug and alcohol use, looting or theft, participation in the sex trade and carrying out political vendettas and other violent behaviours (Salaam, 2011b). Matusitz and Repass found that they are mostly comprised of disaffected boys and girls who lack a definite place in society and tend to respond to disrespect by 'committing egregious acts of violence' as a part of an aggressive, confrontational and racialised 'resistance identity' (2009, pp. 503–504).[12] Their resemblance to the oppositional identities of Cape-based street cultured actors is unmistakable. Common ground between the groups does not end there either. In contrast to the extreme Islamic faith members profess, *Yandaba* 'adopted a style of dress they associated with media depictions of "Westside niggers", or Los Angeles-based rappers' (Casey, 2013, p. 215). In their sunglasses, chains and baggy jeans, they are playing out a 'globalised oppositional repertoire' (Dziewanski, 2020d) that street cultural heroes like American rapper Tupac Shakur have popularised throughout Cape Town and the rest of Africa. According to South African gang scholar Elaine Salo (2005), a structuralist analysis of gangs in the Nigerian context finds identical origins to Capetonian gang subcultures; each is an expression of resistance to the dominant political economy of their societies in the 1980s – apartheid in South Africa and Nigeria under military dictatorship and structural adjustment.

The 'gang' label has been applied to both Lagos' area boys (Salaam, 2011c; Salaam & Brown, 2012) and Kano's *yandaba* (Matusitz & Repass, 2009; Salaam, 2011a). The involvement of both groups in street-level activities like violence is patently gang-like. Yet, the two groups also have important differences. For example, areas boys also have been categorised simply as informal collections of juvenile delinquents that have structures and practices not totally in keeping with the organised hierarchies found in street gangs (Fourchard, 2011; Heap, 2009). Alternatively, *Yandaba* are more likely to straddle the boundary between criminal gangs and political thugs, on one hand (Gomment & Esomchi, 2017; Umar, 2007), and religious rebels, on the other (Casey, 2012). How each is defined is perhaps immaterial, at least in the context of this book. The goal here was not to develop an exact taxonomy of armed groups in Nigeria, but rather to examine their characteristics and to draw connections to gangs in Cape Town. Doing so shows that area boys and the *yandaba* are part of a complex ecosystem of violent organisations that permeates all regions and all segments of Nigerian society. They are connected to a continuum of gangs, vigilantes, terrorists and other oppositional collectivities that can be found throughout the nation, as in all parts of Africa, wherever marginalised men and women come together in an attempt to counter convergent states of economic disrepair, political disenfranchisement and social despair.

---

[12]We should keep in mind that criminal behaviours are not the result of misguided morals and wickedness. There is evidence to show that *yandaba* youth do not easily engage in criminal activities without first taking part in 'strategic intoxication' (Salaam, 2011a, p. 126) to give them the necessary courage to carry out violent acts and to instil fear in people.

2.2 Reconsidering African Gangs

The preceding sections were taken selectively from a patchy literature base on African gangs. Nevertheless, they still present a significant opportunity to explore how armed groups form around the undulating economic, political and social features of the continent's distinctive regional, national and subnational geographies. High birth rates and movement to cities are steadily straining African governments' ability to bring their populations stability and safety. State incapacity also allows transnational criminal networks to take advantage of weak regional regulation to traffic drugs and other illicit goods across the continent. Capetonian gangs are a key link in Africa's illicit value chains. While the coterie of producers, traffickers and wholesalers in this continental drug drama are all brought together by mutually agreeable self-interests, they are best described as criminal associates, rather than as associations of a unified criminal typology. As a rule, the Mother City's gangs are much more prone to public displays of violence, since they go after their enemies and try to take their territory. The rest – be they Tanzanian smugglers or Nigeria drug entrepreneurs – typically favour the profit motive and a low profile.

'Africa is not a country', so the saying goes. The landscape of African criminality is as varied as are the nations on the continent. Communities in different parts of Sub-Saharan Africa have birthed armed groups that are organised differently, and which relate differently to the states and neighbourhoods they are embedded in. Plenty are kindred to gangs, balancing between disenchantment and desire as gangs do, even if they do not fit prevalent ideas of what a 'gang' is or see themselves as such; Nigerian area boys control territory and defend their communities, providing members with status and safety; the *kuluna* in Congo and the *Mungiki* in Kenya use intimidation and violence to achieve local authority; and street children in Zimbabwe band together, seeking strength in numbers. Patterns of collective violence even in individual African countries may not take one particular form. In Nigeria alone, organisations like Boko Haram, the Bakassi Boys, area boys and the *yandaba* all stake their own claim to the country's crimino-political economy in ways and for reasons that are alike as well as distinct. In DRC too, *kuluna* gangs share the streets of Kinshasa with *bashege* street youth trying to make a home in the cracks and crevices of the emerging city.

The variable nature of Africa's violent non-state actors points back to conceptual ambiguities that call into question what kind of fraternity can really be called a gang. The intention of those striving for a standard definition of gangs has been to introduce objectivity into criminology, translating social experiences into predefined objects based on criminogenic traits. Yet, the push to reduce gang members into measurable categories and patterns of social dysfunction has thus far failed to reach any consensus on what a standardised, or 'objective', definition of gangs might be. It is probable then that the problem is not in researchers' inability to find the correct way to be objective, but that the aspiration for objectivity itself is problematic. Truly, there is no reason to believe that short-sighted standardised gang definitions that arose in America would be symmetrical with urban subcultures in Africa (Cunnen, 2012). Predominant criminological frameworks were established in the west, to understand and explore crime and crime control within specific western contexts, argues Cunnen, going on to say that there is a need for a 'critical and reflexive framework that questions the centrality of a western understanding of crime and control' (2012, 252). Armed groups in Africa – be they gangs or merely gang-like – vary from each other idiosyncratically in their social shapes, identities and motivations, and will vary from those encountered overseas. The analysis presented in this chapter gives additional ballast to the argument against so-called 'global' approaches to classifying and addressing gangs (Brotherton, 2015). It echoes Brotherton's call for a 'critical, anti-colonial ethnography' to help understand stigmatised subaltern groups based on 'the premise that social and cultural phenomena emerge out of tensions between the agents and interests of those who seek to control everyday life and those who have little option but to resist this relationship of domination' (2015, 80). Gang formation is more likely, and participation is more attractive, when pathways to legitimate personal, social and economic actualisation are blocked or disrupted by social upheaval or marginalisation.

Deprivation is not a direct cause of conflict. But the appeals being made and possibilities being offered by armed groups are certain to find a more sympathetic ear among a citizenry that is impoverished and downtrodden. Disaffected Africans, from Zimbabwe to DRC to Nigeria to South Africa, are taking to the streets in quickly urbanising settings, as economic polarisation swells and social disorganisation spreads, pressuring state authorities that are too worn out to push back with any great strength or determination. As the excluded seek refuge in violent street culture, they improvise substitutes to legal enterprise, formalised government administration and political participation, in an attempt to make sense of and make the most of their circumstances.

Rather than emphasising the social issues contributing to gang development, African states choose largely to frame the 'gang problem' in terms of delinquency, hooliganism and criminality. At best, stereotyping of this sort undermines the autonomy of poor young Africans. At worst, it provides public support and political cover for repressive policies aimed at 'undesirable' social elements. In Kenya, hundreds have been murdered in extrajudicial killings by security forces. Police executions and disappearances are not uncommon in the DRC either, while Zimbabwean police regularly 'cleanse' public spaces of society's castaways. In South Africa, the army and police periodically team up to attack township communities. Para-militaristic security strategies of this type are founded on and publicise the false premise that armed collectives are made up of sophisticated criminal sociopaths, wantonly preying on the masses. We have seen how far this is from the truth. Gangs and gang-like groups are not the problem. They are symptoms of larger social dilemmas. For the youth that join them, they represent an adaptive – though admittedly aggressive – response to the division, dereliction and demoralisation afflicting African underclasses, something that will be highlighted again and again, as we turn our analysis back to the continent's deadliest city.

Chapter 3

A City Still Segregated

Although apartheid's segregationist policies were dismantled in 1994, its legacy of exclusion unquestionably lingers in Cape Town. Scarcity is the standard for the majority of non-whites, even if a small Black elite has cashed in its anti-apartheid revolutionary capital for political and business connections, and some of South Africa's emerging middle-class Coloureds have also managed to bootstrap their way to better lives. Today, Cape Town remains one of the most unequal cities in the world (Mammon, 2016). But inequality is about more than what different people earn at the end of the day. Who they know is another important source of socioeconomic disparity, as is what they know. Pierre Bourdieu understood this. He developed concepts like 'social capital'[1] (1986, pp. 248–252) and 'cultural capital' (1986, pp. 47–51) in order to account for the important non-monetary measures of societal polarisation. The first concept recognises that personal gains can be made simply from getting invited to the right dinner party, getting accepted to a posh club or getting into a first-rate school. The second concept acknowledges that a great deal of what is taught in elite social circles is intangible and atmospheric; book smarts, good grades and scholarly degrees are all important, but these can only get you so far. The brand of suit you have, how it is cut and the way you wear it can say just as much about you as the letters after your name. So is knowing about what artists are in at the moment, or that one should subscribe to *The New Yorker* and form opinions about its articles. All are important bits of insider information acquired over a lifetime of informal education in high-class social milieus. Ostensibly immaterial, the 'inconspicuous consumption' (Currid-Halkett, 2017, p. 37) of cultural capital is perhaps more vital than ever in paving the way for people to obtain political appointments, professional contacts and remunerative vocations. High-status facts, artefacts and practices are not easily perceived, making them an exclusive – and exclusionary – signifier of symbolic social boundaries (Lamont & Lareau, 1988). The more fragmented a society, the more cut off are the reserves of elite cultural capital to those near the bottom of the social ladder.

---

[1]In contemporary usages, the concept of social capital is often made synonymous with horizontal social cohesion (Putnam, Leonardi, & Nanetti, 1994). Bourdieu's (1986) focus is vertical. Others have also used the concept to explicitly recognise vertical power differentials in social relations (Szreter & Woolcock, 2004).

Gang Entry and Exit in Cape Town, 39–75
Copyright © 2021 Dariusz Dziewanski
Published under exclusive licence by Emerald Publishing Limited
doi:10.1108/978-1-83909-730-020210003

Segregation is still the de facto arrangement of urban planning in South Africa, with cultural groups residing in distinct areas and living according to distinct customs, often with very little real-life integration in terms of whom they spend time with in spaces of living, entertainment, consumption and production (Bray, Gooskens, Kahn, Moses, & Seekings, 2010). As a result, Cape Town's poor and racialised communities often have restricted contact with mostly-white upper-middle-class settings and are frequently left out of the sociocultural networks that link people to educational and professional openings. Naturally, no one neighbourhood is totally closed off from the rest, as township inhabitants regularly travel out to work or to shop, to handle clerical matters, to visit friends or relatives and to enjoy leisure; but territoriality is undeniably essential to understanding Capetonian society. 'Spatial strategies have meant that the [post-apartheid] townships have become a central feature in the everyday lives of coloured people of a certain social standing' (2008, p. 12), argued Jensen. Understood like this, the township is a point at which place and personality meet and fuse through repetitive social interactions in physical space.

All social surroundings form a backdrop to the self in fact. They are the places where quotidian life questions are usually contemplated. How do I pay the bills? How do I acquire social stature? How do I find belonging? And purpose? Every person tries to answer these in their own manner, learning from others as they attempt to do the same. Anybody finding success presses a footpath for the next person. The most efficacious courses of action are encapsulated in memories, gossip and community lore, coming to life through the individual and collective dispositions of folks that live together. Joining a gang is just one available strategy in a township setting. Faith, careers and family are others. All are potential social outlets that compete for people's attention. The vast majority of township residents never join gangs. Nevertheless, gangsters have a disproportionate impact on the consciousness of communities. They find easy money, are respected – or dreaded – and are part of a powerful brotherhood, striking a booming tone that can usually be heard by everybody around them. Even those township dwellers who close the door to gangs cannot entirely shut out what is happening in the streets.

Sociological researchers have long argued that where we live and spend our time nurtures who we are, how we think and what we might mature into. Bourdieusian social theory takes this a step further. It is not just social learning that is at issue here. What opportunities for learning are even available depends on where a person's place of residence is ranked according to the overarching social pyramid of his or her city or town. 'It is the structure of the relations constitutive of the space... which determines the forms that can be assumed by the visible relations of interaction and the very content of the experience that agents may have of them', argues Bourdieu (1985, p. 192). Criminologists have absorbed Bourdieu's ideas into their own research on street culture, in order to draw attention to the fact that concentrations of urban disorganisation often result in a rooted attachment to crime and violence in excluded parts of places like Cape Town. Its downtown and suburbs are full of promise, possibility and choice, while township residents have to compete among each other for the little that is left. Legal possibilities for gaining independence and agency are thin. As individuals attempt to mitigate the deepest schisms of the modern city, many learn that turning to street life can help distinguish them from their friends and neighbours.

The streets represent a marginal social space based on Bourdieu's concept of the 'field' (Bourdieu, 1993, pp. 30–31), where forms of cultural capital are produced and contested. Shammas and Sandberg define the 'street field'[2] as follows:

> The 'street' is that continuum of actions and cultural practices that are centered around various forms of illegalities and crimes that can be understood through what they are not: they are not the crimes of… the state, corporations, and so on; instead, they are the crimes of the dominated. (2016, p. 207)

They are not referring to an actual street, or any other physical locale, but rather an abstraction of social relations from physical space. Social settings are constructed according to the kinds of power, or capital, that are available and favourable in different fields. The life potential of individuals and groups is defined by their relative positions in such social fields based on their ability to collect such capital and power (Bourdieu, 2005). Competition between social actors in 'the street' – as in any social field – takes place in the realm of ideas, language, action, argumentation and the wide range of other modalities of human interaction whereby reputation, rank and prestige are apportioned. Bourdieu frequently calls on the game metaphor (Bourdieu, 1977, 1990) to indicate that contests in social fields have certain rules and requirements that define the terms of play for cultural, social, symbolic and material 'prizes and profits' (Bourdieu & Wacquant, 1992, p. 98). The game Capetonians play is rigged, of course. The ratio of risk and reward favours the rich, as part of 'the invariant, or indeed universal, content of the relationship between the dominant and the dominated' (Bourdieu, 1985, p. 737). Cape Town's urbanites and sub-urbanites have much greater access to the gatekeepers of education and employment that ultimately decide society's winners and losers. The prospects for those shoved onto the Cape Flats, by contrast, are structured by racism, poor pay, gruelling working conditions, state neglect and community insecurity. Dominant society has deemed them expendable. Some have taken this to heart, willing to gamble their lives for a stab at material attainment and a sense of self, however risky or fleeting. They have chosen instead to manufacture their own illicit opportunities by attaching to gang identities and territories, in what amounts to a world unto itself. It is a social sphere that exists in parallel and the rest of Cape Town, moving according to its own rules, ethics and expectations. On

---

[2]Sandberg (2008, pp. 156–157) notes important differences between street culture and Bourdieu's concepts of field and capital. First, street culture lacks formal institutions of traditional fields. Second, street capital accumulation is specific to street culture, lacking the transferability that cultural capital has across social space.

those infrequent occasions that there is overlap, the results can be jarring. Like crossing an imaginary border to another country. In the preface I described the cultural dislocation I experienced arriving in a *kampie* with Gavin. Below we see that the sense of culture shock he feels when venturing to Cape Town's downtown and suburbs is just as harsh, as Gavin too comes into close contact with the opposite extremes of the segregated city.

3.1 Culture Shock

3.1.1 Gavin

The following vignette starts with Gavin (Ottery male, 30 years) making a trip to the west coast suburb of Table View for a job interview. Unfamiliar with Cape Town's suburban geography, he was unsure of how much taxi fare to borrow for the journey. He did not take enough. Left with insufficient funds for a trip home, Gavin decided to walk down from the west coast towards the city. After five hours of slowly watching Table Mountain rise up through the mid-summer haze, he reached the leafy university enclave of Rondebosch where I stayed at the time. It was the only stop Gavin could think of along the way to Ottery. I returned at the end of the workday to find him sitting at my front gate. Exhausted and exasperated, he described how he had attempted to charge his phone at local businesses, solicited the use of other people's mobiles and asked passers-by for taxi money. After all of his overtures were snubbed or met with contempt, he at last conceded:

> I don't know the place bro. It's the city. If I'm at home, I know the hustle. There [in Table View] nobody would help me. And I was even wearing these [professional] clothes and acting proper. But, fuck bro, nobody would help. So, I just kept walking.

City-dwelling Capetonians would probably dispute Gavin's assertion that Table View is really 'the city'. In reality, Table View is one of Cape Town's suburbs. It actually looks across the teal waters of Table Bay at the Mother City's peaks from about the same distance as the part of Ottery where Gavin stays. The difference is that Ottery is predominately Coloured and poor-to-working-class, whereas Table View is an affluent and mostly white beachside area. Its proximity to downtown is defined in Gavin's eyes by demographics and economics, more so than by physical distance.

The cultural gap Gavin had to traverse was much more daunting and disorienting than the almost 20 kilometres he actually schlepped in the scorching sun. If he had still been with his former gang, the Mongrels, the way home would have been much more straightforward. 'If I was a gangster there [in Table View] it would have been different. If I was there for drugs or guns, I phone somebody and have a car in thirty minutes. But, like this, I'm on my own', he said. Gavin's story hints at the calculations gang members are forced to make when exiting gang life: dealing away connections and coinage to beg strangers for a phone charger or taxi fare. It also indicates the sociocultural uncertainties and discrimination that township residents contend with when in prosperous parts of Cape Town. Unsure how to compass their way around unfamiliar ground, many are forced to troop along, one foot after another, hoping to tentatively find their way like Gavin did.

What Gavin felt is the rule rather than the exception. As evidence, let me offer one more example: a story of a visit I made to the Victoria and Alfred (V&A) Waterfront with two young men from Hanover Park – each a member of the Laughing Boys gang. Situated in beautiful Table Bay Harbour, the V&A is one of Cape Town's most popular tourist sites and a busy shopping mall. With its own aquarium, amphitheatre and a Ferris wheel, it is a far cry from the Cape Flats. I suggested that my companions explore the mall's shops and amenities, while I tended to the administrative drudgery that brought us there, supposing it would be a welcome break from the four square blocks of territory their gang controlled at the time. Eager to browse the V&A's consumerist menagerie, they quickly agreed and were off. Almost as quickly, they were back, after being harassed by security and shop staff in each store that they went to. Their only offence was that they are Coloured, poor and were walking outside their neighbourhood. Anxiety and distrust pursue poor men of colour throughout Cape Town's privileged, pre-dominantly white spaces, unless they can manage to prove themselves as 'safe' in order to neutralise suspicion (Lindegaard, 2017). Otherwise, vilified outsiders like the two boys I was with need validation via a white escort to be accepted as anything more than a security threat. After running through my checklist of chores, we happily wandered the Waterfront together.

The passive resignation with which both accepted their fate earlier was curious though. I am well aware that each has a history of considerable violence as part of the Laughing Boys. Yet, neither showed the slightest inclination to square up to the security guards they encountered. A rationale for their behaviour might be inferred from an almost identical story told by another gang researcher. As part of his study of gang life in Heideveld, Jensen commented on the 'difficulty young coloureds from the townships felt when engaging with predominately white space' (2008, pp. 53–54). He recounted the unease undergone by Heideveld youngsters during a visit they also made together to the V&A. As Jensen explained it, their disquiet emanated from an intuition that people of a certain class and colour have stepped into space that is after all these years still 'not for them'. Just like the teens I was with, his sidekicks chose to shy away from the 'white gaze', rather than stare it down and confront it. The implication is that alternative rules of engagement apply to rarefied air of commercial Cape Town than they do to the Cape Flats.

Even seasoned shooters seemed to recognise this, avoiding argument at the V&A, though they readily accepted and contributed to unmentionable acts in Hanover Park on a regular basis. So strongly ingrained are the historical ideological conventions of the city's skewed 'symbolic order' (Burawoy & Von Holdt, 2012, p. 67) that even those at the bottom of its hierarchy abide by it, countersigning their own anguish. This is not, of course, to expect teenagers – no matter how battle-hardened – to be on the vanguard of a fight against structural oppression. It is just to point out that racism and classism eventually settle in the consciousness of the oppressed, as a type of 'symbolic violence' (Bourdieu & Wacquant, 1992, pp. 167–170) that converts subjugation into anger, aggression and assaults enacted against one's own people. The persecuted seek power where they can, even if it sometimes means attacking each other to attain it. Such is the continuum of violence that pushed the two young men into the Laughing Boys, and which ensured that they went back to the gang when they got home from the V&A, retaking their place on the frontlines of internecine gang warfare waged against other Coloureds – poor and marginal just like them.

3.2 Street Capital

If Cape Town is the capital of the South African gang nation, the Cape Flats are its main attraction and financial centre. Gangs operating on 'the Flats' have grown through the decades from small-scale community protection rackets into formidable criminal collectives, exploiting breakdowns in governance by the South African state and failures in development by the formal economy (Standing, 2006). It appears that society abhors a vacuum as much as nature does. Where the government and businesses are unable and unwilling to provide life's necessities, gangs step in with a chance for an illicit income, informal law and justice, and some safety. As Salo noted, mistrust of a corrupt and ineffective criminal justice system meant that residents of Coloured townships 'preferred the gang's kangaroo style court to a formal investigation by the police' (2005, n.p.). Gang membership is also a means of accessing the material goods necessary for minimal well-being, as well as for locating social armour against the buffets of everyday township danger (Standing, 2003). Broadly speaking, involvement in gang activities is a way of obtaining a competitive advantage in poor and unstable communities (Daniels & Adams, 2010). For Coloured men, in particular, membership is a vehicle to relative independence in a society that perceives them as weak, marginal, financially irresponsible and childlike (Jensen, 2008). It assists them in coping with racial stereotyping and systematic marginalisation, deflecting these through the construction of an identity that exists in opposition to mainstream society (Jensen, 2010). Risky and violent conduct is central to attaining esteem as a part of that identity (Cooper, 2009). Crime and violence can offer a short-term source of agency some Capetonians use to try to raise their social and economic status (Lindegaard & Jacques, 2014). Criminologist Don Pinnock, who has studied Cape gangs for more than two decades, concludes that gangs in the city operate in a particular moral universe that legitimises aggression, so that those in their orbit in due course come to 'know that acts of violence against themselves or others are a reliable method for reasserting their existence when life experience has denied it' (2016, p. 200).

What Pinnock describes is an essential characteristic of a globalised street culture that connects the townships of Cape Town to ghettos, *favelas* and slums around the world (Ilan, 2015). Scholars have conceptualised street culture differently. Some have referred to it as a 'code of the street' (Anderson, 2000, p. 33), while some saw it as a 'mindset of "*locura* [emphasis added]"' (Vigil, 2003, pp. 233–236) or a 'defiant individualism' (Sánchez-Jankowski, 1991, pp. 23–28). Every perspective in its own manner strings together 'the complex and conflictual web of beliefs, symbols, modes of interaction, values, and ideologies that have emerged in opposition to exclusion from mainstream society' (Bourgois, 2002, p. 8). At its most benign, talking, dressing and acting unconventionally are a subtle way of giving the mainstream the finger – as punks, goths, skaters or b-boys do. Gangs are anything but benign though. They are both an affront to social order and a hostile call for disorder in general, their members acting rude and combative because it is the pre-eminent way to feel any sense of strength where they come from.

If you are otherwise thought of as socially irrelevant, gangs have room for you. They are always searching for bodies to put on corners or to throw into gang wars, seeking out youngsters willing to convert fear and frustration into rage. Though gang members represent a small minority of people in most areas, they can push overall community norms towards greater combativeness by serving as embodiments of 'street capital' (Sandberg, 2008, pp. 154–157): the skills, knowledge and styles that are the cultural capital of street culture. Amid groups fighting for their lives on the lower rungs of their societies, violence especially is a key cultural competency and accepted and legitimate form of authority – what Bourdieu called 'symbolic capital' (1998, p. 4). A child being abused at home who sees the deferential way a boss is treated might naturally seek the protection that comes with getting involved in a gang. Another may notice the boss' *takkies*,[3] tracksuit, cell phone and fancy car, and aspire to gain the same. He or she might not have regular meals or clean clothes, but knows that the Sexy Boys, Mongrels and Ghetto Kids are open for business round the clock, offering an income and some semblance of material empowerment.

Yesterday, today and tomorrow, gangs will continue to recruit, shoot and sell – peddling not just drugs but also the promise of financial and personal independence. Reputations consecrated through conspicuous consumption and occasional brutality set a high-water mark in their communities, substantiating churlish, criminal and abusive behaviours as 'modes of action' (Hannerz, 1969, pp. 184–191), or 'strategies of action' (Swidler, 1986, pp. 276–277) that can be used for acquiring the elementary units of a decent life; taking on a 'street repertoire' can at any rate concede from others a modicum of courtesy, as well as some cover to get a person from one day to the next. We should not mistake the street repertoire as a fixed set of rules, however, or some form of identity imperialism that constitutes 'a predetermined set of discourses and actions appropriate to a particular "stage-part"' (Bourdieu, 1977, p. 2). Each gangster plays a role in serving as a unique reference point for navigating urban marginality relative to those jostling and competing with each other in the street field. In other words, gang members exemplify a personalised constellation of street cultural strategies that illuminate

---

[3]Sneakers or trainers.

the practical value of street capital. The gang repertoire is a vessel for the aspirations for large numbers of young people in the city. Seeing violent and criminal behaviours, and their effects, demonstrated through such a repertoire brings culture from the realm of abstract signals into decipherable embodiments of action (Lamont & Lareau, 1988). Any person wanting to decipher the bits and pieces of cultural code prevailing in a township environment is simply able to look to gang members for guidance about what survival strategies are available and when they should be called into action. Gangsterism, drug dealing and criminality can thus be comprehended as demonstrable and rational strategic life directions. It is possible to go another way. Most township residents do exactly that. Still, for many, the readily available prospects for self-protection, salary and status offered by street life are too tantalising to resist.

3.2.1 Mikey

The allure of gangsterism is apparent even to the very young. Take Mikey (Philippi male, 10 years), for example, whom I met one afternoon while chatting to some Mongrels in an informal settlement on the southeastern edges of Philippi. He seemed like any carefree kid then, still in his school uniform, kicking up dust around a tattered football with his friends. But shortly thereafter I learned that Mikey was also a Mongrel recruit. The gang called him over to the semi-circle of plastic beer crates they had assembled as seats, addressing Mikey in *Sabela* – a prison dialect that combines a mix of Afrikaans, English, Xhosa and Zulu. To the affirming laughter of the adults around him, Mikey responded by raising his arms and shouting 'son af', with two fingers and a thumb on each hand outstretched in the 28s salute. The phrase means 'sunset' and is a key symbol of the prison gang, which operates by night. Though still just a schoolboy, he was keen to imitate the mannerisms and speech of the gang, presumably to prove just how 'gangster' he was. It is easy to see how tempting it would be to any minor to be privy to clandestine communications spoken only in hushed tones by authoritative adult figures. Little wonder that so many are enticed into gangs.

Although it is difficult to accurately assess the demographic composition of gangsterism in Cape Town, approximately one-half of all gang members might be in their teens (Owen & Greeff, 2015). Some, like Mikey, are younger. Monitoring of South Africa's crime trends suggests that child recruitment has been on the rise for some time (Global Initiative against Transnational Organized Crime, 2020). 'It's cool, it's fun', Mikey said, when asked why he wanted to be a gang member. 'You can be a General and get lots of money'. He was allowed to hang around the Mongrels, and would be sent to run errands to earn pocket money. In the process, the boy absorbed information about the gang and its activities. Youth usually participate in a process of 'trying on' (Brenneman, 2011, p. 67) and testing gang repertoires before they join. Each step in makes it harder to get out. As Mikey gained experience, I was told that he would be given additional tasks: acting as a lookout, holding drugs or arms and then becoming a shooter himself. All are stages in a youngster's insidious progress towards that irrevocable point where a schoolboy suddenly graduates into a gunslinger.

Mikey acquired a fascination for street culture through his father, who was in the 28s prison gang. Children like him are more at risk of gang involvement if their parents have pro-gang attitudes (Cooper & Ward, 2012b). 'Men would come to our house and sit with my daddy, and smoke pipes', he explained. These same men carried out shootings against the rival 26s gang, supposedly to protect their community. 'They shot them dead and nobody touched them. That's how I learned how to act like [a gangster]'. To a boy of 10, the consequences of gang life may not be apparent yet, despite the fact that his own father was stabbed to death two years before I met Mikey. Still, when asked if he is afraid to die, Mikey answered simply: 'no, you must be brave'. Rather than risks, he sees role models. The Mongrel gang that controls the squatter camp he lives in are the ones with cash, cars and clout. 'Sometimes they give all the youngsters money', he told me. 'I like the way they act, the way they ride with their windows dark black'.

Cape Town's gangster elite, especially, make for noteworthy anti-heroes. Street cultural supervillains like Jakie Lonte, Colin Stanfield and Rashied and Rashaad Staggie might have been socialised underground, but they are foregrounded in the collective consciousness of Cape Flats communities as renowned examples of street success. They represent local versions of *Scarface's* Tony Montana, turning subculture into 'high culture', signalling to poor Coloured kids everywhere: 'the world is yours'. Beneath the most audacious gangland personas are scores of street soldiers, who have mobilised around gangs to gain and protect the few advantages available to them, but who will for their entire lives remain at, or below, the poverty line (Standing, 2003). Boys like Mikey have almost no shot at becoming kingpins – a very small minority soar to these heights – but they go for it anyway. At any rate, it is equally as unlikely to think that Mikey might one day leave the *kampie* to sip chilled MCC[4] on a sheltered terrace somewhere in downtown Cape Town or its suburbs. So he might as well settle for what he can get: attention from girls, daps on the block, easy access to drugs and a little spending money. Never mind the thousands of cautionary tales of those shot down before him or lost to prison. These are easily overlooked if searching for a reason to believe, and an occasion to momentarily stand tall with purpose.

The unsanitised reality of it all is that boys just like Mikey are convenient cannon fodder for older criminals, the most powerful and wealthiest of whom live away from gang warzones in the comfort of Cape Town's highly sought-after suburbs. Fortunately, just months after our first interaction, Mikey's recruitment process was terminated. Unlike other susceptible gang recruits, he was never fully initiated. Free from the gang, Mikey is able to safely pursue regular childhood interests; he spoke excitedly about his favourite footballer Cristiano Ronaldo, listed off European countries he aspired to visit and told me about wild animals he liked – especially big cats. However, every now and again our conversations reverted to gangsterism. It is perhaps expectable, given that life in his *kampie* is still so frequently interrupted by gunshots, that the subject of gangs comes up at regular intervals. After these events I often saw Mikey revert to an eager

---

[4]Méthode Cap Classique (MCC) refers to South African sparkling wine made like Champagne.

recitation of the who, where, when, how and what of local gang gossip. During one such dialogue Mikey exclaimed: 'they are hitmen [and] powerful. If they call you and you don't come, they can come to your house and shoot you – dah, dah', firing his hands upwards like pistols, as he once again took on the exaggerated swagger of a gangster. Although the Mongrels were done recruiting him, he could not totally liberate himself from the influences of street culture, which is ceaselessly being role-modelled everywhere throughout communities like his. Street culture is epidemic. Even those living legitimately might dress in street-styled fashion, speak in prison slang or feign the bearing of a gang member, thinking it better to assume subcultural camouflage of a predator than to be victimised amid the sometimes wild environment of the township. Lindegaard labels these people as 'ghetto chameleons' (Lindegaard, 2017, p. 4). Theirs is a real-life application of Batesian mimicry that astutely adopts aspects of street cultural performance – style, slang, handshakes, etc. – but manages to sidestep discord and avoid outright conflict.

But what do you do when conflict stares you right in the face, as it so often does on the Cape Flats? Then street cultural stagecraft of any social actor gets stretched to its breaking point, or past that point maybe. Argumentative posturing and inimical verbal salvos are part of a combative showmanship that is familiar to township residents. I have personally witnessed occasions when mild-mannered teenagers suddenly transform into forbidding figures. The shift can be sudden. Conversation that is breezy and unassuming quickly evaporates, replaced by a string of aggressive *Kaaps*[5] phrases and profanities, spat out through pursed lips and over an outstretched index finger being sharply jabbed forward in warning. Violence is not the outcome every time. But there is an unspoken understanding that it can be. Protagonists, antagonists and their audiences are all well aware of the insinuated ramifications of adopting a street cultural stance – its rewards and its risks. One side plays up how hard and tough he or she is, knowing instinctually to adopt a demeanour and discourse that tells another they should tread carefully; that person must then choose whether or not to call the bluff of the first, knowing that this might mean taking some lumps, but knowing also that the streets are watching to see if they break. Any mistake made today probably means there will be somebody else waiting around the corner tomorrow, the next day and the day after. That is why it is so difficult to resist rising to the bait.

Almost unavoidably, people choose to act out wild, anti-social behaviours in a death-defying pursuit of street capital, which is the street field's reserve currency. It represents safety, status and salary, all manifested as aggression. That is why street culture spreads like wildfire, from person to person, until it engulfs whole neighbourhoods. If you listen closely to conversations in communities from Mitchells Plain to Hanover Park you will hear youngsters 'speaking street',

---

[5]*Kaaps* refers to a form of vernacular Afrikaans that is widely spoken throughout the Western Cape by Coloured people. It is pervasive on the Cape Flats and its history traced back to the seventeenth century.

communicating with one another in slang and *Sabela*, sensing that doing so offers an insider's perspective into the secrets of street gangs. Look closely and you will see young men and women decked out in slick name-brand clothes and *takkies* because they know that 'dressing street' makes them appear cool and authoritative. Most importantly, you will find young men and women 'acting street', trying to build reputations for carrying on impulsively, fearlessly and nastily because it fills them with confidence and potency. The array of street performances they assume creates a commanding archetype through which people can rebel against the structures that repress them, celebrating their own marginality, and finding whatever enfranchisement they can on the edges of Capetonian society.

3.3 Speaking Street

Gang fights – who shot whom, with what type of gun – are a favourite topic of conversation among gang members. Having a gift for 'street talk' (Sandberg & Fleetwood, 2017, p. 366) is part of narrative repertoire that involves telling stories about violence, tough upbringings and selling and taking drugs that earns street capital for storytellers and subjects alike. War stories help to bind the street field together, reproducing social practices and social structures via verbal, emotional and cultural symbolism. Rags-to-riches tales of the local-boy-turned-kingpin, especially, have made legends of Capetonian criminal elite who rose to power through excessive violence, criminal intellect and time spent in prison (Standing, 2003). Narratives of street success do not just give an account of what goes on in gangs. They also solidify gang roles and reputations, and reproduce popular understandings of how streetwise men and women ought to behave (Jimerson & Oware, 2006).

Fascination with gangs is not limited to their members. Lively discussions about local gang disputes, boundaries and personalities hum over tables, around living rooms and on stoops throughout Cape Flats communities. It was often the case that upon arriving in a neighbourhood that the first bits of news I received would be a chronology of the violence that had occurred the previous night, day or week. Gangsterism offers a perverse form of entertainment and a source of vicarious exhilaration. Residents, community workers and former gangbangers I spoke to variously likened community perceptions of gang shootings to a form of entertainment, alternatively calling them: shows, *soapies*,[6] sports and competitions. A conversation with a community worker in Hanover Park described the performative – almost theatrical – aspect of gang violence. He was part of a small team of ex-gangsters labouring to silence gunshots there by mediating gang disputes, hoping that temporary ceasefires would at long last bring peace. But in an area where 45 people were murdered in the first half of 2019 alone, he admitted that finding a new non-violent norm would be a slog:

> Today in the community violence is like a normal thing, you see.
> Because everyday people get killed in front of [their neighbours].

---

[6]Soap opera.

> And when the [gangs are] shooting, the people stand on the corners, maybe, or they stand by the windows, or they stand on the stairs to look, and it's like the Coons[7] coming past, you see. For the people it's like normal, you see. It's like entertainment.

A total 3,787 bullets were fired in Hanover Park in 2018, in 1,222 separate incidents, according to data collected by gunfire detection technology being piloted there as part of the City of Cape Town's gang prevention measures (Peterson, 2019). The consequence is a crackling concerto of attack and counterattack, through which people live in constant fear of bullets penetrating their windows and doors. And yet, denizens still view the crossfires with lurid captivation, treating gang quarrels as one would groups of multi-Coloured minstrels and choirs competing against each other amid the choreographed rhythmic highjinks of Cape Town's famous Coon Carnival parade. Each year more than 10,000 brightly dressed, singing and dancing participants from different Coloured communities take over downtown streets lined by thousands of cheering spectators. That one day every year, Coloureds are no longer the uprooted and unwanted, as they strut jubilantly through heart of a city that is momentarily theirs. In important ways, the performative aspect of the carnival mirrors some elements of the gangs for poor Coloured communities. Marching, shouting and singing through downtown Cape Town are acts of defiance. Steinberg portrays it as a 'giant, raucous fuck-you to whites and the bourgeoisie' (2004b, p. 127). So is shooting. No matter its corrupting and nocuous local impacts, gang fights are explosive displays of a rebellious blaze that consumes attention well beyond the battlefield.

3.3.1 Ryan

Many youths look on in awe of gang leaders and emulate the stars of the street-based soap opera playing out around them, wishing that they too someday may be the centre of their neighbourhood's attention. Remember how eager Mikey was to show off his *Sabela* skills to our small circle of onlookers. Shared linguistic practices underpin insidership in any community, and particularly so for clandestine communities. Possessing a knowledge of *Sabela* is for this reason an important part of any gang member's repertoire (Lindegaard & Zimmermann, 2017). Fluency in prison language implies an intimacy with the history of the number and its rank, structure, symbols and rules – the trademarks of a true *ndota*.[8] It is an essential part of what separates gangsters from the *franse*,[9] or non-gangsters, in prison. 'When an

---

[7]Cape Town's Coon Carnival, officially known as the *Kaapse Klopse*, is an annual minstrel festival whose participants are typically working-class Coloureds. While the word 'coon' has racist connotations in many places, the word is generally used by Cape-based Coloured people without any derogatory connotation (Gaulier & Martin, 2017).
[8]Prison gangster or, more generally, a gangster. *Ndota* means 'man' in Zulu, which shows the significance of gang recruitment rituals as initiations into manhood.
[9]Non-gangsters; insofar as number gangsters are *ndotas* and are considered 'real men', the *franse* are often abused as *wyfies*, or prison wives.

unknown inmate is transferred to a new prison, he is asked a question the moment he enters his cell: "Who are you?"', says Steinberg, in his writings on the 100-year-old oral traditions and violent ideologies of the 26, 27 and 28 prison gangs. 'The question begins a test of authenticity' (2004, n.p.). An initiated *ndota* will know the correct words and references in a well-rehearsed metaphorical exchange that hinges on his proficiency in prison speak. Each number gang has its own idiosyncratic symbols and myths. Anybody unable to answer in the right way is stripped of personhood, along with clothes and whatever belongings he might have; *frans* are robbed and raped behind bars, and can survive only by bending before the *ndotas* who dictate all facets of prison business. Non-gangsters on the outside can to some extent rely on isolation and avoidance as defence mechanisms against violence. In a penitentiary, there is nowhere to run and nowhere to hide.

Merely 'taking a number' offers inmates some protection amid South Africa's heaving inmate population. But prison gangs also have their own internal hierarchies, where members jostle one another for position. *Ndotas* are governed by paramilitary and judicial structures, complete with invisible uniforms and other make-believe paraphernalia. Attaining rank has historically meant spending forbidding years in incarceration, slowly working one's way up the prison gang organogram by committing and absorbing violence. Inmates become *ndotas* through an initiatory ritual process of stabbing a warder and submitting to the pitiless punishments that follow as a consequence (Farrington, 2014). The more you stab, the more you build your reputation in jail, and the further you move up the prison pecking order (Lindegaard & Gear, 2014). Ryan (Mitchells Plain male, 33 years), however, shows that in an environment populated by hardened criminals, somebody with a softer touch can sometimes win out too. He spent much of his late teens, as well as most of his twenties, passing through the revolving door of South Africa's prison system for the crimes he committed on the outside as an American gang member, and later as a part of The Firm. Over the years, he climbed the ranks of the 28s largely by studiously mastering all he could about the number:

Ryan: I was a General.

Dariusz: How did you get to that level?

Ryan: It depends on how interested you are in the number. I thought one day when I became a 28 I will rule this prison gang. I was sure of it. I was into this number stuff. It was *lustig*[10]. I got to know stuff that was not for me – before my time [and rank]. Every time I come [to prison] I just want to *Sabela*. Everyone [in prison] is under observation from the number. They all see how I much I move, how fast, and they have to say: this guy is the right one, he is right for this position.

---

[10]Fun.

Dariusz: It can't be just an interest, you must have done other [violent] stuff too.

Ryan: The prisons have changed a lot to now. Before you had to stab a warder, to get to that [high] level. But that is not like that now. They base it on your interest. When they see you're able in the number, they give you more to do.

Dariusz: You were able to get there [as a General] without blood?

Ryan: Without blood.

Though participants in this study stressed that words would only get a gangster so far, most also accepted that considerable rank and authority can be snapped up by having a commanding grasp of the number; superior knowledge of *Sabela* is particularly important. This is now as true in the 'real world' as it is in prison. The language and practices of South African prison gangs have more recently escaped onto the sandy streets of the Cape Flats, although these two worlds remain nominally separated by barred windows, high walls and barbed wire. Masses of those involved in street gangs have joined prison gangs as a rite of passage into gangsterism, eager to enhance their reputation by entering the number. Gangs outside are themselves now also applying prison gang rituals, symbols and vernacular to solidify loyalty, discipline and networks (Pinnock, 2016). The street presence of number gangs has itself grown in the last decade. The 28s, especially, continue to establish themselves more independently outside of prison. That is why – for street and prison gangsters alike – mastering the number yields considerable street capital:

While I was in prison I was always busy with my number stuff. Because for the three years in prison [in that one stay], I went through levels in the number. I came to a level where I just gave orders and I enjoyed it. I just sat back and then I was just busy with my stuff, with smuggling [drugs] in prison.

By embracing prison culture as he did, Ryan was able to adjust to and thrive amid the hostility of South Africa's carceral system. Perhaps more interesting still is how he adapted to prison culture itself through skilful applications of the number's language and lore:

In prison it's all about the number. You can make a big person so small with the number. You can even be higher than me in the number, but I know more and that makes me more powerful than you by the number. There is nothing I don't know about the number. I made it my mission to know everything −26, 27, 28 − I had friends who were other numbers.

Ryan's comments support studies from Cape Town demonstrating that being knowledgeable in the number, and being able to expertly use this knowledge in your favour, can flatten gang hierarchies. As one ranking member of the 26s said, 'The number is the number. Like, if you're a higher rank, you cannot tell me to do "this", when can I show that – no – the number says "that"' (Dziewanski, 2020a, p. 9).

Researchers in other contexts have also found that controlling narratives about collective criminal exploits can yield considerable personal advantages in unsavoury social circles (King, 1999), if somebody is skilled enough in the art of narration to skew group myth-making towards his or her own selfish motives (King, 2001). The self-serving creative exposition of cultural narratives lays claim to selective justifications for 'what is appropriate, or what an individual can get away with, in any given context' (Bottero, 2009, p. 418). Prison culture in Cape Town is like all culture: it changes and reconstitutes kaleidoscopically, and has significance solely because it has been given meaning by people who believe in it and reproduce it. Moreover, the number is not some singular storyline, but is a subjectively negotiated set of overlapping stories and practices one enacts and interprets relative to others doing the same. *Sabela*, especially, is the mother tongue of Capetonian ganglands. Anybody unable to speak it fluently risks being dominated. Whereas the *ndota* that carefully assimilates its various scripts and learns its competing interpretations holds a powerful weapon – lethal as any bullet or blade, if one knows how to handle it.

3.3.2 William

'Language is one of the most distinctive features of a gang disposition', writes Pinnock. 'It is a particular argot specifically used by gang youths to differentiate between those who are a part of the normal or gang community' (1997, p. 33). But how you say something is as important, if not more so, than the words you use. A quarrelsome attitude, a bullying tone and an angry appearance are part and parcel of speaking street in Cape Town. To hear it described by research participants, speech shifts to a combination of hard *Kaaps* slang and prison vernacular once one is in a gang, in a total makeover of one's demeanour that causes people to become louder, ruder, bigger and more threatening. There is the expectation that gang members speak and act like this. So they do. When repeated over and over, words become habits. After a while, speaking street can turn into a lasting disposition that envelopes one's entire character.

William (male, 32 years) was one of those who described how becoming a gangster changed both his speech patterns and his personal temperament. It happened when he joined Manenberg's Hard Livings following his mother's passing. After he was initiated into the 'HLs', hard speaking went hand in hand with hard living:

> William: There were a couple of times that we were in fights. I was physically attacked, you see. I had to protect myself. So my character

changed a lot. Because the way I start to speak, I speak like a gangster now. So people start to see: hey, this guy is now really a gangster.

Dariusz: So, how do gangsters speak?

William: They speak like: *hosh, salute my bru, wat se jy.*[11] So, that is the way they speak and you can identify that is a gangster... They speak in a more aggressive way.

'*Hosh*', '*salute*' and '*wat se jy*' are gang greetings that broadcast to anybody within earshot that 'this guy is now really a gangster'. Words like *stiek, skiet* and *daala* – stab, shoot, and I dare you – round out a vocabulary of violence that structures, brackets and punctuates life in Manenberg. The subtext of such speech acts establishes those that use them as somebody who is serious about street life. That is why William made it a point to speak street whenever he was in public:

William: It was mostly something to protect me on the street. So, that was the most times I used to speak like that.

Dariusz: How does it protect you?

William: It shows [other people] don't try your luck, because I know what I'm talking about, and I have the *chappie.*[12] So, that is also how they would identify you, in the Hard Livings. So [others in the community] they would hear, and constantly speak of the gang, and that is what would bring sort of a fear in them, you see.

To William, street speech is as symbolically significant as getting a *chappie*. Like having a gang tattoo as a physical mark of his allegiance to the Hard Livings, vocalising violent street culture is part of a set of linguistic acts that identifies him with the gang and with the street capital that gang membership proffers. Most importantly, this protects William, by offering a forewarning to anybody who might want to take a shot at him, cautioning potential foes that he will act adamantly, forcefully and dangerously if confronted.

Playing a gangster character convincingly meant that William had to practice his lines and re-enact his role constantly. Eventually they stuck. 'For some time, you're speaking a particular way and before you know it, it's you like that', said William. 'You obviously have to learn the slang, the way [gangsters] speak. So it develops from a time. So I couldn't speak normal like now, because I was just in that language.'

William went on to explain that he used gangster language most readily 'on the streets, because it is where you must be more aggressive'. This much is expected.

---

[11]A gang greeting.
[12]Tattoo.

Aggression is a keyword in the lexicon of the street field. That the gangster in him would also often come out in other environments – like when he was at home with his parents – is evidence of the stickiness of street practices across social fields. Escaping the deeply buried patterns that embed into people over the course of street socialisation can be a complicated proposition (Fraser, 2015). 'I mean, even with your parents you're speaking usually a normal way. But, like, if they say something, and they made you crossed, then it's like here's [William] the gangster coming out', he said. William's parents insisted that he spoke softly and kept proper table manners while staying in their house. Yet he could not help himself from habitually reacting with profanity and hostility when angered by his kin. A switch flipped, and the soft-spoken son was pulled back into a repertoire of embodied linguist practices that was now his default.

It was when William finally got out of the Hard Livings that he really began breaking down his predisposition for blowing up irately. Deconditioning took a tremendous amount of time though. 'There was a lot of change happening slowly, you see. Firstly, it was the way I would speak to people – calm-like – that started to change. And I would do things I would never do [as a gangster]', explained William. 'I would speak more politely and get more used to this. Sometimes then I would get angry and argue – like sometimes even hitting and kicking people. But then I would come back and try to apologise'. Change was gradual as he attempted to adjust to living anew. 'It was a bit difficult just to change like that. It took some time for me... About 2–3 years for me. In fact, today I could say it's like I'm still learning, you see', he admitted. Given that William was in the Hard Livings for six years, it is unsurprising that he did not metamorphose overnight. Nor is it surprising that he still felt the effects of gangsterism years after disengaging. 'Sometimes William the gangster is still there. When I get crossed – not so much – but sometimes he is there'. William's protracted process of disengaging from street culture dovetails with the narratives presented below. Each shows that a gang persona cannot simply be killed off through de-identification, or even by de-embedding from one's criminal ties. Long is the path to rehabilitation, and many years are needed to pick up the speech patterns and other habits that make up the cultural capital of polite society.

3.4 Dressing Street

This chapter has thus far been commenting on embodied cultural capital, concentrating on those expressions of self that are integrated into the mind and body from lifelong enculturation into street culture. But this section stops to consider cultural capital 'in the objectified state' (Bourdieu, 1986, p. 246): the physical possessions and items that assist in reaching and marking higher social stature in a social field. Dress is one of the most important markers of status in any society, making up much of those all-important first impressions. But street apparel is not just a personal fashion statement. It can also be a statement of affiliation (Garot, 2010). Police pay close attention to what people are wearing, as do gangs themselves. A red or blue bandana could get you murdered in the wrong American neighbourhood; or it could get you props in the right one. In Cape Town, it is Union Jacks and stars and stripes claim sets, bodies and clothes.

Cape Town's biggest gang – the Americans – most obviously borrows and transforms the emblems and icons of the United States, cloaking its members in a sense of nationhood that binds them together when they go to war:

> The American flag, as a symbol of the American nation, defined the 'American' gang's territory: The gang actually call their territory 'America'. According to its members, the six white stripes of the flag are for the clean work (money) and the seven red stripes for the dirty work (blood). The 13 stripes together stand for the 13 presidents of the United States. The 14 stars are the states in America, and one of the stars represents the gang. Both the flag and the Statue of Liberty are used to define a territory around which the gang can mobilise and their territory is marked by elaborate graffiti of the statue and the American eagle. Around these symbols they have also constructed stories and mythical histories that function as a secret entrance ritual. (Pinnock, 1997, pp. 38–42)

Excluded from full citizenship in the Rainbow Nation, the gang has created its own sovereign state. Members of the Americans speak with pride about the Statue of Liberty, White House and US flag; all are key symbols in the secretive lore and rituals of the group. Knowing one's US history can be the difference between being seen as friend or foe when in the gang's territory – or 'America', as they call it. The Americans' aspirations towards a 'land of opportunity' are given significance through a street style that projects a refusal to take part in a society that has shunned them. Street soldiers fight and die for their flag, as would any military force called upon to protect their nation. No inch of the Flats appears to be untouched by the pseudo-statal iconography of gangsterism. I have even seen the US flag shaved into the heads of a young American. His shorn curls matched to a tracksuit, sneakers and silver jewellery in a look that seemingly gave him away as an obvious gang member to the most uninformed of outsiders.

Would this case study then be confirmation of gang stereotypes articulated in South Africa's *POCA* legislation, which states that a gang member can be identified as any person that 'adopts their style of dress' (Republic of South Africa, 1998, Chapter 4, Section 11)? Not necessarily. Taking a walk through a township community on any given day, one will come across countless American and British flags adorning shirts, hats and pants worn by men and women, the young and grown, as well as those with obvious gang affiliations and those without. Itemising the totality of objectified street capital across Cape Town would show that there are just as many people – if not more – who only dress like gangsters, than there are actual gang members. Somebody wearing baggy trousers, a branded cap and shiny earrings might very well be impersonating so-called 'gang fashions' in order to be cool, or as an attempt to blend in and stay safe. The gangster is the fallback fashion icon for a great number of community residents trying to make a way for themselves in the world.

Rather than becoming sheep to the slaughter, young men and women dress themselves up in wolf's clothing, simulating the paradigmatic street practices they behold around them. In associating themselves with street culture like they do, however, it makes it more likely that an individual with tenuous associations to gangs will be policed and criminalised as any official member would be. This illustrates how treating people according to social categories, with fixed social characteristics, can have what Hacking refers to as a 'looping effect', whereby groups of people are created through the 'interactions between classifications of people and the people classified' (2004, p. 279). Unwanted attention from the law enforcement agency only heightens people's sense of persecution and insecurity, making it more probable that more and more of them gravitated towards gangsterism. In the meantime, members and non-members continue to dress street, irrespective of the increased risk of harassment and arrest, because it gives off the impression of some esteem and authority.

3.4.1 Taahir

Taahir (Manenberg male, 26 years) aspired to join the Hard Livings partly because he was enamoured with the fancy clothes they wore and the way they carried themselves. But his way into gangs was about more than a superficial desire to have name-brand shoes and hoodies. Growing up in a working-class family allowed Taahir material comforts poorer kids in Manenberg could not afford. He already had slick threads. What he did not have, however, was safety. Though Taahir's father provided, he also hit him. Growing up in an abusive home will certainly generate a desire for the kind of protection and affirmation that can be found in a gang (Ward & Bakhuis, 2010). For Taahir, he sought out what street styles were tied to – strength, belonging, cash and sex – more so than the clothes themselves:

> First it was Staggie – Rashied Staggie. Everybody knows him. I think he's known [all] over the world... I used to look at him. I got everything growing up as a child, you know, even though I grew up in an abusive home. My father is a teacher, you know, and he had his own businesses. I got everything material-wise... But I always wanted more, and the Hard Livings at the time were known as the most notorious gang because everybody feared them. They had the same tracksuits, and wore the same stuff. They all looked so cool, and had guns and money, and had the most beautiful women.

Like a myriad of Manenberg youth, Taahir looked up to gangster icons like twin brothers Rashied and Rashaad Staggie, who co-founded the Hard Livings, and expanded them beyond their stronghold of Manenberg to an estimated 35 communities throughout Cape Town (Global Initiative Against Transnational Organized Crime, 2020). In their heyday, the two gang bosses used to drive around in their gold BMW convertible raining tens of thousands of rands onto

Manenberg residents as a statement of their largesse (Kinnes, 2000). The Staggies were celebrated for being street smart and well-spoken, but were also feared for being ruthless.

The tracksuits sported by the two folk hero leaders symbolised the ritual objects of success and security in Manenberg. 'I wanted to be around them, to be dressed like them, and to behave like them, to have people give me that respect, knowing that nobody can fuck with you', said Taahir. 'If all you know is abuse, you just really want to be safe finally'. Unable to feel safe at home, he had to seek refuge in the streets, where he faced another type of insecurity:

> Yes, [gang violence] is an everyday thing [in Manenberg]. There are a lot of times you and your friends walk and one gets shot. It's not such a big thing like it would be for other areas – rich areas. There it will be in the news and newspapers and everything, but here it is an everyday thing… Here things are harder for you growing up. Just to prevent being targeted, it's part of a survival thing… you grow up and become a gangster. That's why you want to be like those guys – move like a gangster, look like a gangster, all of those things.

Capetonians rich and poor may point to the same place on a globe to indicate where they come from. But their lives are actually worlds apart. While the rich melt away their anxieties next to a shoreline or pool after the workweek, weekend revelry in Manenberg can easily be spoiled by the very real worry of catching a stray bullet. Taahir juxtaposes the ubiquity of violence in Manenberg with the absence of violent crime in rich areas, implying that the former seems socially acceptable, whereas the latter does not. He has a point. A shooting in the vicinity of the Central Business District would be front-page news, whereas 'It's not such a big thing' on the Cape Flats. Violence in areas like Manenberg is easily ignored or forgotten by the rest of the city. Part of the blame goes to media, which generally skips across the surface of any given incident there, and then hides it in the inner depths of its newspapers. Name, age and cause of death are enough to give an account of the lives of the men and women affected by the violence on the Flats. Overlooked is the fact that a great many of those who are shooting – and getting shot – are adolescents like Taahir who are forced to navigate morality in a context where violence and death are a weekly, if not daily, occurrence. They have often been pushed onto the streets due to problems at home, and into gangs for protection or for respect, in circumstances that are lacking sufficient opportunities for empowerment. Though they may eventually be categorised as 'gangsters' by police and courts, all start out as boys and girls who are merely looking for some sort of shield against the multiple marginalities facing people in communities like theirs. In hooking up with the Hard Livings, Taahir's station in life improved – in the short-term, at any rate. He did not gain full citizenship in the Capetonian social order, but he held some sway in Manenberg.

Years before Taahir ever became a HL, he was already being groomed for gangsterism by his uncle, a Junior Cisko Yakkie and 28s prison gangster, who taught him the number and how to run and gun in the streets. Quite a few participants in this study were coaxed into gangs by relatives – usually by an older male figure such as a father, uncle or brother. Gang elders served as coaches and sources of advice for budding criminal curiosities. For instance, Taahir's uncle imparted on him the importance of the surprise attack in gang wars, a lesson that Taahir applied when he later became a killer in his own right at the age of 12:

> I would go there with my school clothes on and play marbles with their kids there that side and try and blend in with the kids. It's because we were one age, one size, and we would play, and they [in the gang] wouldn't expect me to shoot. So when I see the target, I would go for the target and then I would go back [to Hard Livings territory].

A shiny Adidas tracksuit would have easily marked Taahir as a threat, whereas a schoolboy could move undetected and snipe at his enemies in plain sight. The strategy also provided Taahir cover in another way. 'I go out and do it first. That is how I gained respect from my gang... and stuff and moved up in the rankings and stuff and, [gained] privileges that we got', said Taahir. But he called his ambush tactics 'a trick', an edge gained on the battlefield that garnered considerable respect in the gang, but which disguised the considerable misgivings he held about being a gangster:

> I was always a very scared gangster. I never went like head-on in gang fights. You know, I would be the first one to go and start it. So when my job is done then I go sit back and the rest of them must go fight... So it's going to be easier for you [to use the element of surprise]. Other gang members are going to die there now, you know what I mean?

From Taahir's description of his participation in gang fights it is obvious that it was part of a public performance carried out despite considerable fear. Gangsterism had promised him a way out of an abusive home, along a path that led to a slick and relatively safe lifestyle. As a schoolboy he learned to look up to his uncle and the larger-than-life Staggies, dying to one day be like them. Be careful what you wish for though. The appeal of gangs wore thin with age, as having tracksuits, girls and power lost its lustre. But once he was in the Hard Livings, Taahir was cornered. He had to will himself out of bed day after day to reluctantly slip on the scornful guise of a gangster, which went on over the countenance of the scared little boy he actually was. 'So, now I have this reputation, the clothes, and power, and all this... But it became tiring for me as a gangster because I had to wear this constant mask', Taahir confessed. 'Everyday pretending to be [strong], and every night when I'm home alone in my bed I would cry myself to sleep at night thinking of what I did during the day'. That went on for nearly 12 years, before at last Taahir managed to slough off the hefty demands of street culture.

Being a gangster only brought Taahir closer to the violence he was trying to escape, leaving him bound on both sides. It also removed him from his family, friends and society, making it more difficult to reintegrate when he did afterwards get out. Such are the pitfalls faced by somebody like him. In social spaces where gangs are leading influencers and key market players, young men like Taahir persist into self-defeating acts despite the threat of arrest, prison and worse. 'Once you become part of the gang there is one of two places you going to go: it's either jail or death', said Taahir. 'So if you're willing to take that risk, or live a life like that, so be it'. It is an indication of the dire decisions Taahir had to contemplate as a young boy. But he was not worried about jail or death at that point because he had decided that it was better than being abused by his father. Gangs would teach him differently later, of course. Yet, for the time being he was intent on acting, speaking and dressing like the kind of person who was respected in the house, who demanded deference from the people next door and who was given attention from whoever was watching from across the courtyard. This brought local authorities knocking too – but so what? The dangers police posed were nothing compared to the pitfalls present in his own home.

3.4.2 Emmanuel

'Dressing street' is typically used as a sign of one's attachment to street culture, as was the case with Taahir. But clothes can also signify affiliation to particular gangs. An American gang member's faded red, white and blue sweatshirt unequivocally announces where his or her allegiance lies, just as a Union Jack bandana might give away a Ghetto Kid or Mongrel. These are well-known Capetonian gangs that use objectified cultural capital to solidify and signal collective identities. The Playboys are a minor gang by comparison. Yet, the symbolic functions of clothing in the street repertoire of the group are much the same as those found among larger gangs. Emmanuel (Athlone male, 24 years) believed that his clothes were integral to the identity of a Playboy: 'we're used to like wearing Nike clothes and going to GrandWest [Casino and Entertainment World], getting nice chicks and that stuff, with this *chappie*'. In wearing a recognisable brand name like Nike, the Playboys are choosing a style signifier that is noticed as desirable and expensive, laying claim to middle-class status in which they have no stake otherwise.

In addition, by sporting internationally recognisable brands like Nike, the Playboys specifically separate themselves from their most hated adversaries – the *Stoepa Boys*. The swoosh logo demarcates a Playboy's allegiance like a gang tattoo, fusing style and identity that is projected in opposition to the style and identity of rival groups:

> Emmanuel: The Playboys stands for players and style.
>
> Dariusz: So what was their style like?
>
> Emmanuel: It was just Nike tracksuits, Nike *takkies,* and Nike caps – all Nike. The *Stoepas*, they wear Diamond jerseys and jeans.

Sartorial items play an important role in establishing self-image in every social space. In this case, sought-after clothing labels brand a person either a Playboy or a *Stoepa*, mobilising each group identity against the other via a distinguishable visual representation of their collectivity. 'This was like our thing. It was just *lekker*[13] to see us all like this together – everything Nike. The people there, they can see also', he said. 'It makes you feel like proud to be a Playboy, you see. Like it makes you feel like you have something to fight for'.

In the comments he makes below, Emmanuel also associates clothing with another type of social distinction – between the venerated and the victimised. That is because things that people wear combines with their manner of speaking, body language and violent acts as the constitutive elements of an oppositional 'campaign for respect' (1998, p. 83), says Anderson. Respect is most easily attained in the street through violence. Fashionable clothes are attainable through violent acts as well. Robbing people of their possessions allowed Emmanuel to access symbolic class objects, like sought-after sneakers, which would have been out of reach for him to obtain legally:

> I would maybe get this guy in the club, and see his *takkies* and tell myself: look, he got a pair of 3,000 rand *takkies*, and I got a 200 rand pair of *takkies* on. He is rich, and his mommy will buy him another pair tomorrow... So I would take that pair [he had] and I would tell him: here, you can have my *takkies,* and then I would wear [his] home... If he wouldn't want to give it, there would be hell.

As a young man living in a society urging him to seek standing through stylised consumerism, Emmanuel is just doing what he is able to live up to social expectations. Consumer culture has created a particularly prominent place for sneakers, something unrivalled by other clothing articles and accessories. Sneakerheads buy up new shoe releases as an investment, raking in thousands of rands in profit from a single pair. Others invest in new trainers because having a pair of Jordans turns heads on the street, and lets the person wearing them believe that they too might 'be like Mike'; in other words, that they too might fantasise about life using grand future-tense superlatives in scenarios where they come out as heroes.

Emmanuel was one of a handful of gang members I encountered who spent significant time outside of Cape Flats communities. The preceding quip was the follow-up response to a question about how he felt being so regularly exposed to dominant Capetonian society:

> It did affect me. It made me do things like take people's clothes – or take off their *takkies*... Why should they have all of these nice things, just because they are rich, and I live over there [on the Cape

---

[13]A slang word for cool.

Flats and am poor]? So I just took their stuff sometimes. It was simple.

Emmanuel wants the same things any young man does. He just has limited options to get them. Snubbed from the mainstream job markets, Emmanuel robs the rich as a way of temporarily equalising the socioeconomic power imbalances that keep him poor. His is a self-serving twist on the Robin Hood story, at the end of which he keeps for himself. In doing so, Emmanuel goes home in an expensive pair of *takkies*, as well as the momentary feeling that he has upended the social order that prevents him from buying the branded street gear that rich kids flaunt around him. Taking something from someone from a higher class also knocks the victim down a peg, gaining the aggressor power over that person, by becoming the new owner and controller of that thing. Anderson suggests that 'seemingly ordinary objects can become trophies with symbolic value far beyond their monetary worth. Possessing the trophy can symbolize the ability to violate somebody' (1998, p. 90). Those dope kicks are more than just an essential part of Emmanuel's wardrobe, they are an objectified form of street cultural capital, the having and taking of which adds to his own sense of self-worth and the respect he garners from others.

3.5 Acting Street

Acting street has important immediate payoffs. Among the most alluring elements of gang life are prestige and power. Absent the protection of police and the judicial system, safety comes from demonstrations of belligerence aimed at gaining and keeping street credibility. Frequent and ferocious violence is the surest path towards community celebrity – or infamy. It is this potential to be known and respected that makes gangs so bewitching to the child conscripts queuing up to take up the fight on behalf of the Hard Livings, Playboys, Americans and others.

3.5.1 Marcus

Marcus (Hanover Park male, 25 years) entered the Americans at 11 years old. He had known the raw power of gangsterism for a long time already, having observed and absorbed street culture osmotically through his kin. 'All my family... were deep in the gang. I played with the guns, and that stuff. I was really fascinated. I became a hitman through that. I just wanted a gun in my hand', he said. Once in the gang, he took up gunplay with glee, building a reputation as a shooter and killer that conferred to him significant benefits; 'reputation is like money. So, I had three cars in my life already. When I was very young, 15 years old... I had a car, my own house, girls'. Killing brought repute and prestige, returns on street capital that Marcus cashed in for big dividends. He is living proof of the assembly line that materialises cultural, social and symbolic inputs by converting them into economic capital (Bourdieu, 1977). By Marcus' mid-teens he had already achieved what people around him had been labouring in vain for their entire lives. What teenager would not want that? Especially one indoctrinated into gangs from his earliest years.

'I wanted to be like my uncles – they're driving nice cars and everybody talking about them. My family is that type, everybody knows them for killers', he said. Marcus recalls laughing at his schoolmates for wanting to pursue prestigious careers in formal professions, believing old teachers' tales like: stay in school, put your head down, study hard, and you will become a nurse, a doctor or a lawyer. 'I was like, it's fantasy. They're watching too much TV', Marcus stated sarcastically. 'Where do you get lawyers and stuff in Hanover Park?' Life in one of Cape Town's most gang-affected neighbourhoods hammers home a single incontestable lesson: violent street culture equals power. It is a nearly universal criminological theorem that young children living there learn early on, like memorising the alphabet and their times tables – only way more lucrative. So Marcus came to believe that violent crime could serve him better than any formal education would; he did not see the point of going to school and working hard if there were no jobs anyway.

Because of his family's gang ties, becoming an American was nothing short of a destiny made manifest. 'Some people learn to be *kapadien*[14] and some are born *kapadien*', he declared fatalistically. 'You're an aggressive person who does violent things. You're not scared of anyone. You will do anything'. But of course he was not born *kapadien*, he was conditioned into it. The influence of his family was too overbearing, too fervent and too all-consuming for a little boy to withstand. Returning at the end of the day from his studies, Marcus came home to further his education in the streets: 'I come out of school they would say: hey, this is the next generation, salute the big boy! The Americans and my cousins would do that to me'. By age 10, Marcus was ready to join them, rebutting any insistence that 10 is far too young for such a treacherous rite of passage by saying:

> Yeah, but in Hanover Park that's not young. Once you start having the mind, and you know what *Sabela* is, and you what's going on in a gang, and you know the enemies, you know how to handle a gun, and stuff. You are ready to become a gangster.

Without guidance towards fall-back career options, Marcus enlisted in the Americans, working his way up the gang's hierarchy by building on an already impressive repertoire of street-based knowledge and experience. 'You work through people to learn gangsterism. So, I was taught also... There's a lot of ranks in the gang. I started as a soldier, I worked myself up with blood and that's how people looked at me afterwards', he stated. As with any aptitude,

---

[14]Also a gang rank. But here it denotes the belligerent, attack-oriented state of mind taken on by somebody who is always ready to fight.

becoming a gangster takes time and dedicated effort. Marcus put his head down and studied hard, just not in class. He memorised *Sabela*, schooled himself in street politics and gained a proficiency as a triggerman. 'I won't say it took a long time. I liked to shoot. I liked [having] a gun in my hand. But I still had to grow my own name by shooting all the time, to grow my reputation', he said. So dedicated a shooter was he, that the name Marcus became a metonymic stand-in for bloodshed. 'Even if I come down the road and I don't have a gun on me, they'll still think I have a gun on me. Because they know this is a guy that shoots every day'.

Once somebody gets accustomed to violent street culture it is difficult to stop. Actions develop into habits, values and thereafter into a 'streetwise disposition... that represents the internalization of the experience of marginality and the strategic employment of forms of available capital' (Fraser, 2015, p. 46). This is a subculture-specific application of those corporeal dispositions Bourdieu deemed 'the body schema' – customs, routines and lifestyles that are 'capable of orienting practices in a way that is at once unconscious and systematic' (1990, p. 10). Bourdieu's work dwelled on the embodied and enduring aspects of dispositional schemas. The criminologists he inspired also spend most of their time engaging analysis that speaks to dispositions in the present tense, to show how social arrangements are fixed and reinforced. There is also value, however, in indulging the changing and changeable aspects of the personal disposition, without regarding it as a *fait accompli*. Let us add then to the lexicon of Bourdieusian criminology the idea of street 'dispositioning', to explicitly acknowledge the continuous process by which any social actor becomes dispositioned into social practice, and to more accurately communicate how habits, values and customs can morph and evolve into culture. After all, even someone inculcated from his earliest years into gangs has to be first introduced to street culture before it can ever be internalised and accumulated as a socio-criminological behavioural pattern. Aggression aggregates around action over time, as up-and-coming soldiers self-select away from society and towards the streets, learning the logic, expectations and skills of the street field by shooting every day to grow their reputations by building criminal cultural capital.

For Marcus, street practice eventually became part of a street dispositioning that he went all-in on. 'This is the number one rule if you want to become a gangster: you must be willing to go to prison or die', he said. 'So, you sign your death certificate and you sign your slip into jail. So, that it is what it is, and I believed it.' Marcus soon did land in jail – as predicted – doing time for murder, attempted murder, gun possession and related crimes. In prison he became a 27. Thrown headlong into a bruising fight against warders and other *ndotas*, he hit back wildly at any risk to his reputation, no matter the repercussions. To give one example, following a scuffle with a cellmate, authorities sentenced Marcus to solitary confinement for 14 days. Instead of showing contrition, he plotted revenge on the guard that punished him:

> When I came out, it was breakfast – the morning. You know how
> the warders treat the prisoners. Me, you can't treat me like you

want to. I have a reputation that I must maintain here. Whatever you going to do [to me], I'm going to [do to] you... I grabbed this spoon, hit him in the head so there was blood. So the *ouens*[15] saw it, and that was on my records in the [27] gang. So, I took his *gwinyas*.[16] His rank, I took it. The warder's ranks were placed on me.

Prison authorities retaliated with a vicious pummelling, blurring Marcus' eyesight for months afterwards. From the perspective of somebody not used to gang life, it might be natural to enquire: why would an individual subject themselves to inhumane punishments for the sake of something as ethereal as reputation? Social standing is only insubstantial if there are tangible governance structures and protective institutions working to insulate people from competition with each other. Most people can take such structures for granted. It is evident that Marcus cannot. The world of prison gangs and the real world have few commonalities. A beating is something that hard-boiled *ndotas* are expected to bear without disclosing panic or pain (Steinberg, 2004b). Being regarded as rash and rough bears very real rewards, while refusing to be so comes with a price. 'If you're a gangster and you do not have a [violent] reputation, you will be like a small child. They're going to push you around', declared Marcus definitively. His propensity for conflict was just 'good public relations' (Bourgois, 2011b, pp. 302–303), a perfectly rational move in the political economy of prison gang culture in which self-preservation is a paramount concern.

Violent behaviour was never inherent to Marcus' character. Rather it is inherent to *the character* he played in the street field. Many interviewees similarly revealed that street life required a separate persona. Often this persona was represented by a nickname that highlighted some special physical or psychological trait associated with the attributes, expertise and talents of their street-based roles. The word 'mask' appeared regularly as a descriptor for the psyche a person takes on when in the gangs; recall Taahir using it to characterise how he feigned bravery on the battlefield for the benefit of his Hard Livings brothers, only to go home every night to cry himself to sleep. Marcus put on his own front as an American gangster:

> If I could just take that mask off, and just be what I feel and follow [that], I could have been a much more better person... There's different kinds of masks. You know by the gangster, it's: lie, cheat, and steal. That was me all the time – even if it wasn't me.

Psychologists, poets and philosophers have for some time posited that masks reveal more than they conceal. The social face a person presents to the world is a guise designed to conceal the true nature of the individual so as to reflect back to society a desired impression. If this is the case, masks are as telling of society as

---

[15]The guys.
[16]A prison gang rank; a *gwinya* is also a kind of township dumpling that Cape gangsters say looks like the stars on a military officer's epaulettes.

they are of their wearers. Marcus, Taahir and others were relegated to a social field that denied their better angels, requiring instead that they commit regular acts of lying, cheating and stealing to escape death. The sins they committed are shadows cast over a supremely unfair city. A reminder of the unattended inequities and injustices hanging over sun-revelling urbanites and tourists living their best lives, while those on the outside mask their morals, sentimentality and humanity, thinking it best to victimise somebody else before they themselves are made victims.

3.5.2 Ruan

Disruptive behaviour is never seen as shameful in the street field, and crimes that are prosecutable in the criminal justice system are simply viewed as rational responses to irrational socioeconomic conditions. Neither a court of law nor the court of popular opinion matters much to gangs. Street reputations are what count, as is plainly evidenced in the courtroom antics of Ruan (Lavender Hill male, 34 years). He was brought before a judge in Wynberg Magistrates' Court for the multiple cases he caught as a result of shady street dealings:

> I got called up... and the judge told me: give me a reason why
> I shouldn't send you to prison. And I was like: I don't give a fuck,
> do what you want to. And she was like: if that's your attitude,
> you're going to Pollsmoor.

Caught between acting decent and acting street, he chose the street; he did so in spite of the promise of more jail time, a nod to that part of him dispositioned towards the gang. 'I walked back down to the cells and I was knocking my head against the wall thinking: "couldn't you just have been like decent for once?"', he explained in a post-mortem of his case.

Of course, Ruan knows very well that displaying so-called 'decent' middle-class values will only get you hurt – or killed – in the street field (Anderson, 1998). Courtrooms are liminal zones between gang life and decent life, where those deemed to be society's black sheep congregate to receive punishments and pardons. The nearness of Wynberg to the Cape Flats makes its courthouse an especially important meeting point for Cape Town's underworld; legal proceedings there have in the past been interrupted by shootings and fatal stabbings. Thus, Ruan's outburst was not as counterintuitive as it appeared at first glance. Hurling profanities at the presiding magistrate was not a conflictual expression of 'negative cultural capital' (Barker, 2013, p. 361). It was proof that a contemptible and kamikaze action will be judged differently in the mainstream than it will be in the streets:

> I did it because it was my reputation. Wynberg police station,
> Wynberg court, it was for all the surrounding areas like Lavender
> Hill, and even Athlone. Even the people who are coming to support
> maybe a friend or a brother, the family, they also know me. And
> I still need to portray the same person. It is like a performance.

Prison time was irrelevant. The front was everything. So Ruan could not let anybody think that there were cracks in his façade.

Accepting a longer sentence only elevated Ruan in the eyes of the gallery, reinforcing what he called a 'character [that] was just a crazy guy who didn't give fuck about anything – anyone'. There is a powerful lesson here for anybody that still believes that time in the penitentiary can be an effective deterrent to gangs. Gang prevention based on a criminal justice might not be blind, so much as myopic in its view that mandatory minimums and tougher prosecutions make for effective deterrence. Ruan's wild flayings fly in the face of this theory. Going to Pollsmoor actually made him crazier:

> When I went into prison, I told myself that I'm going to be the craziest motherfucker these people have ever met. Nobody's going to walk over me... I would use anything and everything to win a fight. People respected it and people knew that: this guy's crazy. I fed off that completely. It just made me more crazy.

'The theme of "survival" permeates many of the explanations of why youths go in for gangs and do the "crazy things" they do' (1990, p. 231), states Spergel. He is one of a number of gang researchers to accept what proponents of law and order policies insist on ignoring: strongly and consistently demonstrating an ethos of everyday brinksmanship expands a gang member's social and personal esteem by conforming to a gang ideal of toughness and fearlessness (Vigil, 1988). Doing 'anything and everything to win a fight' is a functional adaptation to both the do-or-die prison environment and the prison gangs' value system. There is little hope besides being crazy, if one is to sustain oneself in a cell filled with cons and killers.

For a teenager socialised into a spartan standard of living in Parkwood, who found himself approaching adulthood on the wrong side of the tracks, fighting always felt like the best way to get ahead for Ruan. 'Parkwood itself is poor... There's a border road that runs through Parkwood, Parkwood on the one side, Fairways on the other. So Fairways is the working-class, Parkwood is the ghetto', recalled Ruan of the community where his single mother raised him. Mom struggled valiantly to bestow upon her boy an acceptable childhood, but could not finally offer as much as the neighbourhood gang did. Ruan blames poverty and inequality. But he also blames himself. Bluntly stated, 'I wanted to get rich fast', he admitted. The Junky Funky Kids had a monopoly on street capital in Parkwood. So he joined them at the age of 12.

The ongoing wrangle and hustle of 'JFK' membership landed him the case referred to above. From the Wynberg Magistrates' Court he was transferred to Pollsmoor Prison. While serving his sentence, Ruan fell in with the leader of the rival Corner Boys through their common prison gang affiliation:

> We slept in the same room, and just for some reason we hit it off. Things that happen on the outside [stay there], you are not allowed to bring any [outside] animosity inside the number. He was like:

> you're a Junky Funky, I'm a Corner Boy, outside we're going to
> have to kill each other; but I have a proposition for you: go with
> me, and I will make you rich. And I just decided I was going to go
> with him.

Just like that Ruan pledged allegiance to a new gang. After being discharged
from Pollsmoor he migrated south from Parkwood to their home base in neighbouring Lavender Hill. Though an avowed Corner Boy now and right-hand man
to the gang's boss, he still had to convince the gang's other membership of his
loyalty and worth. 'First thing I did to prove myself was to kill one of the
Mongrels', he said straightforwardly. Criminal violence is lifeblood in the street
field, flowing through it like current in a wire, generating and regenerating relations between people. Violence is even generative of people themselves, who make
their names by killing with abandon, and who understand how a sworn foe – who
was previously dead to them – might be reborn as a brother after making the right
sacrifice.

Ruan got a shot to prove himself shortly after making the move to Lavender
Hill. Though he lived within walking distance from the gentle eastern curve of the
False Bay coast and Muizenburg's popular Surfer's Corner, Ruan whiled away
the days bouncing between the cookie-cutter council flats and battered courtyards
of his new neighbourhood. One afternoon he came upon a member of the
Mongrels while taking a turn around this territory with some fellow Corner Boys.
The Mongrel gang member was the lone remaining witness in a pending triple
murder against a Corner Boy. So the man had to die:

> I'm not known with the Mongrels. They just saw me walking with
> these guys. On the way back, they gave me a gun in F-Court, and
> said if you want to prove that you're with us, you'll do this for us
> now. And I did it without blinking, in broad daylight, and that was
> the start.

A lack of remorse ruled the rest of Ruan's tenure with the Corner Boys as well.
As the muscle that made good on the gang's drug bills, he apportioned street
justice to anybody found owing. Violence committed against a delinquent client
upheld a corporate model that requires panic and terror as deterrence to unpaid
debts. Broken down doors, busted up homes and cracked bones are just a cost of
doing business with the gang. From Ruan's perspective they are a necessary part of
a communications strategy that served as fair warning for anybody else sourcing
buttons, *tik* or *unga* from the Corner Boys' stash:

> If you don't pay… Men, women, children, it didn't matter to me.
> Mothers, fathers, grandparents, I'd go in with my baseball bat and
> I would just fuck shit up. Obviously I'm not going to shoot people
> who don't need to be shot. So maybe I stab you. I hit this guy with
> a hammer in his face for 60 rands… just to say don't fuck with me
> and don't fuck with us.

But Ruan's case is illustrative exactly because it is unexceptional. There were plenty of accounts like it in this study. His was not the only score settled by bashing somebody's face in. Hammers, bats, bricks, fists and firearms are all instrumental to gang violence. By mainstream society's standards street conventions probably seem gross and disproportionate. But the demands of the drug economy are unrelenting and unforgiving, and make no exceptions for the very young, the very old or anybody else. Enacting these demands unflaggingly leads to a powerful reputation. 'To me that kind of reputation – that fear people have – is almost like a currency in a certain environment, isn't it?', I asked, after listening to Ruan for a couple of hours. 'Yeah. Because of who I was I had women. I had drugs. I'd come into a drug den, and I don't even need money', replied the former Corner Boy. 'And I don't even need to tell you... if I do tell you, there's going to be a slap involved in me telling you to give me your stuff, if you're not going to come and give it yourself'.

There is perhaps one anecdote that best encapsulates how deeds and consequences are ordered in gang-controlled drug economies. It starts with a business dilemma: in a weekend-long bender with his girlfriend, a member of the Corner Boys had smoked up a stockpile of methamphetamines he was sitting on. Ruan was called upon to resolve the issue. The snag in the story is that it was the nephew of the leader of the Corner Boys that had transgressed. Family or not, he still had to pay:

> [The leader] told me to break both his legs. I said: but this is your nephew. It's your brother's son. He was like: I don't care, where's my money? All I'm worried about is getting rich, you break both of his legs now, or I'm going to break your legs. I broke both his legs with a baseball bat – his own nephew.

This is just further evidence of the grotesque acts that are accepted and justified to keep a drug enterprise churning. Ruan himself unenthusiastically acknowledged that if you fuck up 'you pay your dues'. 'It's all in the game', after all, he said nonchalantly.[17] Just as Bourdieu frequently invoked the competitive nature of social 'games', research participants often also analogised 'the game' and 'the streets'. The rules and stakes are firmly established and well known to street hustlers – or 'playas' – all over the world, who bet against long odds that the right combination of fearlessness, shrewdness and craziness wins them enough street capital to beat the competition (Harding, 2014). By continually acting crazy, assailing all that messed with him, aligning closely with the Corner Boys' leader and knowing enough not to get high on his own supply, Ruan became a dominant player in the gang. He was simply doing what any professional would

---

[17]This same catchphrase was imprinted into popular culture by *The Wire's* Omar Little, a fictitious Baltimore stick-up man making a living robbing street-level drug dealers, perpetrating crimes not pursuable or prosecutable in any extrajudicial system because 'it's all in the game'.

do: working hard, playing the cards he was dealt to the best of his abilities and taking calculated risks in order to earn a promotion and a higher income.

'Me and the guy whose legs I broke, the two of us, started basically running the whole operation – the whole *tik* operation – of the Corner Boys', Ruan went on to reveal. No human resources offices, labour laws or workplace insurance schemes were there to aid the injured gang member. Having taken his lumps, and without viable alternative livelihoods, the nephew returned to dealing. Once he was able to walk, he again worked collegially alongside Ruan – his associate and attacker – to distribute drugs throughout Lavender Hill. What appears irrational from one vantage point might be anything but from another. Context matters. Society's notions of fairness are made by and for comfortable people, people who have been lucky enough to have lived lives defined more by certitude than by ambiguity. Passing laws that ignore the moral, cultural and circum- stantial relativity of the streets, and then acting surprised when they fail to produce improvements in public safety, is probably as crazy as anything any gangster might be accused of. It is just as objectionable too, when one considers the many people that unnecessarily die every year because of an unwillingness to tackle gang-related violence on its own terms.

3.6 Street Habitus

Cape Flats residents are surrounded by killing fields of human design, planned by the apartheid government and maintained under neo-apartheid. Outright antag- onism has succumbed to state apathy. The results are just the same. Disparities, divisions and discrimination are still the baseline. It is normal that people search for pathways out of such circumstances wherever they can. Street gangs are one route many people take. Boys and girls take a look around them, and take note that to be *kapadien* and crazy is to be feared and respected. Thinking they have no real chance at legit wealth or fame, some will settle for infamy, joining gangs and gradually growing into gangsters. In the process, each is dispositioned in a combative personality that will serve as their most trusted weapon in a fight for self-preservation. However, absorbing oneself too fully in gang practices increases the likelihood of coming to a bad end too (Lindegaard, Miller, & Reynald, 2013). Gang members might not be passive victims any longer, but long-term adherence to street culture is dangerous and self-damaging for them. Poor Coloured men like Gavin, Taahir, William, Marcus and Ruan unfailingly target other poor Col- oured men. They will be targeted in turn.

The same reputation for going out and gunning every day that protected Marcus, also made life miserable for him. 'What people spoke about me, it's going to automatically be a trigger to them. When they see me in gang fighting, then this person's going to shoot me', said Marcus. Although he was among the few I talked to who were fortunate enough to never catch a bullet, Marcus could not escape being hurt in other ways. 'I was lucky I was never shot. I was shot at but it missed me. But they were beating me… There were a lot of times I was beaten bad'. Emmanuel was not blessed with the same 'good fortune'. At 16 he was shot up badly by a *Stoepa Boy* seeking revenge after being maimed in a gang fight with the Playboys. 'He lost his eye in a gang fight, then he blamed me. I told him it wasn't me that [took] your eye out. Then the friend next to him told him shoot him and so he shot me', Emmanuel stated. Bullets pierced his arm, chest and back, sending Emmanuel to the hospital for six months. 'When I got out of hospital I went to go shoot the guy that shot me'. Gang norms require that acts of violence against oneself or one's brothers are followed by 'picking up blood' – the Capetonian underworld's version of 'an eye for an eye'. This edict is at the heart of a requirement for revenge that is proverbial and unquestionable. Emmanuel went to war as soon as he physically could, in an attempt to transform himself from being the victimised to being the victimiser – even if the line between the two is seldom clear in the chaotic, chronic inertia of the street field.

Gangs offer life, and gangs snatch it away, using a sleight of hand that is ignored by the many thousands of young Capetonians that turn to gangsterism. We would have perhaps done the same, if we had come from an abusive home like Taahir's, or had to grapple with the trauma of a mother's death like William did, or had grown up around gangs as in Marcus' case. Add to this anxieties around joblessness, hunger and lack of housing, and we start to see their choices more honestly. Suddenly the danger, drugs and destabilisation are not such a high price to pay. People take what they can, when they can, from whom they can, accumulating street capital by shooting one another, stealing from family and selling drugs to their neighbours; the outrage and grief flowing from their marginality is internalised and converted into an interpersonal everyday violence that predominantly harms themselves and their loved ones. William got into various fistfights and shootouts, dodging blows and bullets, while giving back as good as he got. Everybody else in this study did likewise. Without a single exception, all interviewees described being beaten and shot at. All also found that being in the streets is closely connected to stress, trauma, isolation and addiction. 'You think I'm skinny now, you had to see me on drugs, I was like a skeleton. I had no face. It was just that I was crazy', recounted Ruan, when speaking of the many years he was under the spell of *tik*.

What began for him and others in this book as an adaptive retort to urban marginality, in time congealed into 'street habitus' (Fraser, 2015, pp. 43–44); this is another key street cultural concept transposed from Bourdieusian sociology to illustrate how the repetition of gang behaviours structurally attaches crime, violence and poverty to people and places. Bourdieu situates habitus alongside cultural capital and the social field, in an exhaustive theory of practice, saying that:

> The habitus... produces strategies which are objectively adjusted
> to the objective situation, even though these strategies are neither
> the outcome of the explicit aiming at consciously pursued goals, nor
> the result of some mechanical determination by external causes.
> (1988, p. 782)

Habitus is meant to balance agency and structure in a dynamic dialectic interplay between the two. Through it, Bourdieu wanted to explain how the subjective experiences of social agents mediated the objectifying forces of social structures, through a vision of social life that can at once be considered both improvised and instinctual. But Bourdieu's detractors pointed out that he was inclined to overemphasise the structuring effects of habitus, subsuming agency as a genuine condition of practice (Chouliaraki & Fairclough, 1999; Evens, 1999; Gartman, 1991; Schatzki, 1997). Giroux, for instance, claimed that Bourdieu's theory of practice is in effect a theory of reproduction 'that displays no faith in subordinate classes and groups, no hope in their ability or willingness to reinvent and reconstruct the conditions under which they live, work, and learn' (2001, pp. 95–96). Even Loïc Wacquant, a protégé and collaborator of Bourdieu's, matter-of-factly appraises the defects of Bourdieusian sociology by admitting that 'while it contains a creative and powerful theory of social reproduction, it falls short of offering anything close to an equally comprehensive *theory of social transformation* [emphasis in original]' (1987, p. 81). Caveats raised by Wacquant, Giroux and others are given credibility by how Bourdieu's work has been transfered elsewhere. Academics overwhelmingly use it to focus on how sociocultural processes contribute to the reproduction of structural inequalities[18] and power imbalances, without affording the same attention to the transformative potential of individual agency.

Gang scholars tend to fall into this trap too, even if it is not their intention. True, they pay lip service to deviance and criminality as acts of agency. At its best, street cultural literature 'brings "the gang" into the realm of structured agency, and resolves some of the tensions latent in social theory surrounding the gang; specifically the issues of continuity, change, diversity, and difference' (2015, p. 53), writes Fraser. At least this is what it is supposed to do in theory. In practice, however, the conditional and messy nature of street life has mostly been lost because such preeminence is given to the reproductive elements of gang culture, all but negating the possibility for personal and social transformation. Writings on street culture overwhelmingly present the 'homologies of [street] habitus' (Fraser, 2015, p. 46) as hardwired, preconscious and cyclical, and gang members as inevitably complicit in reinforcing the very structures that pushed them there into gangs to begin with. In short, the transformative effects of street culture for individuals are limited to oppositional action that in the end keeps them ensnared in the streets (Bourgois, 2002; Fraser, 2013). Continual hypersensitivity to disrespect and frequent violent performances in due course come to endure as the long-term dispositions of the street-cultured individual (Sandberg & Pedersen, 2011). Residual bad temper colludes together with drug addiction, lack of gainful employment and criminal records to keep people and places mired in everyday violence (Bourgois, 2011a). Shammas and Sandberg write that street habitus has a 'generative grammar' that

---

[18]Studies have shown how variations in sociocultural resources reproduce societal stratification in subjects as diverse as: health (Collyer, Willis, Franklin, Harley, & Short, 2015), agroforestry (Raedeke, Green, Hodge, & Valdivia, 2009), education (Colley, James, Diment, & Tedder, 2003) and organisational management (Konecki, 2006).

can reproduce activities within the street field, keeping whole cohorts of society perpetually poor, confined and underprivileged 'through a locking-in effect' (2016, p. 209). Getting into street culture might be easy; but barriers to departing the street field are high – too high it seems. Sometimes it can truly feel there is no way out.

Yet, there is life after gangs, as we will see shortly. Street cultural scholarship needs to better account for this possibility. Casting blame on social structures in a manner that gives so much power to dysfunctional coping strategies, to substance abuse, to economic disenfranchisement, to racial prejudice, makes it hard to envisage how people can do much to resist the socioeconomic institutions that surround and act upon them. Explanations of what ails broken cities like Cape Town surely cannot ignore social structures. That is not the point. But they also cannot foreground structural analysis so much that it trivialises the agency of social actors. Writing more about gang exit can help return agency – and hope – to the young men and women trying to disengage from street culture, showing gang membership for what it is: something subjective and ultimately surmountable. This will also restore agency to street scholarship itself, by pushing back against a presumptive bias that favours the reproductive forces of street habitus – and habitus in general – towards a more complete picture that also makes room for social transformation.

3.7 The Practical Dimensions of Street Practice

Bourdieu famously developed 'the habitus' as a theoretical resolution to the subject–object dualism of sociology. He aimed to show that all social actors are at once cultural products and cultural producers, by framing social life as something that is continually forming people, but which they also contribute to forming. What King deemed as the 'practical dimension' (2000, p. 418) of Bourdieu's work may be subordinated in his social theory, but it is there. It addresses the fact that people do not solipsistically consult a priori social rules that independently determine their actions. Social action is guided, not pre-determined, by a practical sense of what is appropriate in any given situation; a 'feel for the game' (Bourdieu, 1988, p. 782) is interactionally – or jointly – established by individuals through the give and take of 'regulated improvisation' (Bourdieu, 1990, p. 57) with other individuals. One plays in any social field with an array of personal strategies, adjusted in a day-to-day manoeuvring to the strategies used by one's peers.

What appears to be 'so-called "structure"' is actually the simplified reification of complex, negotiated, and ever-changing relations between individuals, who are constantly renegotiating their relations relative to each other' (King, 2000, p. 421). Society is interminably changing, adjusting and evolving, though it looks stable on the surface. Habitus itself is only the aggregated sense of how life has been, is being and can be played according to the miscellaneous moves available in any field of power relations (Kloot, 2009). It too is contingent and changeable. The same is true for gangs themselves, which are organised and reorganised by their membership, under the constant strain of internal and external struggle. This is equally true for long-standing social patterns, like lamentably high homicide rates or intergenerational gang structures. These are just the sustained performance of individual gangsters adapting to what allies, foes, neighbours, civil society, police and other government stakeholders are doing over the long-term. Even the successful execution of the most routinised social practices – be they in a society, a gang or an orchestra – must adjust the rehearsed performance of individual functions towards some collective objective (Barnes, 2000). Bourdieu and Wacquant (1992) argued that to think in terms of social fields is to always think relationally and interactionally, prioritising the exchanges between people and renouncing interpretations of life that force a choice between objectivism and subjectivism, by allowing space for both.[19] The upshot is a world view based on 'constructivist structuralism' (Bourdieu, 1989, p. 14), whereby any field – street field included – 'is a field of forces and a field of struggles' (Bourdieu, 2005, p. 44). Lovell is correct to conclude that '[w]hat Bourdieu offers that is most powerful is a way of understanding both the arbitrary, and therefore contestable, nature of the social, and its compelling presence and effectiveness' (2000, p. 31).

If the Bourdieusian perspective on the social world is accurate, neither street culture nor any other type of culture can be read like a recipe, or as some baked-in ideology. There is evidence that this is so, if we look in the right places. For example, D. Harding (2007) finds that disadvantaged neighbourhoods are permeated by a wide array of competing and conflicting social models and forms of cultural capital, not just street capital; they have what he calls 'cultural heterogeneity' (Harding, 2010, pp. 144–146). Street culture may be primary while a person is a member of a gang. But mainstream cultural capital can still be socialised through family and non-gang peers as a secondary source of cultural learning (Rodgers, 2003). Anderson (1998), for instance, showed that youth in America can assimilate and switch between the codes of street culture and middle-class values of wider society, depending on what their context calls for. Researchers in Cape Town have shown too how youth in townships use 'flexible cultural repertoires' (Lindegaard & Zimmermann, 2017, p. 194), which dynamically combine multiform elements of suburban propriety and oppositional street culture to balance competing social interests in separate settings.

Already we can see that street culture is not as fixed as sometimes made out to be. A more discordant and less certain version of street habitus also starts to materialise once we start to pay more attention to the internal conflicts, clashing preferences, differing strategies and changing expectations of gang members. For anybody that is still unconvinced, there are even more examples from emerging

---

[19] Let us also acknowledge that Bourdieu himself sometimes appears to double back on his own practical theorisations; for example, he suggests that the virtuoso is socially institutionalised through some 'objective intention', softening his stance a few paragraphs later, pointing to the way that social institutions are changed through 'the revisions and transformations that [their] reactivation entails' (Bourdieu, 1990, p. 57).

gang research in Cape Town that offers further evidence: young township women participate in gangs by improvising 'typically masculine'[20] street cultural performances (Dziewanski, 2020c); men and women alike improvise inspiration from gangster rap in different ways depending on their individual life situations (Dziewanski, 2020d); and 'street virtuosos' (Dziewanski, 2020a, p. 14) challenge the accepted rationale of gangsterism to survive and thrive as mercenaries against the city's 100 or so gangs. All are exemplars of how gang culture is creatively changed by members playing 'on all the resources inherent in the ambiguties and uncertainties of behaviour and situation in order to produce the actions appropriate to each case' (Bourdieu, 1977, p. 8). This is proof that an array of cultural moves are possible within the Capetonian street field, and that the path into gangs is neither clear-cut nor inevitable.

But it never was. A teen may start hanging out with gangsters as a way of dealing with boredom or to feel cool, and may then dabble with drugs and crime, until such a point where this youth takes a gang tattoo and commits a murder. Or he may never take that final stride towards gangsterism, as with Mikey above. Even the stories of those who do step into the streets are not a foregone conclusion. For sure, significant barriers impede their way out. Enemies' grudges, employers' suspicions, community stigma and criminalisation by cops all must be negotiated by anybody aiming to quit. Most transitions out of gangs are onerous and are hampered by setbacks. But some do have happy endings. With enough time, effort, lots of luck and a bit of mercy, a hardened felon can end up an ex-gangster, confirming that street culture is just a means to a better end, not an end itself. Even those apparently locked into street habitus – who insist defiantly that being crazy or *kapadien* are the best paths forward for them – can manage to salvage their lives and get out of gangs. Street culture theorists are yet to properly take account of such perspectives. This book tries to fill this knowledge gap, by showing that street cultural practices are neither simply nor statically constituted, but are innovated in a situationally variable manner that depends on their interlocutors and their context. In the coming pages we will re-centre Bourdieusian field analysis away from 'dispositions', and towards 'dispositioning'. The intention is to tell more vociferously those life histories that speak to the struggle of the street field in Cape Town and to amplify the practical aspects of agency that have been thus far overlooked both in street cultural writings and in the social theory that inspired them.

---

[20]Street culture is typically presented as masculine in its essence (see Bourgois, 1996; Ilan, 2012; Fraser, 2015). Mullins, for instance, describes the 'gender capital' that can be accrued through the violent performance of 'street masculinity' (2013, p. 153).

Chapter 4

Leaving the Streets

The preceding pages spotlighted the significant generative strength of the street field, in what has thus far been a pretty typical interpretation of street culture. Flexing one's muscles, talking loudly and taking on antagonistic airs are forces of habit for populations trying to cut it along the sharp and jagged edges of a splintered society. But bodies and minds are never totally and decisively dispositioned towards gangs. It is disingenuous – not to mention disempowering and disheartening – to insist that members' futures are indelibly written once in the gang. The individual histories that follow attest that some of the sternest and most taciturn personalities have erased pasts rife with addiction, arrest and aggression to show that alternate endings to gang enrolment are imaginable. Steering clear of an overly objective representation of habitus in our reading of street culture requires that we soften somewhat how we speak about gangsterism, inflecting towards narratives that substantiate the possibility of leaving street life for normal life.

Not enough has been said about the potential for people to remake street culture. Too little has also been published about disengagement from gangs in low-income environments, with virtually nothing written in this regard in Cape Town. This chapter overlays Bourdieusian criminological concepts with global literature on gang disengagement and criminal desistance. It finds inter-linkages between seemingly divergent theoretical traditions in a way that raises the analytical utility of their respective self-contained, esoteric efforts to show that getting out of gangs is not impossible. Bourdieusian sociological theory has already been put to good use to solve numerous real criminological problems. In its dialectical focus on agency and structure, it may especially prove constructive to understanding gang exit too. Imaginative agentic action can deviate from structured street practice, situationally contesting how habitus shapes the street field. The result turns a field of forces into a field of struggles by re-emphasising the 'practical dimensions' of Bourdieu's social theory.

4.1 What Is Normal Anyway?

Early research posited that processes of maturation were behind most gang exits (New York City Youth Board, 1960; Suttles, 1968; Thrasher, 1927; Vigil, 1988). As people grow older and wiser, they also grow less inclined to stay in gangs.

Gang Entry and Exit in Cape Town, 77–105
Copyright © 2021 Dariusz Dziewanski
Published under exclusive licence by Emerald Publishing Limited
doi:10.1108/978-1-83909-730-020210004

Later studies showed that various exit paths are in fact possible. These indicated that a portion of people withdraw just after joining (Thornberry, Krohn, Lizotte, Smith, & Tobin, 2003), while some disconnect well after they reached the age of maturity (Spergel, 1990); others stay in the gang forever, go to prison, are killed or die of natural causes before they can get out (Sánchez-Jankowski, 1991). So there is no single prototype for disengaging from gangs. For this reason, there is also not one framework for understanding disengagement (Decker, Pyrooz, & Moule, 2014). Leaving is the result of a personalised array of pull or push factors (Pyrooz & Decker, 2011a); these may include growing discontent with gangs (Roks, 2017), moving communities (Bolden, 2013), experiencing violence (Decker & Lauritsen, 2002), new parental roles (Hunt, Moloney, Joe-Laidler, & McKenzie, 2011; Moloney, Mackenzie, Hunt, & Joe-Laidler, 2009), turning to religion (Kolind, Friis Søgaard, Hunt, & Thylstrup, 2017) and a myriad of other reasons (Carson & Esbensen, 2016). Members may leave after 'triggering events' or simply 'drift away' (Decker & Lauritsen, 2002, p. 66). Change happens distinctively for every person. But change is conceivable.

However, let us not insinuate that putting down one's pistol, relinquishing one's street fame or isolating from one's gang brothers is a simple matter. Disengagement requires much more than the proverbial 'change of heart'. Denouncing a group is one thing; leaving behind established street practices is another; and finding new opportunities and forming new social bonds and habits is another still. What makes leaving the gang so difficult ultimately comes down to those same risk factors that influenced gang participation in the first place: indigence, adversity, racism, separation, etc. The drivers of initial gang entry will then be further compounded by delinquent socialisation, social isolation and institutionalised criminalisation, which are all attached to gang membership. If you have been ensnared in the street for years – or decades – where do you locate fresh cultural capital? Or how do you access more social capital? The chapters show that most ex-gangsters find answers in family, profession and religion. Each represents a single node in a triad of options for reorganising one's inner world. But the utility of domesticity, work and spirituality is perhaps even more important in the social world, authenticating to allies, adversaries, family and community that gang quitting is in earnest. By drawing on such sociocultural assets, gang-leavers in Cape Town are able to find both personal resolve and interpersonal validation, in the long walk to finding freedom from the streets.

4.1.1 Ruan

In the only published study that focuses on gang disengagement in Cape Town, Dziewanski (2021) found a number of commonalities between the motives, motivations and modalities of local exit histories and global gang research on disengaging (Decker et al., 2014; Pyrooz & Decker, 2011a). Being targeted by violence, or having loved ones targeted, proved an important reason for quitting gangs. Some got fed up that the gang cut them off from relatives and friendships; others grew up, grew doubtful about the integrity of the gang or simply grew tired of the gangster lifestyle. We will consider a few specific disengagement cases below. In Ruan's (Lavender Hill male, 34 years) case, he merely grew bored of the streets. As he tells it, his turning point is conspicuously unexciting when compared with some of the hardcore aspects of time spent first as a Junky Funky Kid and then as a Corner Boy and 27:

> Honestly, I got bored [of being a Corner Boy]. I got bored of only being in this specific part of Lavender Hill, as you're going up to Retreat Station [which is about four kilometres away], there were [the enemy] Junky Funkies all over. But nobody owned Retreat Station, so my life was that area and Pollsmoor. It was all that I did – that I was.

Rather than leaving the Corners Boys as the kickback of some spectacular shootout, Ruan got fed up with the day-in and day-out circumscription of the street field. Sell, shoot, smoke and repeat – that is all his life was. 'In those few blocks I controlled, I could go into this person's house, sit down... give the mother 10 rands for beer, smoke a button with the father, [and] then have sex with the daughter', said Ruan. He had a kingdom. But it was a tiny kingdom, and ruling over it was growing more and more unfulfilling:

> I saw family, friends, everybody's always doing something cool. But I can't, as there's always that risk of someone seeing me. Or there is the risk of me actually doing something [with family or friends] and somebody harming the people around me.

Ruan's turning point was not blatantly violent in nature, in that no individual incident made him abandon the gang. The threat of death or injury did, however, separate him from meaningful moments with his family, which is what finally motivated him to drop out. As he explained:

> I was like: where am I actually going? Yes, I don't have to work, people fear me... [but] I said: I can't do it anymore. I want to have a relationship with my children.

The typical way of picturing a 'turning point' is as an 'event that mobilises and focusses awareness that old lives of action are complete, have failed, have been disrupted or are no longer personally satisfying' (Ebaugh, 2013, p. 123). But viewed another way, a turning point is less a single incident, so much as a creeping change that occurs as a 'part of a potential causal dynamic over the life course' (Sampson & Laub, 2005, p. 34). In the Capetonian context,

> ...transitioning from gang roles is not an event, or even a set of easily identifiable stages. It is rather a blend of helping and hindering events and processes that, when taken together, are manifested as disengagement. (Dziewanski, 2020b, p. 10)

This fits the general view among criminologists of desistance from delinquent roles, criminal associates and illegal opportunities as a progression that is usually fluid, sporadic, lengthy and fraught with pitfalls (Maruna, 2007). Quitting gangs usually has two parts: declaring non-membership through 'de-identification' and 'decreasing gang embeddedness' (Sweeten, Pyrooz, & Piquero, 2013, pp. 475–476). While de-identification is an instance that announces the cutting of group ties, de-embedding has a 'succession quality' (Vigil, 1988, pp. 106–109) that comes about from incremental decreases to commitment and association with group activities.

Under the pretext that detoxing would make him a more competent gangster, and therefore more valuable to the gang, Ruan was able to 'knife off' (Maruna & Roy, 2007, pp. 106–109) his ties to the Corner Boys by telling them he was leaving Lavender Hill to attend a rehab in Observatory. 'Obs' is a bohemian part of Cape Town that is populated by students and known for cafés, bars, second-hand clothing and vinyl shops. However, this was not Ruan's first trip there. He had visited five years prior, actually checking into the same rehabilitation centre during another aborted effort to stop drugs. So while his eventual exit appears to be the result of a knifing off of gang connections, it was actually the outgrowth of a process commenced years before, which he described here when talking about his first attempt to leave gangs and drugs:

> Ruan: [My mom] asked me to go for a drive with her, and the kids, [and] the kids' mom. We went to Observatory, the rehab that I went to five years ago. It was the same rehab in the same house [where I eventually got clean], under a different banner. They took me there and asked: me do I want to go to rehab? Do I want to stop doing drugs?
>
> Dariusz: So they did like a mini-intervention, I guess?
>
> Ruan: They told me I could start immediately… I said: I'm coming back now, I just want to fetch my things from home. I didn't come back. I went straight to the gang, I left my kids and their mother at my mother's place. They saw me like 7–8 months later.

At that point, the attractiveness of the streets was too magnetic. 'I loved drugs. Also, I loved people fearing me. I loved being crazy', said Ruan. Being with family did not have the same appeal then as it would five years later. As a person matures, their cognitive development favours non-delinquent connections – to family, for instance – that act as the 'hooks for change' (Giordano, Cernkovich, & Rudolph, 2002, p. 992). Criminal connections turn out to be less personally and socially advantageous with age, adding to the opportunity cost of crime, and further reinforcing desistance (Moffitt, 1993). Relatively less association with law-breaking peers is in time replaced by greater engagement with law-abiding peers, who model and reinforce non-delinquent behaviours (Akers, 1998).

Sad to say, disengagement does not always go smoothly for ex-gang members. The limited opportunities members have for accessing legal forms of economic and social empowerment are a critical part of what sustains involvement in gangs (Hagedorn & Macon, 1988). Those without the right social networks may find it especially difficult to access formal work (Brotherton & Barrios, 2011). The challenges ex-members encounter finding employment are further compounded by the threats of violence, criminalisation, diminished social options and stigma that can follow gang membership (Feavel & Pyrooz, 2014). Someone can announce an intention to leave a gang, but still be treated as a gangster by collaborators, foes and the police (Pyrooz & Decker, 2011b). That person might then come to occupy a disengaged 'grey area', formally departing the gang, but remaining socially and emotionally tied to it (Moore, 1994; Pyrooz, Decker, & Webb, 2014).

Fear of violent victimisation is a particular concern among ex-members (Roks, 2017). When Ruan eventually returned to make his peace with the Corner Boys after that second stint at the rehabilitation centre in Observatory, he did not receive a warm welcome. 'The Corner boys were like you turned your back on us, fuck you, you need to die', he stated. But Ruan pleaded his case to their boss, the same man who had recruited him in prison so many years before. 'I told [him] everything, sat there crying and told him: I'm out, I'm done... He was angry, but he said he was going to call on me when he needs me.'

The Corner Boys did let Ruan leave, with a caveat. 'I was [to be] readily available always. If anything breaks out now and they call on me I have to go. So I'm out, but I'm not out... That's why I live in this area where nobody knows me', he stated. Caught in a conditional departure that kept him in the group's grip, Ruan moved to Rondebosch. He was the only person in this study who was able to leave the Cape Flats. Ruan was also fortunate to land a paid gig at the rehab he was at in Obs, after volunteering there first. With his salary he was stretched to make ends meet living in the burbs. But cost was not a consideration at that point. Keeping out of the streets was his main concern. 'Doesn't matter what the rent is in this small shitty place I stay in. If people see me too much in a certain area. I move out of that area. Nothing's happened in this five years [I've been out]', said Ruan.

His exit story is indicative that the violent street act need not be explicitly present in the lives of gangsters for the indirect, oppressive ramifications of street culture to have powerful consequences. When he was a gangster Ruan had to self-isolate from his family for fear of putting them in harm's way. In doing so, he was kept apart from everybody he cared for most, missing his two baby girls' first words, their initial steps and many of their birthdays. Only now, can he embark on re-establishing a normal and steady relationship with his girlfriend and daughters. Children and romantic unions, along with employment and religion, were regularly listed among interviewees as essential to pulling people out of gangs. These roles gave participants a crucial sense of empowerment and direction and were paramount to validating people's non-street personas to former gang mates, enemies, family and acquaintances. Other researchers of Cape gangs have equally suggested that being a good son and father (Salo, 2004) and a good Christian or Muslim (Jensen, 2008) positively supports new non-gang identities. Domestic, professional and spiritual successes are the metrics by which disengagement is measured. If mainstream cultural strategies can be accessed enough times, with enough conviction, a person will eventually come to believe in himself or herself as an ex-gangster – and have others believe in that too.

4.1.2 Prince

Working, worshipping, loving and childrearing were also instrumental in the disengagement of Prince (Mitchells Plain male, 35 years), as he suggests below. Prince gradually adopted street culture as a way of finding success as a thief and robber in the Black township of Nyanga. He would eventually graduate from robbery to gangsterism after moving to Mitchells Plain, a massive Coloured township about 30 minutes from Cape Town's centre. Although he was recruited by Cape Town's biggest street gangs, he refused to join one, not wanting to subordinate himself before a gang boss. Instead, he used extraordinary violence and took risks that others would not even consider, squaring off single-handedly as a mercenary among the estimated 100,000 others that populate the city's ganglands. For almost 20 years he stole, murdered and dealt drugs in his ambition to hold the title of 'the greatest hitman and biggest drug smuggler in the Western Cape'. With age, however, street-based aspirations became less salient, and family and stability became more important, as Prince explained here:

> I was at that age where I wanted to have a normal life... But to come [to] that life is a process. I distanced myself of everyone and everything in the gang-world and I focused on [my girlfriend][1] and her children... That's the lifestyle I chose for myself... It means no more violence, and [in] this woman that I'm with I'm starting to see now a family life. I'm seeing I'm a husband and a father – a man.

Prince's experiences accurately illustrate what other research participants also conveyed: he or she who embraces normal living disassociates from street-based activities in the interests of family stability, modesty, respectfulness and non-confrontation. In the passage above, Prince projects his future into his partner and her kids. Later he would add labour and faith to complete the assemblage of identities by which he defined his new 'normal' self.

Kolind et al. (2017) found that, for members looking to transition from a gang, 'A "normal life" worked as a metaphor, which represented both a break from their past, their activities and values, and a belief in a future free of major problems and concerns'. (p. 11). Elements of the normal life are analogous to 'decent' social orientations associated with an adherence to middle-class or sub-urban values epitomised by: being professional, speaking properly, dressing nicely and not being conflictual (Anderson, 1998; Lindegaard & Zimmermann, 2017). While acting decently is typically presented as a failing strategy in township settings, which leaves those utilising it dangerously exposed, this book asserts the

---

[1]She later became his wife.

opposite. The repertoires of normal living can actually be beneficial behavioural strategies for those shifting out of gangs. To argue, this, however, is not to give primacy to the non-economic, normative aspects of labels such as 'middle class', 'mainstream' or 'normal' (Pattillo-McCoy, 2000). Cultural repertoires represent strategic pursuits, not moral positions (Hannerz, 1969; Swidler, 1986). The sociocultural maneuvers somebody takes on can change with their objectives and outlook. To the men and women in this study, for one, gangsterism initially seemed like a track towards empowerment and dignity. After trying on the street repertoire for some time, they discovered it was a dead end.

What is – and is not – 'normal' is not by necessity self-evident. Normality is a discretionary and idiosyncratic social construction. For a person like Prince, what might be considered normal stood in contrast to his former way of living, a lifestyle in which he had lost count of how many people he had killed. Harmony and incorruptibility were long leaps away from the atrocities he was used to. So he started by taking small steps. 'It means less gun activity and less being out there. Everything is in the house. And the life I'm going to be in is a life with children, so I have to put these people first before myself', he said, of his changing life.

Good intentions do not pay the bills though. Since Prince could not find legitimate work right away, he continued to sell drugs in small quantities. After all, he understood the inner workings of the drug industry, had credibility on the streets, hook-ups to suppliers and knew how to market product that could attract clients. Prince was not totally legit at this point, but it was a start. 'The adjustment was for me to stop living a reckless life, and try to fit in a safe life – though the safe life had smuggling and cops in it', he said. Lack of legitimate professional connections and employment kept him stuck, one foot in society and one foot still in the streets. It is with good reason that associations with drug dealing are often referred to as the 'trap' in the American inner city. Ghettos, townships and other spaces of urban poverty are all places where deleterious markets, segregationist planning and apathetic government conspire to obstruct an income earned within the law, even for those striving to find one (Fraser, 2015; Ilan, 2015).

Prince did not have the luxury of making a defined distinction between right and wrong, because food needed to be put on the table and school supplies had to be purchased. The result was a moral middle ground where a bearing towards legal living coexisted with petty illegality. When one considers that mass murder was the counterfactual, the lesser of two evils does not seem bad at all. South African Police Service (SAPS) officers still monitoring Prince at that point seemed to understand this too. 'Even if they get a small quantity of drugs they would say: you're lucky we know you, we're going take [the drugs], but we're leaving you', he revealed. 'The cops were a little bit more acceptable, after the past I had'. They gave him a free pass on drug charges, fearing that criminalisation could nudge Prince back into the game. The reaction of law enforcement in this particular instance is an example of on-the-ground officials who recognise that keeping the streets secure from crime and safeguarding officialised criminal statutes are not the same thing. Public safety requires that police read the street to adapt to subjective situations that are highly changing, contextual and relative. What is particularly cogent about this anecdote is that Prince did, a few years later, completely disengage from gangsterism – no more killing *and* no more selling. Had he been put back in jail just then Prince might have gone back to the number – where he was a high-ranking 26 – and back to fighting to become the greatest hitman and biggest drug merchant. In giving him the leeway that they did, officers accepted that the liminal space between street life and normal life is a sensitive spot to be in, acknowledging also that the change Prince had already made was itself extraordinary.

Prince's character arc evolved even more over the following three years, taking a line that suggests 'that leaving the gang, as well as desisting from crime, is a complex process replete with pushes and pulls to conformity and back to the gang' (Pyrooz, Decker, & Webb, 2014, p. 508). It is not about being perfect. It is about making an effort, every single day to be better. That is where transformation happens. Real change took time for Prince – time to examine and process, time for growth to take hold and time for his old self to die and fall away. 'That [normal] lifestyle had to creep into me', he explained. '[Soon] I was thinking of marrying. I was thinking of normalcy'. To even make it to his wedding day, Prince had to abide almost-arrests and would-be wars. By the standards of most townies, Prince the low-level drug dealer would likely have been written off as just another figure in Cape Town's sinister netherworld. But gang exit is not an out-and-out process. According to his own account, Prince was leading a comparatively quiet way of life, away from shootouts and wholesale smuggling – no longer busy with what he called 'real gangsterism'.

However, Prince also conceded that being connected to any gang activities at all placed him in continual jeopardy of being dragged back into the gang lifestyle. For this reason, he did abandon drug-dealing altogether, marrying his girlfriend and joining a church. Shootouts and drug sales were not an option anymore. 'We have taken now another form of lifestyle… We must cease selling drugs now. But children must eat and clothes must be bought. Now we are sitting asking: what now?', he said. Prince got a contract as a cleaner at a mall in Mitchells Plain. With the career change came a sizeable pay cut. 'Now I'm getting money in one month that I used to get in an hour', said Prince. There is less money for pushing a mop than in pushing powders, pills and crystals. But there is also less of a likelihood of being shot down or locked up. In the abstract, this compromise makes sense. Amid the daily drudgery of dirty floors and overflowed toilets, it can be difficult to tolerate. Prince squeezed just enough out of a janitor's salary for a single-room shack and basic provisions for himself, his wife and her two children. He had family and stability now, but not much else. Yet Prince was content with the quaint life he had cobbled together. 'That other gang life was a gamble… I can die, or go to hospital, or I can go to prison', he opined. 'This, it is stable. Yet it is less than the money that I used to make when I was in the [gang] world. But I choose to live this life'.

One cannot help but wonder, however, if Prince's experiences attest to a larger truth: somebody like him can strive to be physically safe and stable, or he can strive to have status and success; but he cannot have both. Naturally, I am not implying that there are no examples of status and wealth in Mitchells Plain; there are. But Prince is an ex-convict with few professional prospects. From his vantage point business people and professionals are an invisible minority, overshadowed by the towering images of the almighty crime bosses who capture the imaginations of township residents. They are the heroes their predicaments allow for, personifying independence and influence in a pastiche of violence, drugs and flash. All of that now seemed to be off the table for Prince, who was fighting for scraps, trying to eke out a livelihood by the narrowest of margins.

Mindful not to upset Prince's fledgling conversion, I gently posed my dilemma to him. The reply he gave was revealing of someone that took ownership of his past and represented himself with dignity and autonomy in the present:

> I don't see it that way... I have chosen a new life, which I am busy building. I hope that maybe what I have been through, my experiences, I can use as a testimony to benefit others. Maybe telling my story can even be a benefit to me. You never know what opportunities can come.

His reply also betrayed a hope that represents other Cape Flats gang trope: the gangster-turned-preacher. Just as gang members draw from ritualised public displays of street culture, providing personal testimony of one's recovery through proselytising and public speaking is a way of gaining acclaim for an ex-hustler. There are a number of high-profile religious leaders who, in particular, embody ideals of triumphant reformation and who have taken advantage of criminal histories to grow large followings and find funding for neighbourhood-uplift initiatives. Standing over congregations and controlling church coffers provides an impressive vision of the possibilities after gangs. It resonated with Prince. Other ex-gangsters expressed corresponding ideas of who they might be after disengaging. Most wanted to be motivational speakers, social workers and spiritual leaders, hoping that their redemption narratives could be exchanged for social and material benefits. Of course, few retired outlaws ever head up a church or a community organisation. Most settle for just getting by, consoling themselves with the knowledge that living normally leads to living longer, even if it also means living poorer. Prince originally aspired towards the gang because he believed in his own heroism, imagining wholeheartedly that he too was entitled to a big house, fancy car, nice meal and financial prosperity. On some level, longing for the regular life means letting these dreams die, accepting a sort of defeat by once again taking a place near the bottom of the existing order of things in Cape Town. I am not arguing here for a reversion to violence for Prince. I am purely pointing out the social contradictions of a society that offers too little to Coloured men and women living in townships, and which is then surprised when they agitate for something more. If their agitation is to abate, much work is required to expand the opportunities available to someone like Prince. So that he too can endeavour to live well and live safe – without having to compromise one of the two.

4.1.3 Patrick

Let us consider one more narrative to get a better sense of what normal life means and how it compares to street life. Patrick (Hanover Park male, 29 years) could have inherited an empire. His family started and still runs much of Hanover Park's Laughing Boys gang. Patrick was intent on taking over the family enterprise when he was young. The excesses of gangsterism gleamed and glittered at first. However, about four years before this book was written, he consigned danger and decadence to his uncles and cousins:

> They can have their flashy cars, lots of money, and tons of girlfriends, it doesn't interest me. I don't want to live my life looking over my shoulder every day... I just want to be fucking normal. I don't want to have nothing fancy. I don't want exotic friends. I don't need to be rich. I just want to be normal for once in my life. Just try to live a normal life and serve my purpose here on earth, as the head of a family. I got myself a reasonable job.

For Patrick, Prince and other interviewees, satisfaction with quiet living was portrayed in contrast with the insecurity that consumes a street-based lifestyle. Crime pays, and brings with it easy women, cars, clothes, cars, etc. But this all comes at a hefty personal cost. Tension, anxiety, stress, insomnia and distrust were words frequently used to describe what it feels like to be in the streets. No rest can come when ceaselessly keeping one eye open, moving nervously through a world where everybody is a potential adversary. It is not hard to understand how Patrick would grow weary of such unabating turbulence and want to leave it.

Still, simply getting out of the Laughing Boys did not automatically mean that Patrick could totally abandon his old life and habits. Especially in the early stages of his transition, he continued to display aggressive tendencies, getting into confrontations, picking fights and attacking anybody that confronted him. Rancorous outbursts were the norm among study participants shortly after disengaging gangs, many of whom also struggled to keep their tempers from bubbling over. Of that initial period, Patrick said:

> At first, I used to struggle with it. I used [to] get into a lot of fights, just with people in my area that would try me. People here do that... I would even stab guys a couple of times, because I was still that stubborn guy who wasn't going to let anybody step on him – even just step on my toes, for that matter.

Patrick embodied the fact that taking the man out of the streets does not necessarily take the streets out of that man – not right away anyway. He was still very much a live wire, the charged current of street life flowing through him. Announcing that a person wants and plans to change is the easy part; the real work is in translating words into action:

The more it happened to me the easier it became, I guess... I knew that in order for me to able to survive this process, and come out in the end successful, I need to be humble as shit. That was the kind of things I was practicing every day – little things... It's not easy to just put a finger on these things, it's things you mostly learn by personal experience.

Patrick spent 12 years selling, smoking, stabbing and shooting. He could not just erase his past, no matter how much he hoped to. He needed to practice change, so that his intentions could be tested and validated via in-the-world interactions. With each day away from the Laughing Boys, Patrick proved to himself that a different way of being in the world was obtainable.

In general, the greater the period of time that research participants spent out of the streets, the more likely they were to routinely handle interpersonal problems without flying into fits. All the same, issues with anger could still remain for many years after an exit. The body's memory of the streets lets go of its grip begrudgingly. 'Up until today I have issues with my temper. I got into an argument with my manager not too long ago, and I almost hit him with a spade',[2] stated Patrick, who is today working as an electrician for the City of Cape Town. 'But I just left the site that day'. While hitting somebody with a spade is a way to flex in the drug economy, it will get you fired from any other occupation. A year or two earlier, Patrick very possibly would not have been so restrained and could have ended up unemployed and possibly in jail as a result. Left dejected, criminalised and without pay, there is a good chance that he also would have gone back to the Laughing Boys. Instead, Patrick was rewarded with keeping his electrician's post.

To the passive observer it might seem strange to applaud another for not bludgeoning a co-worker. It is up to Patrick – gang past notwithstanding – to control his impulses and do no harm, after all. But it is also up to us, who are writing and reading about him from cosy nooks, tranquil balconies or artisanal coffee shops, to appreciate how far he has come in a few years and how easy it would be for him to go back. His road forward is ragged and there are pitfalls everywhere. Patrick belongs to a family famous for lawbreaking and lives in a community where confrontation is everywhere. Making things worse still, he continues to be chained to his past, dragging it around as the residue of an aggressive disposition that risks getting him into the types of confrontations that could land him back in prison. A failure to read his narrative with sufficient compassion might mean he falls back into the streets, after losing a job or taking a charge. This does not require anybody to pardon foul play, just to remember that decomposing the constitutive behavioural material of the street-self requires time. The half-life of testiness, wrath and militancy appears to be years, rather than days or months.

---

[2]This incident occurred at a public works role Patrick has been working at two years prior to these interviews. He got this work subsequent to the catering job described below.

But if a gang member can make the right moves and stay out of prison for a while, he or she may put sufficient distance between himself or herself and old habits, so that these recede into distant memory. Getting to that point is not without peril, however. Like most interviewees in this study, Patrick has neither the funds nor the social networks to move out of his home community of Hanover Park. So he stays out of harm's way by keeping updated on a mishmash of intersecting gang territories and ever-shifting rivalries, doing what he can to bypass them. Avoidance tactics are not foolproof, unfortunately. Patrick was ambushed and almost assassinated by a local American leader when walking to mass one Sunday through the gang's grounds. 'He didn't have a gun fortunately, that day he wanted to kill me. I actually came from church on a Sunday walking with my Bible. I had my shirt on, and my slacks, and my shoes', Patrick explained. 'He jumped out his car and said: you taking chances to even fucking walk here. I tried to reason with him. He didn't want to accept anything at the time... So your past can come back to haunt you'.

Places where the Laughing Boys reign are safer, but come with their own entanglements. Going to work, attending church, visiting with family and friends and participating in the fundamental aspects of social life inevitably bring Patrick into contact with the gang. This puts his recovery in danger as well:

> I went to church this Sunday and I'm walking past them with a bible tomorrow, they would come and *Sabela: jy, my bru salut*[3] and as much as I would feel obligated to speak in such a way I would not. I would greet: hi, how are you? Are you alright? I would say: I'm good, my brother, even if that makes me look like a wuss sometimes... It's easy for them to say: ah you want to keep you like this, like a *bekeerde*[4] brother, you a *kerk broer*[5] – try to look down on me.

Gangs in Cape Town usually do not attack former members. That does not mean they make it easy to get out. Verbal barbs cut differently than do physical assaults, but they sting nonetheless. Stigma and distrust from neighbours is another stumbling block. There is an intensified social scrutiny facing the ex-gangster that compounds the usual – and already-demanding – pressures of township life. Without adequate state-provided security, Patrick's ability to act and speak freely is policed by former gang brothers, close relatives and anybody else residing around him. To show he no longer associates with street life, Patrick responds to their overtures with words befitting of a *kerk broer*. In presenting himself with a Bible and a brotherly greeting, he reaffirms that his transformation is heartfelt. Failure to display sufficient investment in the practices of normal living

---

[3] A gang greeting.
[4] Saved.
[5] Church brother.

will cheapen in the eyes of the community any new cultural capital Patrick tries to pawn off on them:

> I don't associate with them [in the gang] because it's easy for someone else to spot me and think: *naai*,[6] he's with them having a beer; yeah, he says he's not part of that [gang] anymore, but now we know about him also. Tomorrow they get me at another place, then I'm dead. So I want my change to be visible, to be known by everybody that I'm not that type of person anymore.

Recovery must be visible to be plausible. Performing social ideals such as the 'man of God' (Flores & Hondagneu-Sotelo, 2013, p. 480) allows former gang members to detach themselves from their past. We will see below that religion is an important part of normal life. If adopted properly, this religious repertoire probably provides somebody like Patrick his best chance of keeping alive through the risky early stages of his out-of-gang transition – the period when his gang history remains hottest to the touch.

Eventually things cool down. With time 'it gets easier', said Patrick. 'Now I don't face these tests anymore – [only] sometimes... Even though it took a while, they eventually saw that it wasn't my scene anymore'. But until new forms of speech and action are second nature and the loafers, khakis and polo of a *kerk broer* can be worn like a second skin, ex-gangsters make do with willpower, determination and good fortune. Patrick passed through numerous tests withdrawing from the Laughing Boys, surviving violence done against him and avoiding prison because the people he did violence to did not press charges. That took four years. Gone today are the dreams of 'flashy cars, lots of money and tons of girlfriends' that are associated with his drug-running family. Ruan also traded drugs, women, wealth and notoriety for the peace and stability of a 'small shitty place', whereas Prince now tallies in a month what dealing used to bring in in hours. They just want to be normal, to work hard for a promotion, to spend time with their nearest and dearest, to keep the faith that better days are on the way; most of all they want to live with the certitude that they will not be dispatched unexpectedly to a prison cell or an early grave.

While Patrick and others are no longer at the epicentre of township violence, they also cannot ignore that each is still living along Cape Town's various spatial, economic and racial fault lines. Where they were born, what class they were born into and what colour their skin is all continue to interfere with their life chances. This too is 'normal' in Cape Town. That is why they take what little is offered to them at this point. In doing so, they are making the statement that the violent, poverty-stricken and drug-dependent cul-de-sac that is gangsterism is even more exploitative and dehumanising than the warped racialised social architecture that gives birth to gangs. So they stick to the small slice of the city apportioned to

---

[6]A slang expression of distaste or disagreement.

them, tending it as best they can, hoping to one day build a solid home for themselves, their spouses and their dependants.

4.2 Making a Home

Maturing gang members often begin to feel like settling down and getting married (Hagedorn, 1994). The family feeling they once got from the gang becomes less prominent (Fagan, 1989) and bonds to one's actual family start taking precedence (Laub & Sampson, 2001). This makes home life an important inducing influence for gang disengagement (Hunt et al., 2011; Moloney et al., 2009; Pyrooz & Decker, 2011a). All participants in this study mentioned motivations to create a family as an important factor in the decision to leave the gang. Loved ones were also a loadbearing support structure when it came to providing financial and emotional assistance and an avenue for social re-integration back into communities. More than that, moving from raising hell to raising children provided practical evidence to all and sundry of the shifting priorities in gang members' lives, in a way that words alone could not.

4.2.1 Jayden

Jayden (Hanover Park male, 41 years) is a veteran member of the Americans, and what you would call an 'original gangster'. When he was coming up in the game, gangs were still brawling with bricks, knives and *pangas*. Usually, two groups from opposing neighbourhoods would meet in a field to enact a form of ritualised inter-gang warfare. What followed was a choreographed proto-battle in which rampaging gang members contained violence among themselves. That was the antecedent to today's scattershot firefights, before guns and meth were everywhere. With them spread a predatory regime of terror that serves new drug-related economic interests rather than any sense of community solidarity. 'That time the knives were popular. As the gang grew stronger, they are making money from drugs, and they would buy guns', said Jayden. A true 'OG' like him finds the current chaos contemptible. 'We not stabbing each other anymore, now we stand from a distance and now they shoot each other from afar. There is no discipline'. The result is frequently a spray of shots indiscriminately directed towards civilians and gangsters alike.

As much as some things about gang culture have changed on the Cape Flats, they have also stayed decidedly the same. Jayden's fascination with gangsterism started for the usual reasons and in the usual ways. He followed his friends, first smoking marijuana with Americans members and then moving on to Mandrax and eventually to harder drugs. One person was especially influential. 'That time there was this other guy – "Ore." He is also [now] an ex-gangster. I wanted to be like him. He was an Ugly American. The clothes they used to wear, I liked them', Jayden recollected. 'There was a lot of respect for him. The people listen to what he says, so I think now: this is the way'. For a while gang life was '*lekker*', he said. 'You met girls and you went to nightclubs. Sundays you see now the enemy and you fight, like Sunday after lunch there is a gang fight'. Then things turned. Jayden murdered a man one Sunday afternoon, getting 12 years for the stabbing. He finished eight of them.

That all happened back in the mid-1990s. This is how long it took him to finally leave the Americans. Jayden had been out for about a year and a half at the time of our first interview. He said his family was the primary reason he left:

> For the first time I began to act like a parent should be. My children come to me, this is happening at school and that is happening at school, and I am thinking I must go to the school now, and not stay here [with the gang].

Decamping from his role as a local American shot caller meant making a claim on new identities and practices by 'trying to become [what he called] a proper man'. Jayden's desire to live properly centred on his wife and children and the goal of providing for them by earning an honest buck. 'I got a family and I can focus on that. You earn money in a proper way, and you give it to your wife to use it for the kids. You realise the gangster life is not for you', he said.

As a first step, Jayden convened the gang's inner circle to inform them he was finished. 'From now on you will know me as [Jayden], and these are my kids and my family', he explained to his brothers in that meeting. By boldly professing his independence, Jayden meant to de-identify from the gang and knife himself off from his street persona '*Lange*',[7] who was once known for his ability to smuggle arms and drugs, and who now served as the foil to Jayden the newly reformed man. On one hand, separating from one's gang persona is a symbolic personal act. On the other hand, it is a necessary survival practice that allowed Jayden to dissociate from the risks of street life. 'Don't call me for gang-related things', he told the Americans. 'Because the enemies see me with them, [and] they're going to come to me'.

Though de-identification is an initial step to de-embedding, one cannot construct a new existential edifice by simply knocking away the old one. Something must take its place; new company must be found, new priorities articulated and new tendencies built up, if a new lease on life is to be secured:

> I am now thinking in a proper way. Because there are many things I have learned from the past. It is hard to change some stuff [in the way I behave] *mos*. But I can see the difference between this life and that life. This life now is a *lekker* life... No more focusing on [gang] friends and selling drugs, now focus on my family.

The family life is '*lekker*' now. It brings stability, support and meaning. All are essential to Jayden's successful transition. But it is not all good. Domesticity also comes with new responsibilities. 'I have got a wife and she is worried about

---

[7]His nickname while in the Americans.

Friday. So I must focus on bringing in the money, and she can sort her things out', said Jayden. Accepting and successfully fulfilling his traditional breadwinning role necessitates that he earn a steady income. Making money to feed their family is a significant burden for anybody from a poor township. But it might be particularly weighty for someone used to easy cash. Jayden claims he would earn four times more previously – drug dealing, robbery and housebreaking – than he could legitimately. 'When you try to change it's not easy. Sometimes you will try, but no man, the things don't work out. Then you fall back [into gangsterism] again... It's all about money', stated Jayden.

Financial frustrations had many times undermined his previous withdrawals from the gang, a number of which failed due to cash flow shortages. 'When I stopped [before with gangsterism] I had to budget. You bought a TV. Now you must earn money. Otherwise the shops come collect all the things. Then I said: no man, I cannot manage with this, I must earn money again', said Jayden. There are always profits to be made in the streets. Two decades as an American taught Jayden that gangs operate in an industry exempt from analyst's reports, employment forecasts and economic recessions. Whenever he fell back into his old ways of living – and earning a living – he could provide as a breadwinner. Yet, using the methods of *Lange* the gangster put him into conflict with Jayden the family man. Embodying the domestic repertoire of a husband and father is not just about having funds, it is also about where those funds are sourced. 'In this family life you are in now, the criminal things like that don't work; because then you go back [to the gang life] again', he concluded. 'You must choose for yourself, what is best now'.

It remains to be seen whether the changes Jayden is making can finally – and totally – take hold, or whether financial pressures will pull him back into the Americans again. The amount of time spent on the streets and the ability to support oneself through legal income are two important factors influencing whether a gang member can permanently transform his or her outlook, priorities and future orientation (Moloney et al., 2009). Jayden says he is prepared for what is coming and seems to understand that dispositioning the normal life will be a laborious task:

> You must face life. When you wake up, you wash your face and brush your teeth, and everything like that. You go out and think I got kids at home and a wife, and I must go out there and work and earn money in a proper way. You do your work, don't let anything bother you, and finish and come home. Then one day you do the right thing. Then you do that every day. I am trying to do that now.

His family may be the main reason for his gang leaving, but his obligations towards them can only be met through the contemporaneous, proper and consistent enactment of normality. This is not easy to do at first:

> They [the non-gangsters] are talking Afrikaans to you and you have to talk back to them in Afrikaans. But you use a gang word

in between. You *sommer*[8] *Sabela* in between. At first it was very difficult. I struggled to fit into the society, because you're used to the gang life and now you must get used to the community.

It can actually be quite a struggle to even speak normally, when you have passed a whole decade bunking with *ndotas* in prison and spent another decade dealing with the Americans in the streets. A mix of *Sabela*, gang slang and in-your-face *Kaaps* becomes your *lingua franca*. If Jayden is able to persevere in a performance of domesticity without letting up, perhaps then he can finally bring about a permanent move home by learning the language of legitimate life.

In general, the domestic repertoire served as an important behavioural guide for interviewees, which also gave them a resource to signal to others that their change could be trusted. Being a spouse and parent are one-third of a three-part performance of normality that gang-leavers relied on. As told by one research participant: 'there are only a few things the gang can understand [to justify leaving]: serving the Lord and getting married and finding work'. He cautioned, however, that the gang is watching all the time, and that by adopting and per-forming the normal life 'only *maybe* you can go from gangsterism. But you can still die. Trouble and enemies is everywhere'. The women who participated in this study also emphasised embracing paternal responsibility as a mode of moving away from gangs. This is consistent with research that shows that becoming a mother offers gang girls alternative identities as 'respectable women' and as 'good mothers' (Hunt et al., 2011). There are too few females in our sample to draw definitive conclusions in this regard. But it is notable that none spoke about their domesticity as a source of externalised role validation, like males did. This might relate to differences in gender parenting roles: because women are typically expected to be mothers, seeing them turn to domestic life is not as impactful as it is when men do it. It may also be that women might not need to corroborate non-gang roles to outsiders because they are much less likely to be on the frontlines of gang wars and therefore less likely than men to be perceived as still a threat when disengaging. More research is needed about female gang leaving in the Capeto-nian context to say for certain.

4.2.2 Prince

Let us consider two more examples of domestic life before moving on. We wit-nessed already how Prince's aspirations of becoming 'the greatest hitman and biggest drug smuggler in the Western Cape' were derailed by the desire to be a husband and a father. However, he quickly found that becoming a family man is a difficult endeavour. There is a harsh contrast between the composed demeanour needed to succeed at housecraft and recklessness required while participating in street-craft:

---

[8]Used colloquially to mean: just, simply or only.

> I'm used to a reckless life. So now, the difficulty that I am facing is
> to be normal, and to act normal, accordingly. When people like me
> are put in a situation, or pushed into a corner, we react violently...
> But now we must get into that place of being calm and patient and
> understanding.

The same man who opened fire on a family of three, burned down their house
and threatened to murder anybody who tried to do anything about it was now
championing patience and paternal understanding. However, Prince also revealed
that 'it is very difficult for a person who is used to violence only, to get to that
space. Those are the things that a man is struggling with now, and being now a
husband and father'.

While street capital was previously earned through risk-taking and hyper-
aggression, domestic capital calls for the opposite. 'Fatherhood and being a husband is not a thing you can say that you studied for in your previous [street] ways.
It is a thing you gradually learn to do better', he stated. 'I have to change everything. At this moment, I'm trying to be the best I can... until those ways are no
more'. We have already noted repeatedly that perfecting the practices of normal life
requires resolve, effort and time. But to leave the analysis here tells an incomplete
story, one that risks cementing the idea that 'grit' or 'willpower' is what separates
the ex-gangster from an active one. The urban poor already have grit aplenty. The
fortitude and commitment needed to tough it out of gangs is next-level. Prince, for
one, traded street success for a small *hokie*[9] at the back of a Mitchells Plain residence owned by a member of his church. The dwelling was barely big enough for
two beds, a television and a hotplate. With no other place to sit, we would conduct
our interviews positioned opposite one another on a bed while his wife and her
children bustled around us.

Very quickly it became palpable how the stress of such cramped lodging
arrangements could send somebody running to the streets for refuge. 'Imagine what
it's like for two people [living with two children and] quarrelling for four days in a
box like that, it's hell. It can make you crazy', whispered Prince. On top of Prince's
own background of violence and substance abuse, his wife is also dealing with her
own recovery from taking and dealing drugs. Although they consider themselves
'blessed' to be renting the shack at a discount, it is in the middle of Eastridge, the
same locality that many of Prince's former drug associations and gang animosities
also still reside. The Americans, Spoilt Brats, 28s and others are constantly fighting
to carve up the community. Because of this, Prince tiptoes through his new world
on a tightrope stretched taut between the out-of-control violence of street life and
the claustrophobic craziness of home life. He is left with little room for slippage,
since a fall back into gangs could very well be the end of him.

Ironically, he is most preoccupied with prosaic day-to-day concerns now. 'The
only thing that attacks me is my nearest family, with the home life. I'm not used to
the home life. I'm not used to being around the people I love all the time', Prince

---

[9]Shack.

confided. Those aspects of violent street culture that would make any normal man cower or retreat in terror, by contrast, fail to faze him. 'There is nothing off the street that it can throw at me to shock me, because I know everything off the street. The things that gangsters fear, I can handle that'. As a husband and father, however, he is a novice, every day straining to keep a lid on the destructive street habits that threaten to tear down his peaceful home; he said that 'there are times, for instance, when my wife rubs me the wrong way, and I just get so angry and I just explode at her'. At first glance, the struggles of a husband and father seem trivial in comparison to the life-and-death fight of a triggerman and drug smuggler. However, hardship is relative. After more than 15 years in the streets, he had mastered the art of killing. Today, Prince is facing an unfamiliar challenge, he must master the art of living. 'These are the small things I'm busy with now', he said. Maybe if enacted over time, the tendency to walk away from conflict will one day totally overwrite Prince's preconditioned street sensibilities.

4.2.3 Jerome

Jerome (Mitchells Plain male, 31 years) is another 'street virtuoso' I encountered in this study.[10] Both he and Prince challenged accepted gang norms by refusing to declare allegiance to a group, defend its tattoo and die for its turf. Without the protection of an armed posse, they had to fend for themselves, relying on tremendous violence and dangerous risk-taking to survive – and thrive – in Cape Town's underworld. As an example of the brutality he would resort to, Jerome outlined to me how he taught a criminal colleague a lesson for almost botching a robbery. 'We were doing a job. It was very easy. But the guy didn't do what I said he must do, and I beat his head up with a hammer... I beat his head like a milk sachet', he said. In a place where violence is the norm, it takes a really heinous offence to catch people's attention. This might mean 'taking a hammer, hitting the person over his head, to make an example for a small thing; to say that that is the way you are; taking a knife and stabbing the person in the face', explained Jerome. 'Do it so that you don't have to do it again... I must make an example for everyone, so that my space for working, for making money, is broader'. Atrocities of the highest magnitude send a message, showing bystanders who is boss and bestowing status onto the perpetrator through the rumours and street gossip that follow the incident.

But Jerome's account indicates that nobody endures horror like this unscathed, something that is true not just for the victim of a violent act, but also for the person perpetrating it:

> Because of the permanency of the pretence   fighting always and
> hitting people – that became part of my character. When we came
> home, I was very angry and I hit him, again and again. He went to

---

[10]See Dziewanski (2020a) for an in-depth discussion of Jerome and Prince's experiences with street virtuosity.

hospital… And he came out again, and he still just came [back]
and he was loyal to what we was doing.

The incident illustrates the complex interaction of factors that define street
dispositions, showing how the strength and intensity of street-based acts
combust when catalysed. The more times this reaction takes place, the more
likely it is that violent criminality becomes a compulsive action that will alter
the composition of the perpetrator's character. 'People do not simply "survive"
violence as if it somehow remained outside of them, and they are rarely if ever
ennobled by it', writes Bourgois (2011a, p. 433). Jerome, for instance, claimed
he had become 'possessed' by a warlike nature, to the point where he was
unable to fight off 'this demonic force that's in you, and makes you aggressive
and evil all the time'. Indeed, his street dispositions haunted him for some time,
nagging, pestering and pulling him back into gangsterism on many occasions
before he finally got free.

The man of family and faith he would eventually come to be when we met had a
different spirit. It took a dispute with the powerful Hard Livings gang to definitively trigger a turnaround for Jerome; the HLs came after him when he carried out
a hit on one of the gang's high-flyers, which brought the whole gang hunting for
him and jammed Jerome into a very tight corner. He had never backed down from
such threats prior to this, and through the years he had built his street cred with acts
of wild bravado. A few years before his exit, for instance, he was almost beaten to
death. Rather than taking time to convalesce, Jerome fled hospitalisation after a
couple of days and, still burdened by casts and bandages, almost single-handedly
went on the offensive against his assailants. Yet, he was now inexplicably running
away from the Hard Livings. That is because things had changed for Jerome. Just
prior to the conflict he had reconnected with his parents, after his girlfriend had
given birth to their first child. He had previously been almost totally cut off from
this type of family connection for six years, just to keep his small clan from
becoming collateral damage of the different gang wars Jerome was waging in
and around Mitchells Plain. 'There is always a weakness in any gangster. If it's
not his family, it's a woman; if it's not woman, it's his head. But there's always a
weakness', said Jerome. 'Family was the weakness [I had]… It was a weakness then.
It's a strength now'.

Reversing course back to the streets by going to war with the Hard Livings
would have likely meant severing ties with family again, and the prospect of
killing off these nascent connections was more than he could countenance:

> I thought this will be very dangerous towards the family that I now
> have, and at that time it was crucial making my decision… I have
> stirred up a lot of hatred again, so will I be responsible for more
> murders? So I would then be responsible for that? My decision was
> then to retreat.

The week after his fight with the HLs he moved into his parents' home,
stopped doing drugs and joined a church. From that point onwards, Jerome spent

as much time as possible with his loved ones. 'I was more with my family. That's what I was all about', said Jerome of his change. But living under house rules was no simple feat for a man used to taking risks that made the gangsters around him think that 'no normal, sane human being would do things like this':

> When I came back [to my family's house], I had to now conform to the family values and it was quite hard... Aggressiveness would pop up, say, where I would explode... I would repent and say sorry, apologise, which we gangsters do not do. You do not ask forgiveness and do stuff like that, so that's also a new thing that's part of the new pattern that I've learned after some time.

As we have already seen above, the first step to ditching the brotherhood is de-identifying from street capital. After that, many subsequent strides are needed if disengagement is to stick. 'Short temperedness I had to cut off, and get more patience... I'm speaking about getting experience now', Jerome stated. 'That thing is key to [overcoming] your short temperedness and the patterns you had in the gangsterism – when you say something it must happen, or else. When you come here [back home] there's more patience needed, and new patterns'. Mastery over normal life is gained only by trial and error. Domestication is a long-run exercise that engenders competencies, practices and dispositions that might in the long-term lay the foundations for a happy home.

'I would say that the cure for the gangsterism thing is, the pattern changing... Like a computer hard drive, you format it. Then you start a new pattern', Jerome explained. 'This gangsterism makes you believe you're strong. [But] you are alone... So, for me to change from there, it was really a family and spiritual thing that happened with me, to show what things are [really] valuable'. Family and faith helped 'reformat' his old street operating system into a new set of beliefs. Jerome also confirmed the important role that being a family man played in signalling change to others. 'One excuse that they [the gangs] understand is: I'm busy with my family', he said, presenting the following example as evidence:

> Like the other day, an Inspector[11] came to me and says: hey, [Jerome], I miss you... and he would say: when you going to come around, like old times? We [are] still here waiting on you man. So, I just said: you know I'm with my family now, [I told you] I was going stop this life. Then I tell him: why don't you just do the same I'm doing? But then he stopped me and said: don't preach, just go. I'm then out and away [from the situation].

A gang-leaver like Jerome can expect to navigate a series of such trials, whereby his non-street credibility is checked and the reliability of his renewed character is tested. Getting the gang to let go of its command of you means overcoming each

---

[11] A prison gang rank.

test by persuasively personifying your commitment to your family, to your work and to your religion. While familial baggage was a burden before, it lightens his load now, giving him focus, purpose and a repertoire for himself and others to buy into. 'I just stay inside the house, and then move to church and to the job. That is what is safest now for me. People can see that this thing I am involved in now is really real', stated Jerome. Too much street talk could jeopardise his disengagement process entirely, sending Jerome back to the trenches, where he would yet again be dug in along old battle lines.

4.3 Work Makes the Man

We have already witnessed the ways that family and work fit together practically: steady and sufficient economic capital supports the acquisition of domestic cultural capital. This section shows further how buckling down at a day job can bond an ex-felon to normal life, just like focussing on family does. Consistent employment is a proven determinant of criminal desistance (Sampson & Laub, 2005). Without a legal occupation, gang-leavers can be pushed back to street hustling (Hagedorn, 1994). The unemployed are also denied the legitimate forms of social and human capital offered in the workplace, leaving them undertrained and socially isolated (Sweeten et al., 2013). Although it is doubtful that every gang member would simply disengage if they were given jobs, the centrality of employment in role transition was noted by all interviewees in this study. However, few were able to find steady work. The streets may offer no quarter. But neoliberal capitalist society is cut-throat in its own way. In a country with a high unemployment rate, and even higher youth unemployment,[12] professional markets are intensely competitive. What jobs do exist pay next to nothing and are often found in precarious 'flexible' labour that brings inconsistent, occasional and insufficient livelihoods. Anybody without stores of social and cultural capital is at a further disadvantage when trying to obtain work. Somebody with a gang past, criminal record and a history of drug abuse is doubly – or triply – excluded. This leaves loads of people awkwardly straddling gang life and normal life, their intentions to leave the streets sabotaged by the difficult realities of getting somewhere in South Africa's saturated workforce.

4.3.1 Joanna

Joanna's (Hanover Park female, 35 years) story is a testament to how draining the job hunt can be for reformed gangbangers. At the age of 15, she became one of three female members of the Backstreet Kids. The Hanover Park gang no longer exists. Most of its members have since been lost to violence or long-term jail sentences. Joanna also went to prison, serving four-and-a-half years for her involvement in a robbery and murder. It was while imprisoned that she decided to

---

[12]World Bank estimates that the total unemployment rate in South Africa was 28.5% in 2019, with youth unemployment estimated at a staggering 57%.

get out of the Backstreets, finishing high school by sleeping and studying in the showers of her cellblock – the one place she could access 24-hour light. When she was released, Joanna had a matriculation certificate,[13] but no idea about how to translate her education into gainful employment. 'I knew for a fact it won't be easy for me to get a job, because I've got a criminal record. I never worked in my life... I didn't [even] know what to do, where to start', she admitted. Lack of skills and work experience are major obstacles to finding financial stability, which increases the risk of criminal recidivism (Glaser, 1964). Joanna struggled greatly in that initial year outside, making money working sporadically at odd jobs around Hanover Park before finally getting hired permanently. 'It was tough, seriously. If you come from prison, you've got no clothes to begin with, you've got nothing to your name. So everybody wants to take you for a nothing', recalled Joanna. 'You've got nothing, you mean nothing. That is life today outside... and that is how I felt – [like] I'm nothing. I'm doing people's washing, just for roll-on – for stuff like that – not even for money'.

As ex-offenders, former gang members are consigned to the very fringes of an already ailing economy. Any application form attached to a rap sheet will almost certainly be rejected from a pile of job seekers (Standing, 2006). Joanna, for example, has been out of the Backstreet Kids for over a decade, but she still regularly gets refused the most menial of positions because her gang background has been inescapably etched into government records. Her only option is to apply for formal expungement of those records, something that can take years and costs thousands of rands in lawyer fees. Others in this study were worse off still. After a lifetime of living informally, many lacked even the most basic forms of identification, which further precluded them from official opportunities. In such cases, employment was available almost entirely via personal networks and off-the-record appointments. All but a select few were able to find any sort of income via applications tendered inside of traditional channels. Most jobs were procured through a friend, or a friend of a friend, who got them a posting as a cleaner, factory worker, labourer, etc. The reward for such employment was usually long hours, backbreaking work and small wages. Nonetheless, anybody who could find even the most exploitative nine-to-five job considered themselves 'lucky'. At least it kept them off the streets. A large portion of people interviewed did not have any work at all.

Joanna was one of the so-called lucky ones. She managed to find a job via a contact she met once through a prison church ministry. Tracking down and getting a meeting with this person required that Joanna find the phone number for the ministry in the newspaper, cold call her contact and then pester the woman every day for two weeks. That tenacity finally led to an interview at a small printing business in Ottery. Although Ottery is a mere four kilometres from Hanover Park, navigating this new social space still proved difficult for Joanna. There are some township residents that rarely leave their communities

---

[13]High school diploma.

(Jensen, 2008). When they do, the change in geographical and cultural context can be bewildering:

> The first day I had to go to the interview, I walked to Ottery. I was getting lost. And the people [I asked for help] did not look helpful. I spent like three hours looking for this place, the meeting was supposed to be for 9 o'clock, I got there past 11 [o'clock].

The social dislocation sensed by Joanna was compounded by the stigma she felt as an ex-gangster. 'The day that I went for the interview, I put on gloves [to cover my tattoos]. That is what I normally do. People look at these [tattoos] first, and they judge you', she said. Hers was one of a number of mentions of the stigmatisation and criminalisation that linger after abandoning gangs – not just in one's permanent documents but also on one's person.

Joanna did get the job in the end. That is when the hard work really started. 'I didn't know what it was like to go wake up in the morning, or how to dress or behave. So I didn't know what to do, where to start', said Joanna. Being punctual, being professionally attired and being compliant are not imperatives for gang members. Going from street glory to the insults and indignities of normal life can also prove wearying. 'Even the people that worked there were judgemental, because of the tattoos. They didn't know my story', explained Joanna. In the owners of the print shop, she found a couple of sensitive souls who ignored her criminal past. Colleagues were less magnanimous, gossiping and hiding their belongings. 'And that is the one thing I told myself, I'm not going to take somebody's 2 rands, because that's stealing... I'm not going to be locked up for eighteen hours [again]. They don't even treat the animals at the zoo like that', Joanna stated defiantly.

Ottery is a predominately Coloured area, like Hanover Park. So it was not racial relations that were at play in the print shop, as much as class dynamics. 'In Hanover Park people have got certain ways. Now you come from Ottery, now you got your own ways there. I'm going to pick up these ways don't come from Hanover Park', she said. Ottery is mostly working class, whereas Hanover Park is predominantly poor. Joanna's co-workers sensed a difference in her. This is because culture gets distorted through the fractures and fragments of social class divisions. People know to judge outsiders via vesture, footwear, jewellery, accents, turns of speech and points of deportment. Street culture, especially, embeds in people, giving away where they are from through their words, clothes and etiquette. 'There [in Ottery], people are different from here. It's also a Coloured community, but there the people are not so loud as here. Here you're going to see people sitting on street corners drinking. There people don't do that', concluded Joanna.

Unable to change her environment, it fell back to Joanna to rearrange herself to fit the expectations of the situation. She decided to be single-mindedly submissive in the face of suspicion and stigma, keeping the promise she made to herself to never be caged up again. There were others I met who encountered insults and insinuations and slipped back into old ways, letting their street dispositions lead them into on-the-job conflict that got them canned. But Joanna bit her tongue and kept her head down. Menial as it was, her labour laid the groundwork for a normal life. By earning a small income, Joanna was stabilising the foundation of her still shaky new identity. Every bank deposit, rent payment, food purchase or acquisition of a household appliance reinforced a belief that she was on the right track, as Joanna explained here:

> For me, my life, I could see that I'm growing, because I bought myself a bed, bought myself a TV. It's mine... I bought it with my money. I worked for it... It makes you feel human... It gives you more dignity and pride. So that builds you as a person and makes you stronger. Because you come out of the prison and your pride is gone.

These words are a testament to Joanna's newfound self-regard as a working-woman. Labouring, having a legitimate income and using it to make the most basic of purchases validated her place in the world. Small was her foothold in the formal economy. But it was enough to make her feel she belonged there – and to make her feel that she too could manage to make it through lawful means.

4.3.2 Declan

Transitioning towards a headspace where a functional response to keep at it overrides the dysfunctional desire to fight or flee does not come effortlessly. The experiences of Declan (Mitchells Plain male, 42 years) illustrate further the tribulations associated with going from pushing drugs and pulling off hits to pressing on with proper work. Just two years before we spoke, he bludgeoned his own brother-in-law within an inch of his life with a hammer simply for playing a prank on him. What was meant as comedy quickly turned tragic, when Declan turned on the man for punking him in front of family and neighbours. 'The enemies might see I was caught off-guard, and I told him you don't do something like that. So, I had to show the community that I was still on-guard', said Declan. 'I meant to hit him once. But I was hitting him all the time, and the blood was all over the place, then police was coming, and I ran away. It was a whole commotion'.

If the only tool you have is a hammer, everything looks like a nail; not to be flippant, but one would be hard-pressed to find a truer and more poignant application of this famous phrase than to Declan's mindset in the streets, where he was defined by the alter ego *Duiwel*.[14] It was a persona he developed as a member of the Americans in Athlone and Mitchells Plain. 'This other guy was very bad, and he don't care. [As *Duiwel*] I just do stuff and I don't care about the consequences', said Declan. The nickname *Duiwel* obviously communicates amorality, vice and rancour. It is a self-styled moniker that Declan actively created as a rebuke to another nickname derisively given to him by schoolmates when he was

---

[14]Devil.

young. 'At school, the children mocked me – hey "Pastor"! You a pastor! – And all that, because my parents were like pastors. I didn't like it. I did feel out, and so I wanted to be in like [the gangsters]', remembered Declan. He was going to church with his mother and father, but secretly looked up to and aspired to be like his gangster brother, a founding member of the Americans gang in the neighbourhood where Declan grew up. '[My brother] was drugged and drunk and his dress code was not like ours. His dress code was like nice *takkies*, and jeans, stuff like that, and my clothes were boring. I wanted to also wear Nikes and [Converse] Purcells', Declan said. 'Sometimes I stole his clothes and wore them to school and I also dressed like the others in the gangs, like I was that [*Duiwel*] character'. Declan would go on to raise hell with the Americans for more than two decades, stealing, robbing and spilling blood in the same streets and for the same gang as his sibling.

Jumpy, cynical and always waiting to strike – that was Declan's demeanour when he found work as a farm labourer many years later. The working world was unlike anything he was used to, as his early travails on the job attest. Case in point, Declan described an interaction he had with a superior during one of his first days in the fields:

> I worked in the garden and one of the authorities he was scolding me [saying]: hey, look how you look, Pollsmoor is written all over your face, and this is not Pollsmoor... And I thought to fight him right there, then take my bags and I wanted to go.

The subconscious of an old street soldier distorts everyday conflicts into contentious provocations, prompting aggression as a reasonable reaction, regardless if a situation presents an existential bodily threat. In rebelling against his boss, Declan could boomerang back to a domain of street practices where he was the authority. By comparison, staying at work meant deferring to superiors, something that was anathema to the basic tenets of his gang dispositioning. Before Declan had a chance to act on the impulse and lash out, a colleague familiar with his background intervened. 'You going to let the same *Duiwel* get you down again? Just for that simple thing? Instead, just submit under the authority [of the supervisor]', she advised. To his credit, Declan heeded her counsel, but went on to disclose that exorcising the devilish part of him was the most strenuous labour of his entire life. 'This is the right path. Where I can break down from the old path and focus on the new. So when I go one day I'm a new person', he said. 'But it's the hardest thing I have ever done, more hard than even [being] the hardest gangster'. He also acknowledged that rediscovering Declan 'the pastor' would take time. 'I was 25 years in gangsterism and it's not going to go over in a couple of months for myself. I thought maybe three years to break down these old habits, and maybe adapt new habits in life', he admitted.

The logic of the street demands that respect is earned through violence, while on-the-job recognition is gained through trust, humility and compliance, sentiments that can feel wholly unnatural initially for an ex-gangster:

I took time [to listen to bosses]. In the beginning it was very difficult. I was watching them carefully, because I knew how some white people are. I did speak to them, and I thought they're going to keep [the things I told them] against me because I was used to that... I had goodness, but I had to hide it away. Because if one of my gang members had to see that goodness, then I would be a target for them. It works *mos* like that in a gang. Your own members, they are enemies and they watching each other closely. I couldn't dare to show there was a softness in me.

'Trust no one but yourself' is a key rule that gangsters live by. A gang member puts himself in danger each time he or she confides in somebody. So having confidence in colleagues seemed totally out of place for Declan. Instead, he kept to himself, as a way of protecting against getting betrayed, humiliated or taken advantage of, no matter the consequences professionally.

This was not the first time Delcan had tried to adjust to a new work role. For example, he previously had employment as a day labourer when hired to 'move the rich people's furniture from the one house to the other house'. He was compensated a paltry 40 rands for a full day of grunt work. This did not even include the hours spent struggling to get to and from the job. He woke at five in the morning, to be at the worksite at eight. 'When you arrive to the job you are already tired of struggling to get there. Fighting in the train, [where] there's a lot of people in that small space', he said of his morning routine. And there was no guarantee that there would be work waiting for him when he arrived either. Every day Declan lined up with tens of other hopefuls, as part of the anxiety-provoking selection process on which the day's income depended. 'I have to pray the whole time that they pick me... It affected me by sometimes a lot, watching other people eat nice. I also have a taste for nice things. But I sometimes can't even get one plate', said Declan forlornly. If not chosen, he and his family might go without food that day. 'It does something to you. You don't think much of yourself because the way life treats you'. He too wished to have a crisp suit for the office and a nice car to go to work in. But he did not even have enough money for a train ticket. Declan said, 'it's stressful. These full trains, and sometimes the trains are not working; or then I decided I won't pay for a ticket and must watch out [for security]'.

Many poor- and working-class Capetonians toil with considerable effort for very little. All the while, their poverty is compounded by grinding uncertainties, indignities and discrimination. So it is no small wonder that someone like Declan might relapse. On top of that, somebody simply struggling to come right may also be subjected to mistreatment and abuse by their employers. 'They're looking down on us because we're coming from the bush, we're coming from the concrete jungle', he said of his managers and their customers. Delcan compensated himself for those daily degradations by thieving from the clients whose furniture he was lugging around, creating an artifice of decency in order to gain some cover for his sticky fingers. 'I just knew I had to be humble under these people... just submit, and manipulate them by stealing their stuff. That is how I got my power back over them in the end'.

As a mover, Declan was still relying on his criminal instincts, refusing to really yield to his bosses without gaining something over them. The manipulative application of the workplace repertoire was prompted by the instrumental and adversarial version of life he believed in then, an existence extracted from a zero-sum world of unremitting power contests between gangsters. It was a direct extension of experiences in a street field where there is little room to trust or to be trusted. But trustfulness and trustworthiness are the social wiring that connects people to each other in other social settings. This is something Declan came to later realise when employed on the farm, where he tentatively tested the waters of workplace relationships. 'First, I will just go by greeting the person, and go on and do my own stuff, not keep conversation with him. The next day I will again greet him and see what is his reaction then', recalled Declan, describing the demonstrable suspicions he had of his colleagues. 'If I will see he will greet me back, I won't go to him trying to "buy face." But the next day I will maybe ask him how was work stuff today'. Progressively, he learned that lessons based on hustling and shooting proved dissonant in a professional environment:

> That I never did because by me asking a guy how was work today was like *soapies* in my eyes – like *Days of Our Lives* and the *Bold and the Beautiful* – because that is like weakness, and I'm showing now a soft part of me, just by being interested in what he did for the day. It may sound small now, but to me it was a big thing to just ask a guy how was work today and or ask him: how is it?. I never spoke like that. [In gangs] it was just *Sabela* or blood all the time.

After those early faltering steps into the workplace, he gained firmer footing. The stumbling blocks he described are indicative of the size of the gulf between the social fields of street life and normal life. Much work is needed to cover this gap. But Declan is sanguine about his tempestuous past and composed about his potential future, relating lessons learned on the farmstead to his attempts at decent living. 'It's all about farming, to get the weeds out of my life, by destroying the bad habits I picked up – to get that out of my life', he said. With this moral in mind, he remains clear-eyed about the task at hand, bowing to authority without trickery or thievery, as he labours to sustain himself as an ex-gangster.

4.4 Working It Out

Living the normal life requires that ex-gangsters change the way that they speak, dress and act – even how they refer to themselves. As this happens, nicknames are erased and overwritten by new identities, *Sabela* is supplanted by solicitousness and scripture, shirts are buttoned, pants are pulled up and *takkies* are exchanged for Sunday shoes. Most important is the way that a reformed gang member approaches conflict. Violent eruptions were the gangster's way of dealing with things. Now they must find another way forward: humbling themselves, walking away from discord and seeking forgiveness. That being said, out-of-gang conversions are a labour of great effort and much time. As a starting point, a decent and steady livelihood is needed to sustain a stable home life by sourcing food, paying household bills, sending children to school and the like. Absent economic opportunities, being normal becomes very tricky. Disconnection from social networks and mainstream cultural resources makes it twice as difficult to access employment. Despite everything, ex-fugitives quit fisticuffs and shootouts to knuckle down at work and at home. The next chapter adds to the analysis introduced above, by describing the important role that religion plays for individuals leaving gangs. Attending mass or going to the mosque helps them keep the faith that sticking to the repertoires of normal life might eventually lead to something resembling a lasting change in their living conditions.

Chapter 5

Walking the Righteous Path

As important as family and work are to disengagement, it is perhaps the redemptive role of religion that is paramount to normal living. Most South Africans affiliate with one religion or another,[1] and many interviewees' turning points came as a result of a spiritual awakening. Almost all practiced some form of faith as a central part of their non-gang identities. A godly life provided them with structure, guidance, forgiveness, acceptance, a support system and deliverance from lives spent amid depravity and disrepute. These findings are consistent with other studies on gang disengagement (Kolind, Friis Søgaard, Hunt, & Thylstrup, 2017) and criminal desistance (Giordano, Cernkovich, & Rudolph, 2002), which have described how ex-gangsters all around the world are weaving their way up from the penitentiary to the pulpit in the hope of being saved. According to international research, a spiritual conversion can help a gang member switch tracks to a life course that would have otherwise been off limits (Brenneman, 2011); faith provides a way of atoning for past crimes (Maruna, Wilson, & Curran, 2006), a critical resource for alleviating everyday problems in a non-criminal manner (Schroeder & Frana, 2009) and a purposeful place to redirect energies previously applied towards illegal industry (Flores, 2014). Creed is community, culture and counsel all in one package, and one of the few social resources accessible to people holding on in unwelcoming environments (Deuchar, 2018).

'Religion, like any youth programme, offers a trajectory, a pathway or line of development. It also holds out the possibility of transition... a new trajectory or turning point – seeing the light' (2016, p. 266), writes Pinnock, of the role spirituality plays in gang exit in Cape Town. Getting a job requires that one rise to the top of a list of prospective applicants; high marks are a prerequisite for attending any good school, and the right contacts are needed to skip the line at a trendy club; but the local church and mosque accept all willing supplicants. Accepting Jesus Christ, Mohammed or some other prophetic figure is a way for former members to signal the sincerity of their disengagement from gangs (Johnson & Densley, 2018). Piety projects powerful signs of personal restoration to anybody who might be suspicious of the freshly converted. In Cape Town, there is at least some social acceptance among gangsters themselves of religion as an exit strategy.

---

[1]Only 5.2% of South Africans do not affiliate with any religion in particular (Statistics South Africa 2015).

Gang Entry and Exit in Cape Town, 107–123
Copyright © 2021 Dariusz Dziewanski
Published under exclusive licence by Emerald Publishing Limited
doi:10.1108/978-1-83909-730-020210005

But people's allowances for absolution are not absolute. Too many have backslid into gangsterism after supposedly finding God. Hard Livings co-founder Rashied Staggie is one high-profile example. 'While Staggie had supposedly left gang life behind and converted to Christianity, actually, he was more active than ever in various criminal markets across Cape Town' (2020b), reported the Global Initiative Against Transnational Organised Crime. Few people believed that Staggie's conversion was genuine and his new fraudulent image upset many gangsters. In late-2019, he was assassinated outside his home in Salt River.

Memories of failed conversions like Staggie's still linger, creating great scepticism about anybody else trying to claim higher ground. So it is not enough to simply be saved. One must convince naysayers by providing a credible counterpoint to all of those who have tried and failed to walk the righteous path before them. In this sense, churchgoing is a strategic practice and not a spiritual one, drawing people in as a cultural resource that acts *for* them, rather than as a moralising force that acts *on* them (Campany, 2012). Recall the '*kerk broer*' that Patrick presented to the Laughing Boys in the preceding chapter; he sought to subvert the brotherhood of the gang by infusing it with what Flores calls 'brotherly love' (2014, p. 186). Walking past his old crew every Sunday with a Bible was essential to reminding them where his allegiance is now. The good book is a ritual symbol of the religious repertoire, just as *takkies*, name brand clothing and a cell phone are cultural objects associated with street success. Unable to move out of his community and into more secure circumstances, religiosity gives a gang member like Patrick his best chance at finding sanctuary from the challenges inherent to his transition. As a result, many ex-gangsters ardently take up pious poses trying to prove that they have truly found peaceability.

5.1 Religious Repertoires

5.1.1 *Ryan*

Ryan (Mitchells Plain male, 33 years) is a good example of an individual who relied on religion to leave street life. He was initiated into the Americans at 18, not long after both his parents died in a car accident. 'My parents died and I was not focusing straight. I took it hard man. I started smoking drugs because of the pain inside', he said. 'You know the people that sell the drugs are gangsters. I went to the gangs to get the drugs and they influenced me to become an American. Then I stayed with them so that I could smoke my drugs'. Things escalated from there. 'I am part of the gang now – an Ugly American. We went on smuggling. From smuggling it went to: my bro here's the gun, the gun works like this. So now I'm shooting like a cold-blooded killer', Ryan recalled. Smuggling and shooting inevitably led to prison, where Ryan joined the 28s. 'I was a 28s leader too'. Because the Americans are usually affiliated with the 26s and 27s, his gang brothers felt betrayed and went after him. So Ryan switched sides and jumped in with The Firm, a street-based brotherhood connected to the 28s. The years that followed were defined by drugs, crime and jail.

'I only made it out alive because I gave my heart to God', revealed Ryan. 'That is what gave me the strength to no longer be a gangster'. It was not easy though. He was repeatedly harassed during his disengagement. 'The only change the gangs understand is spiritual change. But they will not just believe it. So they test you, like mocking you – calling you like "pastor" or even making threats – to see what you do'. But, just as Patrick had mentioned above, Ryan stuck true to his new course in life in an attempt to demonstrate to the gang that he had redefined what it means to be a 'brother':

> They still came looking [for me] – saying: where is that *ndota*? Where is 'Stripes'[2]? But I said: I am now brother Ryan… the people in the number also needed to get used to it. And I had to get the number out of me. Sometimes a word still slips out – a *Sabela* word… I must get used to normal talking. The whole mind-set, my way of speaking, my whole character must change.

While Ryan was resolutely attempting to quiet the voice of 'Stripes', his persona over many years in the streets and prison, The Firm and 28s were actively inciting the gangster in him – or trying to anyway. 'They come *Sabela* with me, to ask when I am coming back', to which he responded: 'my brother, I serve the Lord'. He admitted though that rehabilitating and re-habituating took determination. Street culture is a conviction so essential to the gang that it could itself qualify as religion. 'I was long in gangs and the number. And now everything is new… So, I must get used to this church stuff'. Ryan applied himself to the Bible just like he had studied the number, attempting to discipline his spirit, his mind and his body to a renewed way of living:

> When I changed my life, I had to be disciplined. My pants were not anymore hanging [low], down here. I don't walk with a vest anymore [to show my *chappies*]. I had a long *bokkie*[3] that I took off. There was a time I made dreads [in my hair] also. Everything changed. The way I speak, the way I talk, the way I do everything… I used to swagger, and now I walk straight.

What garments you wear, how you wear them, the gait you walk with and the words you choose are a way of refashioning one's identity from gangs to godliness (Garot, 2010). Ryan even changed the way he wore his hair and beard, cutting his dreadlocks and the *bokkie* he had kept with pride over the years.

Low-hanging chinos, a nice vest, etc., were an exemplar of a street style that proved that 'this man, the way he looks, he is a boss; he has *discipline*; he can lead'. His new style, by comparison, he said exhibited '*discipline* with my religion'.

---

[2]His nickname while in gangs.
[3]Beard.

All were part of an act through which Ryan tried to convince others of the seriousness of his undertaking:

> Ryan: You will never see me stand on the corner. They will just see me – the gangs. They think I am coming to spy on them. I always try to give them the message I am no longer involved in this... You get guys, they say: we kill the 28s. They want me to hear that stuff. I tell myself: they want me to say something, so they can have a reason to kill me.
>
> Dariusz: That must be very difficult to deal with.
>
> Ryan: I just show them I go to church, and I come from church. They share information with each other. They ask: what is that guy doing here? They looking for that one mistake, and they will kill you... I don't give them a reason. I just show them I am by my church and family.

With minimal room for error, Ryan cannot but be totally committed to what he calls 'making a real change', assuring that 'people will not see you with the gang, and even people cannot see you still smoking drugs and drinking'. Though I insisted that neither cigarettes nor alcohol make anybody a gangster, he countered by saying that 'the gangster's mind works differently. They think: this guy, he can still come back [if he is smoking and drinking]'. Illicit or illegal behaviour conveys the impression of a man unserious about normal life. Gangs can sense weakness and will try what they can to chisel away at any cracks in the character of a recently restored soul.

'Especially in these [gang-affected] communities like Mitchells Plain, if they see when you walking with the bible, or going to the mosque, they will test you – threaten you – to see if you get angry', said Ryan. 'Then if they see your change is genuine they will respect you'. Thus, Ryan keeps going to church, sticking steadfastly to his religious repertoire. Even spiritual intervention may not be enough though. I have personally known numerous young people that zealously embraced God in their lives, only to be mercilessly murdered afterwards. One story that comes to mind is Dillon's. He had completely left the Laughing Boys, found faith and had mediated his exit with the rival Americans through a local organisation. None of that mattered. Six months later he was dead. Whether the hit was sanctioned through the gang's leaders remains unknown. Perhaps it was simply a mournful case of being in the wrong place at the wrong time. In the end, it makes little difference. The streets are unrelenting, and there is certainly nothing to be taken for granted when trying to depart them.

5.1.2 Byron

The gangster aggressively stands up for what is his (or hers) and takes offence at the slightest provocation, 'picking up blood' where it is spilled by foes. Conversely, the righteous individual lives by a different set of commandments. Thou shalt not kill; more than a moral imperative, pacifism is itself cast in opposition to the centrality of violence in street culture. Repentant sinners make clear who they are by trying to put as much distance as possible between who they are now and who they used to be. The case of Byron (male, 25 years) illustrates this well. Getting baptised as a Born Again Christian was a means of washing away the dirt he did in his five years as a member of the Mongrels in Hanover Park. It could not totally purge his past, however. Byron had already been out of the gang for about four years when he got caught in the middle of a war between the Americans and his former gang. 'I come here around the corner and two [Americans] are just there... [One of them], he grabs the gun. I run in here by the flats, to the people. Three shots he shot on me', Byron recalled. In the wake of that near-death encounter, he had no thoughts of hitting back. 'I can't do anything, I must just be strong and go on with my new life... Born Again Christians don't fight back. I must pray to God for his protection. So it's a little difficult', said Byron. That things are 'a little difficult' for Byron is the grossest of understatements, when his difficulties include the possibility that death is quite literally waiting around the corner. If he could move to Cape Town's fortified City Bowl or the verdant serenity of its suburbs, Byron might be buffered from such insecurity. Because he remains ensnared in an unsafe neighbourhood, he must fend for himself. Faith provides him some protection. Whether this will be enough to keep him alive is up to higher powers.

As an ex-Mongrel no longer protected by the gang, Byron is easy pickings to other gangsters. 'I can't retaliate. Imagine if I retaliate, then I'm back in it', he stated. 'Now I can also do that [and pick up a gun]; it's easy. But I think to myself: I can't go back into that life again'. Turning to violence is no longer an option. Byron has to turn the other cheek rather. 'The gangs, they can come shoot there. They can come and stab me here. They can hurt my family. I must just stay with this new path', he explained further. 'A Born Again Christian cannot attack back'. The hope is that if he gets by like this for long enough, the threats made against him will be worn away a little more every day, eventually receding altogether, as other people's recollections of Byron the Mongrel fade and are replaced with an acceptance of Byron the Born Again Christian.

Theological takes on gang violence prevention in Cape Town assert that religion 'bears the power to disarm, subvert, and even redeem the powers and principalities that seek to keep communities captive' (Bowers Du Toit, 2014, n.p.). This is true to some extent. But it is not divine law that keeps Byron from fetching a firearm. He is restrained by a real-world acknowledgement that this is what the rules of disengagement call for. In speaking of a former Mongrel brother named Clayton below, Byron clarifies the motivations behind his own performance of religiosity:

> Byron: When Clayton fell back [into the streets], he didn't go back to the gang. He went a little with the alcohol and girlfriends.

> Dariusz: So if you get back with the alcohol and girls, partying, eventually it may lead to....
>
> Byron: The enemies, they can hear about this and check [that] you're playing [with disengagement]. So they can come shoot you. That happened too. They did shoot. The Americans did, and the Laughing Boys wanted to shoot on Clayton because they say: hey, this person he's playing. He's not serious with a new life.
>
> Dariusz: So, the idea is, if you go into the church, and you live things the proper way, then people are more likely to respect that?
>
> Byron: Yes, but if you start playing, then [people think] it's just an excuse, you know. So you must be 100%.

If folks see you drinking, partying and cavorting, it taints their perceptions of your purity – rightly or wrongly. They see these behaviours as being inconsistent with a repertoire of righteousness. As in the streets, the façade is all there is. You always have to be '100%'. Byron remarked that plenty of gang members have 'played around' with religion, using it as a way of covering criminality – like Rashied Staggie purportedly did. This builds distrust about bids at redemption like Byron's, making it all the more important that gang exit be performed precisely.

He has foregone earrings, chains, *takkies* and other aspects of his previous street style and changed into that other well-worn uniform: a buttoned shirt, tucked into smart slacks, on top of polished shoes. So complete is Byron's conversion that he has gone as far as switching the soundtrack to his life from gangster rap to gospel music:

> People that have earrings and chains, *takkies,* and whatever, they can just dress like this, and not be a gangster. But other people in this [street] life, they don't see it that way. They think: this guy, he's still the same... You must change everything: the ways you speak, even the music you listen to. That time [when in the Mongrels], I used to like a lot of Lil Wayne rap. Even that you must leave, as well. There's more stuff even. The way I wear [my clothes], I mustn't actually wear [them like that], because the people will see: this boy's still a gangster.

One's conduct, one's threads, one's tunes and even one's thoughts all must be remodelled according to cultural signifiers associated with normal life. Not to say that old street dispositions are simply expunged and replaced, as has been shown already. Personal dispositions from distinct fields can come into conflict, competing in any given situation to determine what course of action is taken. Different people can react differently to similar circumstances. Even church-goers might reach again for their guns when threatened. This strategy is hazardous though, as it risks pulling a person back into violence. That is why Byron insists on shunning street culture in every way possible, even if it means pardoning attempts made on his very life.

5.1.3 Emerson

Disengagement is a dangerous undertaking. One can actively avoid playing with fire. But it is hard not to get burned when residing in a tinderbox. Each person in this study had their own run-ins with resentful former brothers, indignant foes, police officers and others wanting to do them ill. Some were hurt in such altercations. Even those who got away without a scratch were not unaffected. Every external conflict brought with it an internal one, leading them to question why they were consciously choosing to go from being powerful to being disempowered. To some degree each subject in this study, at one point or another, questioned whether the decision to withdraw from the gang was the right one. There were many stories like these. One of the most gripping came in the case of Emerson (Elsies River male, 43 years). He had been with the Americans for over 20 years before he disengaged. Emerson was also a self-described, 'respected' and 'high-ranking' member of the 26s, who earned his *gwinyas* during 16 separate stints in prison. The majority of his convictions were for violent crimes. 'If we get into an argument I won't still finish talking, I will pull out my gun or knife', he asserted. After a nine-month rehabilitation programme, Emerson was able to quit both gangs and drugs, swapping aggression and addiction for the normal life.

He leaned heavily on scripture to guide the way forward during his disengagement process, especially when facing personal ordeals. Emerson described, for instance, a robbery attempt against him in Parow, a fly-by northern suburb on the way toward the charming Franschhoek Wine Valley. The altercation brought him up against a mugger, who tried to relieve him of his wallet and phone by threatening to smash Emerson's face in with a brick. The incident brought the gangster in Emerson up against the religious man, creating a tug-of-war between the two that almost dragged him back into the streets:

> I got into this situation when a guy tried to rob me. Then my ego, the mindset I had, kicks in. Does this guy know who I am? Who I am in the number? That was a big challenge to me. Then I knew I have to rely on God. His word says: no weapon formed against you shall prosper. The bible tells you about meekness. You know what you can do [in retaliation], but you don't.

Both the sinner and the saint stood up to the threat. The saint ultimately triumphed. Although he previously would have pulled out a gun or knife before he finished talking, Emerson was now ready to martyr himself as a robbery victim. 'He's standing over me with this brick. And I'm thinking in my mind that this guy is going to hit me. My teeth is going to, you know, be knocked [in]. I just relied on God', he said. 'I cannot operate like I used to if I get into situations like with that robber. Because people are watching to see how I react. The gangs are watching. I knew I had to resist and forgive this guy'.

As luck would have it, the attacker simply stalked off. Perhaps he was taken aback by his victim's impassive reaction. Emerson was surprised too. For most people, the violent event is exceptional. Yet, if one is used to wanton cruelty, pacifism lands the hardest blow:

> It was hard for me... When I walked away, that's when it started. I thought: how can I let that guy do that? Does this guy know who I am in the number? My mind was like turned around. I don't even have to hurt that guy. I can just give an order to the [gang], saying: look here guys, this guy tried to do this. They would have sorted him out... It was very hard. I started crying also, thinking that this thing happened and I did nothing.

Although he got through the robbery safe and sound, Emerson was still shaken. The aftershocks he registered thrust to the surface underlying anxieties about interpretations of himself in the world. Emerson had to evade two threats that day. The first was the robbery itself, which could have left him broke and broken. The second was the emotional chain reaction that followed it, which threatened to derail his commitment to ceding the street life.

The ordeal provides persuasive evidence for disengagement as a process and not an event. Human interactions might be manifested in the moment, but no one experience is isolatable from others. Emerson experienced disengagement, not as a singular instance, but as a string of events – a continuous confluence of deliberations, doubts, hopes, introspections, traumas and resolutions – that tangled together in complicated and sometimes contradictory ways. The effect was a dynamic, time-varying and indefinite commitment to gang exit that was never simple, static or sure. The rest of the research participants in this study had similar experiences. Eventually each got to the point where he or she was more out of gangs than in. However, regress was always a possibility. To a certain degree, any person is on any occasion in the midst of his or her story. How it will end up is always unknown. But disengagement from gangs is particularly uncertain. Religion offers some semblance of order and certitude amid the tensions between: jobs and joblessness, security and insecurity, empowerment and disempowerment and life and death. Moreover, adhering to a sacral script creates internal and external continuity during outgoing transitions, shielding new non-gang identities from the forces threatening to batter them into relapsing, until such a time that the ex-hoodlum can stand solid and strong on his or her own.

5.1.4 Declan

Initiations into normal life can be intense. They call for radical conformity to harmony, forgiveness and humility, no matter how ominous the circumstances. This point is brought home in Declan's (Mitchells Plain male, 42 years) struggle to cope with the murder of his son, who was shot by the opposing Hustlers gang in Mitchells Plain three months before our interview. At first, Declan had a strong urge to avenge the killing. Later, he realised that the social landscape of his new peaceable life necessitated a recalibration of his moral compass towards compassion:

> With my son's death, I did go find out who is the guys that shot him and I went up to them with the car. I told myself that I was going face them [and kill them]. But when I came there I couldn't retaliate because of the step I took in my life; and I knew [then] I must forgive them, and try to do that every day. Sometimes I [still] want to go see who are these people [that killed my son] and what are their mothers are doing... But that is stuff that wants to take me back to the gang. It's easier for me to go the gangster way, take a gun, go up to them, and just go finish them off. Then you know you 'go get your blood', also. But now I can't do that anymore, because I'm in life the normal way.

Imagine having to confront your child's killers as Declan did. It would be hard for anybody to find forgiveness after an agonising attack on one's child. Declan had to do this while also trying to override his socialisation towards a long-held belief that he *had to* retaliate. Remember, this is the same man that almost killed his brother-in-law with a hammer, just for playing a prank on him in front of family and friends, and he was now being asked to exonerate the gangland killing of his own son.

Not only was Declan willing to look past his son's murder, he decided to meet the killers in person to offer them peace. To boot, the attempt at reconciliation was being navigated through the direst of straits. It took place in a part of Mitchells Plain where Declan had throughout the years left a trail of spent shell casings and plundered property. It also centred on a meeting with his archenemies the Hustlers, a gang that he had bitterly battled for years. He had to confront all of this head-on, with faith as his sole weapon:

> I was afraid of the gangs, because I thought they are going to kill me... It was very difficult. The life I lived made it seem impossible for me to find peace. There were times when I knew I can't go to church because it was another weak point, and other gang members would see me go to church and target me, and now I'm showing weakness. So when I came there [to Mitchells Plain], all the stuff that I learned as a child [in the streets] I got to learn again in the church... At the meeting, [the Hustler's leader] named all the things that I did... but in a harsh way; and I told him in a humble way: yes I did do it. I asked that he please forgive me, and so he said alright, and he was also asking me for forgiveness for what he did.

Declan's split from the streets is nothing short of miraculous. 'That guy is still today in a gang. That gang fight is still on. There's still people dying. He gave me his hand in front of [the other Hustlers and] the community', said Declan. 'What we sensed there was the Holy Spirit. Because something like that doesn't happen in the community – the enemy going to his enemy to make peace. Usually they do it the other [gangster] way'. Violence and vengeance are so centrally entrenched in the modes and motives of the streets that mercy seemed wholly illogical without a sense of something of biblical proportions as having occurred. That the meeting ended without bloodshed was profound to be sure. But the reasons for this are probably more practical than they are spiritual. A religious repertoire provided Declan with a road map for navigating years of accumulated resentment and trauma, so that he could pardon and be pardoned for some of the most egregious sins imaginable. To his enemies and to Mitchells Plain residents, the religious repertoire also offered a cultural frame that explained how bitter enemies might meet to find peace rather than seeking violence. That all walked away from the meeting alive was perhaps a small reason to believe that a normal life might be possible for Declan after all. Indeed, today he is fighting only his own demons, focusing on work, family and faith to live 'the normal way', in spite of a temptation to sometimes lapse into his old gangster ways.

5.2 Returning to the Streets

Disengaging from gangs usually means also decreasing one's delinquent behaviour (Sweeten, Pyrooz, & Piquero, 2013). Research suggests that violent offending, for example, declines among ex-members (Bjerk, 2008; Gordon et al., 2004; Melde & Esbensen, 2013).[4] Most of the research participants in this study managed to abstain from gang associations, criminality and violent behaviour, something that grew increasingly true the longer they were out. Nevertheless, totally avoiding aggression was sometimes impossible. The township environment is a social space with porous frontiers, meaning that street life and normal life can overlap irrespective of a person's intentionality towards the law. Whether a person is a gangster, an ex-gangster or has never been in gangs, living in an unsafe community means regularly dealing with uncertainty. The following are two examples of ex-members – Ashwin and Joanna – who had each been out of gangs for over a decade. Neither can be said to be in immediate danger of regressing into street culture. Both now work in the area of gang violence prevention. Nevertheless, each described instances in which they went back to street-oriented behaviours to deal with threats made against their person and their possessions.

---

[4]Former members may, however, resort to violence more readily than those never in a gang (Melde & Esbensen, 2011).

5.2.1 *Ashwin*

Ashwin (Athlone male, 49 years) is a former American and 26. Having spent much of his life in gangs, he now capitalises on his experience in the streets as an anti-gang community activist. Despite dedicating himself to promoting peace, Ashwin still cannot escape intimidation, crime and the like, as is evidenced by an altercation he had with a phone thief on a minibus taxi traveling to Hanover Park:

> There in the taxi, I did see my phone is gone. You know *mos*, the taxis they can be jammed up... I turned and am asking the people around. I then see that there is this young guy close behind. And I think: no man, this guy is not coming correct. He has my phone. So I started on him. But first I asked to see if he has my phone. Like not too much angry, but just to test him. He said no [he didn't take it], but I see he is like *skelm*,[5] man. Because I've seen characters like him many times.

Already there are indications of Ashwin's street instincts. A person cannot assess anything accurately without first knowing the subject in front of him. Applying a litmus test for what is and what is not *skelm* implies an expert's knowledge of criminal proclivities and practices.

I met Ashwin early on in my stay in Cape Town, and I am aware he possesses a rap sheet that stretches from wholesale distribution of drugs to murder. Although he is now long out of the gang, and getting on in years, Ashwin is still a man of considerable stature, who presents an imposing challenge to any would-be crook:

> It continues like this. Now I'm applying even more pressure, [but] still talking to him, and the people [on the bus] start to be interested too. I say: *naai*, this cannot go [on]. I am mad, you see. There is only one way to now handle this thing... I smacked him hard – like with the backhand... You know, I am working against these violent things. But I come to a point where that [violence] is all this man [can] understand. I hit him then very hard.

A sudden flash of ire was enough to dislodge the truth and recover the stolen phone. It must be observed, however, that Ashwin's immediate response was not hostile. The altercation begins with him speaking to the thief, reasoning with him, as would be expected in any 'normal' exchange between two people. When words failed, decisive action was required. That is when the situation escalated from an interaction to an altercation. Feeling that his hand was forced, Ashwin clapped back more aggressively, calling into action the only form of persuasion

---

[5]An Afrikaans word directly translated as 'sly', which insinuates something or somebody villainous or crooked.

a thief could understand, in a surgical strike that points to the dexterity of a man adept at treating social complications with his fists. Even knowing to target a particular person in a bus full of people, by simply feeling 'he was not coming correctly', implies a sixth sense that most people do not possess.

Ashwin had been out of the gang for as long as he had been in one at that point. Still, his street skills had not disappeared. They are seldom used now, but still come out when called upon, like when he is on the job and working with gangsters:

> There are times in this community activism work, where I come to the guys [I'm working with] by the number. Because I was long in the number [26], I can use it to my advantage then, you see. But it is a dangerous... You do not know how they see you now. Do they think: this man is pretending in this activism business, but you see how he talks the number to us.

Ashwin is well aware that street capital is double-edged; its rewards appear shiny, but its repercussions can be sharp. Applying it too sharply can imperil the ex-gangster, re-associating him with a world he had previously cut off. Ashwin is worried that any additional scrutiny of him could result in added threat. Protecting himself from what comes next – a fight, a hit, a proposition to re-join the Americans – might in turn require him to channel yet again that same energy that helped him get his phone back. Before you know it, he is in the gang once more.

Street capital is devalued in mainstream society, as reasoned dialogue is given primacy over striking somebody or speaking *Sabela*. But street practices are never totally forgotten. They lay inert, like a language one was once fluent in and has not spoken for a while. Although a past gangbanger may not want to speak street anymore, sometimes it slips out. With so much of Ashwin's character shaped by experiences in gangs, it is easy to imagine how this part of him is not so easily put out of his mind. After all, the community activist grew out of the tough guy, in a nested identity made up of both his past and present selves.

Long ago, Ashwin chose to walk an honourable path, burying the gangster in him into the recesses of his character. It is hard to totally leave that part of him behind since Ashwin still remains chained to the same forces that coaxed him into gangs originally. For instance, he has struggled financially over the last two years, as the funding for the community project that pays him has fluctuated. At times he has gone months without a paycheck, which left him hustling to scrape by. Without his job as a community activist he has few places to seek income. Doors to the majority of the city's office buildings, shops and factories are closed to him due to his prison record; that is assuming businesses would hire a Coloured man with few skills and no matriculation certificate anyway. So it is inaccurate and wholly unfair to imply that Ashwin's past is ever really his past; it lurks behind him still, as looming and menacing as it ever was:

> I have conversations with some of my old [gang] friends. They also experience these challenges. Even though we're so long outside, it's

always coming from the back of our minds. It's always that you can make a mistake and go back to prison, even though you don't want to be there... Because sometimes the treatment by society and the challenges get too much. We struggle in our communities to get something to survive on. Yes, so that feeling is there. The fear comes, and it goes, and it comes – that anxiety. Now we have started a family, you know, all of these responsibilities, and life is just tough for an ex-convict. I think I have it better off, but even through my own [financial] crisis, I think: hey, I hope I can be in self-control and not go back to prison, for doing a wrong thing that will look right at the time that you do it.

Though much has changed in Ashwin's life, much has also stayed the same. He is once more caught trying to make ends meet. It is for this reason that he does not take for granted any betterment in his circumstances, believing he is at any time just a financial emergency or wrong move away from doing a U-turn into the streets. Should he get caught up in crime to get some stopgap cash, a judge is unlikely to consider his long record favourably. He would, no doubt, be in prison again. And then what? 'I think sometimes: what must I do if I go back to prison? Because, you see, these things can happen, even now', said Ashwin. 'Will I then return to the number? Or will I enter with my spiritual or activism side? I was one of those [prison gangsters] that was threatening the religious guys that are leaving the number'. Ashwin has come far. Yet, he is in some ways also not that far from where he started. He still knows deep down that, if worst comes to worst, he might find some reprieve from his travails by going back to gangsterism.

5.2.2 *Joanna*

Like Ashwin, Joanna (Hanover Park female, 35 years) has been out of gangs for more than 10 years and is also working for a community-based organisation to assist young men and women in withdrawing from gangs. I have watched her strive tirelessly over the years to use her own experiences in street life to assist others in need: providing them with mentoring, linking them with rehabilitation and training programmes, supporting them in court, visiting them in prison, helping with reintegration after prison releases and providing assistance as a case worker, role model and friend. But the project that she worked for was also defunded and she was left without work, struggling to subsist as Ashwin was. That was almost two years ago, and Joanna is still unemployed, lugging around a criminal record from 2001 that blocked options for the most basic employment. Joanna, for example, passed an initial application screening and two subsequent interviews for cashier work at Pick n' Pay, which is one of South Africa's largest supermarket chains, only to be denied the position after a background check, betrayed by mistakes that she made as a punk kid and which she has long ago atoned for.

I met Joanna for an interview a few months before this book was finalised, in her poky Hanover Park two-bedroom apartment, its contents virtually sold off in a last-ditch effort to bring in some cash. 'I know I can go to the gang for money. But then I'm back again. Believe me, I don't want to do that. I've come too far. But I don't know what to do – really', she said. Everybody in Hanover Park knows that the gang is a lender of last resort. The strings attached to a gang loan are also well known. Pay it back, and you still incur a high premium and the stigma of gang association. That is the best-case scenario. Failure to manage your accounts might mean a visit from a loan shark like Ruan or services rendered in lieu of payment – stashing money, drugs or weapons. For the downhearted and demoralised, the pains and humiliations of destitution might be too formidable to consider any such fine print. Where else can you go when you are unable to pay the bills or put food on the table, especially if your family and friends have an abundance of expenses as well and too little money to support you too? That is the question Joanna now faces. Despite leaving the Backstreets such a long time ago and striving to aid others overcome poverty, gangs and prison, she is now confronted with these same challenges – for the second time in her life. She no longer brandishes a knife or gun as a member of the Backstreet Kids. Yet she is nonetheless mired in violence – structural violence – trading punches every day against an unrelenting assault that beats her down through unemployment, hunger, stigma and an accumulation of other aggressions enacted on her body and psyche. As a person slowly takes on stresses, indignities and injuries, death comes by way of a thousand tiny cuts, rather than as the result of a single fatal blow.

Her financial hardships notwithstanding, Joanna is intent on staying off the streets. Once a girl gangster who leveraged street cultural performances to gain security, income and status (Dziewanski, 2020c), she now disavows her street persona:

> I tell people, my name is Joanna, but I've also got my nickname *'Skim'*. Those two names carry different weights. If you call me Joanna, then you're going to call on the rehabilitated person. But if you call me *Skim* then that person was rude. Like I tell people a lot, don't call me that name again because that is who I used to be. And for me, if I think back now, me, myself, I didn't like that person. Really, because that person was rude, nobody fucked with that person, that is how she was... Joanna has a way more softer approach. *Skim*, a fly must not even sit on her nose.

To bring home the distinction between her current and previous selves, Joanna summons *Skim*, a gang nickname and street-generated persona once regularly called upon as part of her Backstreets identity. Although she insists that people not refer to her as *Skim*, the gangster in her can emerge when needed. 'Sometimes *Skim* comes out... Even with some of my participants [when I worked for the local gang prevention organisation], I couldn't be [Joanna]. I must be *Skim*', she explained. 'I must show you who I am otherwise you're going to take advantage'.

As with Ashwin, who sometimes used his expertise in the number to gain advantage when working in anti-gang community activism, she also went back to her street sensibilities in a workplace setting where street life overhangs professional life.

Street practices can bleed into everyday practices in other ways, as well. In Hanover Park, being pulled into a confrontation can come from something as innocuous as relaxing outside your front door. This was the setting for an altercation between Joanna and a member of the Ghetto Kids, the gang that took over the territory the Backstreet Kids once occupied:

> It was a hot day like today, everybody's outside… That was really a huge fight. That day I told myself I had to prove myself… because there were too many people in the street. Who are you to disrespect me like that? Tomorrow they're [all] going to do the exact same thing. This is Hanover Park. If you don't stand up for yourself in Hanover Park, everybody's going to walk over you. You think you're all that because you're with the gang [so you can disrespect me]. I had to make a point that day, seriously. And she never spoke nonsense to me since that day.

For Cape Town's urban underclasses, the social fields that define gang life and normal life are not completely exclusive of each other, as Joanna described above. She is an ex-gangster, but still cannot take being disrespected in front of family, friends and neighbours. That afternoon Joanna turned into *Skim*. It was a form of street theatre that was anything but play-acting. With the community's eyes on her, Joanna had to strike back then and there, frantically and unapologetically, or risk being victimised over and over again later. So she fought, and she won. Temporarily stepping into the streets again that day gained her some space to exist more safely outside of them in the days that followed.

That was not the only challenge she had to beat back in this manner. 'I fought with a lady one day, a woman that lives here around the corner. She was no gangster though', she told me. 'But I fucked her up pretty good'. Again, Joanna doubled back to *Skim* to shoot down disrespect aimed in her direction:

> I was sitting here in the yard, she came to talk her *kak*[6] with me. She came in here [to my yard], she was forcing for a lift to Elsies [River], or wherever, [with a man that lives with me]. The more I tell her the man is sleeping, and then [the more] she started swearing, I was *lekker* tipsy already. I hit her outside the gate. It told her: no man, you're rude. You're sitting on your premises, somebody comes and talks nonsense with you, what are you going to do? I told myself: no man, if I allow this other people are also going to do it. There are times when you still have to act tough.

---

[6]Shit.

This time *Skim* had to deal with a quarrelsome neighbour. Acting tough had nothing to do with securing turf or fighting for a flag. It was required just to safeguard some clout in the community in an incident that illustrates the insidious nature of the street field. Fights between civilians are generated by the same set of values that inform street culture. Gang members are perhaps apex predators in the social ecology of township violence, but the food chain includes several other actors as well. Competition among them takes no prisoners. Neighbour is pitted against neighbour. The strongest wins. In lieu of wealth, higher education and social status, they are fighting for control of some of the most valuable symbolic currency their communities have – respect.

5.3 Still Searching for Salvation

Cape Town's gangs have become part of its social psyche. Tales of hitmen, generals, drugs and wealth have all been rendered in blood, as part of a narrative repertoire that communicates what is possible for those dismissed to the fringes of the segregated city. Such stories represent real-world incarnations of street habitus and cannot be ignored. However, it was shown above that the street field is far from a settled account. It is an ongoing negotiation of what life can imaginably be. Changing the narrative for those that are in gangs shows that alternatives are available, countering the accepted notion that there is no way out of gangs. This is more than just semantics. The stories told in any social space establish 'schemes of perception' (Bourdieu, 1990, p. 13) that define what is practically possible in that setting. Telling stories of successful gang leaving illustrates that living on the Cape Flats is not synonymous with dying in the streets.

Of course, disengagement is a gruelling process that gives no guarantee of safety. So retreating members take what precautions they can to mitigate the risks of gang exit. Performing repertoires of work, family and religion gives them room to ride it out for long enough that their gang mates forget about them and beefs with their rivals wane. Sadly, many do not make it that far, either getting killed or sucked back into gangsterism. For those who manage to leave gangs and live to tell the tale, like the participants in this project did, there await even more challenges. The ex-gangster must ultimately confront the hard reality that he or she remains planted in the same tainted ground in which street culture is rooted. The very problems that brought them into gangs are as present as they ever were upon departing them: the ache of poverty stays as acute as before; pangs of hunger remain just as upsetting; and the everyday pains of inequality, racism and segregation structure their lives still. For good measure, uncertainty and insecurity are still the norm for former gang members living in communities like Hanover Park, Elsies River, Mitchells Plain or even the relatively better-off Athlone. So sometimes they are forced to fight, as with Ashwin and Joanna, or they might be compelled into petty criminality like Prince was. But they must be careful. Regressing too far back into street life might mean totally losing one's way eventually.

Every altercation opens the door a bit more slippage back to the streets. Ex-members eventually need to step fully over the threshold of normal life – through work, family and religion – if they ever hope to totally shut out the streets. Performances of normality are crucial for validating to oneself, as well as to observers, the kind of person one is trying to become. Most problematic perhaps is persuading allies that one is not functioning anymore in service of turf or tattoo and proving to adversaries that the past really is the past. The religious repertoire helps here, especially. Spirituality also offers a model for handling conflict, as well as instructions for repairing relationships with family and community. It is a personal schematic known widely – even among gangsters – to embrace diffidence, virtue and composure, all traits that are antithetical to gangsterism. Maybe if the ex-thug can answer the call to prayer with enough devotion, he or she can in time convince friends, neighbours and foes alike that their transformation is authentic.

Chapter 6

Gavin

In this final empirical chapter, we will revisit the story of Gavin, the former Mongrel and 28 introduced at the very outset of this book. His life history will tie together the different theoretical threads explored earlier, showing how they fit into a single personal narrative. Gavin is someone who I came to know well during my time in Cape Town. When we met in 2013, he had spent approximately half of his life in gangs, and was just out of Pollsmoor Prison after serving 10 years for murder. Laying on his bunk in the maximum security facility, Gavin frequently daydreamed about the prospect of returning to lawful living, as he attempted to drown out the chaos coming from the 30–40 cellmates that were imprisoned with him. The plan was to have his own home, his own car and his own money, he hoped, 'made in a legal way, not drug money like in the past'. Prison is a place where there is ample time to contemplate past mistakes and future plans. Naturally one's thoughts may wander into doubts about gang life. However, the presence of South Africa's notorious prison gangs makes it hazardous to disengage while inside. Deserting the number just then would have left Gavin exposed to the brutalities of the carceral system. But staying in meant still acting as a 28. Rank and responsibility, for instance, dictated that he continued to liaise with other *ndotas*, to address disputes and to dole out punishments.

So he attempted a compromise. Gavin enrolled in a high school equivalency programme 'just to get away from the cell for a few hours'. It provided some breathing room, a short period each day during which he could cease being a 28, and just be. A small break from the madness is all it was at first. Eventually, however, Gavin would learn to like school. He passed an exam or two, then a couple of classes, and in the end managed to achieve a matriculation certificate. 'I started believing in myself. I started reading the Bible. I started reading everything… I started to develop myself. I started investing in me', he told me of that time. Gavin's scholastic successes surprised him. But they should not have come as a shock really. You do not make your way up the Capetonian criminal hierarchy by being stupid. Once you are on its higher rungs though, it is difficult to get off, especially in a prison cell, where there is nowhere to hide. 'I was also still in the gangster game, but I kept building myself in classes', said Gavin. 'I was too much in to escape that – you know, this is Pollsmoor'. Unable to leave the gang just then, Gavin continued in the game, playing both sides. When with the 28s, he studied the number. When he could get away, he studied for school and read the Bible, preparing to get totally free as soon as he was out of jail.

Gang Entry and Exit in Cape Town, 125–146
Copyright © 2021 Dariusz Dziewanski
Published under exclusive licence by Emerald Publishing Limited
doi:10.1108/978-1-83909-730-020210006

However, his horizons outside were significantly less sunny than those he had envisioned from his bunk. Finding work proved unfeasible for a former felon with few networks outside of the underground economy. Reality soon clouded out his early optimism. Every day he was re-introduced to a city that was no more hospitable to him than when he entered Pollsmoor. 'When I came out of prison I wanted a job. I got a matric [certificate] but couldn't get a job', explained Gavin. Of course, the Mongrels welcomed him with open arms. 'And here I get this big job to sell drugs and make money... and I felt bigger than ever before – bigger than before I went to prison'. He was back at the beginning – more mature and perhaps more resolute, but still in a society that had no meaningful place for somebody like him. Even the promise that a matriculation certificate might make life easier was quickly dispelled. Significance is placed in South Africa on education as a pathway to prosperity.[1] Indeed, lack of education is cited as a risk factor for gang participation in the country (Cooper & Ward, 2012a); for those already in gangs, not having schooling or skills can also hinder disengagement (Cooper & Ward, 2012b). Yet, even young South Africans that possess those much-coveted high school credentials still struggle to find employment.

One reason is that the focus on qualification neglects the practical knowledge and support needed to capitalise on a diploma.[2] But there are other important reasons why an ex-con like Gavin struggled to find work. First, he has a prison record. Second, he did not have access to the type of social and cultural capital needed for finding a legit job. I have seen it all before: a young man or woman coming out of the gate running after being released from prison, taking a victory lap and telling whomever will listen about the promise that tomorrow holds – no more drugs, no more gang friends, no more mistakes. It seems simple enough. 'Just say no'. How hard can it be? Yet this ignores one fundamental fact: a person must also have something to say 'yes' to, some alternative to drug money, gang rank and the sense of approval that comes from being a Mongrel and 28. Without other options, rehabilitation and reintegration turn into nothing more than an act of will. It is an uphill undertaking that is not fully apparent to a convicted felon dreaming about how good life will be once he gets out of the pen. Gavin found real life to be far less rosy. Nobody would hire him, so he went back to the Mongrels with this tail between his legs. 'I couldn't get work when I was released. I was just like [I am a] gangster. I was like I don't give a fuck about life anymore. I had nothing to lose', Gavin stated. His hopes of living legally were no match

---

[1]The suggestion is that, in South Africa, education policy reform plays an important role given that youth unemployment co-exists with an under-supply of skills in certain areas of the labour market (Gustafsson, 2011). A 2016 statement by the Government of the Western Cape that announced the launch of a three-year project to employ youth stated that a 'better educated and more highly skilled workforce is the most pressing long-term priority for the South African economy and for the Western Cape Government' (Schäfer, 2016, n.p.).

[2]Students get little career guidance and support (Branson, Clare, Joy, & Needham, 2015) and school career guidance programmes are not comprehensive, particularly in socioeconomically disadvantaged schools (Mudhovozi & Chireshe, 2012).

compared to the need for food, shelter and dignity. '[The Mongrels] gave me rank in the gang and said I could run the gang of youngsters. I took the job, seeing it as my only way to survive'. Just like that Gavin was a gangster again, leveraging the significant rank, networks, expertise and reputation he had built up in half a lifetime as a street and prison gang member.

6.1 Born into the Streets

Gavin's original point of entry into gangs was an older brother – also a Mongrel and 28 – whom he described as his 'everything'. They were raised in an impoverished, overcrowded and under-resourced slum community located on the fringes of Ottery. His sibling modelled a way of achieving stability, security and self-assurance. 'We stayed in a shack, but he always provided', Gavin recalled. Because Gavin's father was mean-spirited and abusive, big bro stepped into a paternal role. 'I wanted to run away because of my father. But my brother advised me not to run away but to stand like a man – face the challenges. He built me very strong as a boy'. Socialised into strength from early on, it was not long before Gavin followed his sibling into gangs and prison:

> I used to tell my brother I wanted to be like [him]. He then told me: no, I don't need to be like him because I'm a good football player. But I wanted all the things he had, because I saw it every day… He told me: it's very dangerous. But I didn't give a damn. I also wanted money… And I saw how they were stabbing and shooting people. I saw [the gangsters] giving life to the kids. They were like role models to all the kids. Despite him telling me of the negativity, I still wanted to be like him.

Gangs were Gavin's aspiration. They seemed as good as any livelihood on offer, putting money in your pocket, food on the table and earning admiration in the neighbourhood. All are emphatic arguments for a life of crime that can easily stifle even the most well-intentioned pleas that baby brother stay off the streets. Anyway, 'do as I say, and not as I do' has little meaning when licit options for attaining symbolic and economic capital are virtually non-existent. So Gavin was lured into gangsterism. The turning point came when his sibling was slain by a rival gang. Thirteen years of street socialisation made the young boy believe that avenging the killing was his one and only option. He joined the Mongrels to do just that.

Although it was the bullet that claimed his brother that sealed Gavin's fate as a Mongrel, he was already well on his way to becoming a gunfighter by that point. He just needed a push. 'I grew up my life in it… I knew too much and I said to myself I understand [gang life] because I witnessed it and it was the easiest way [to survive]', he said. Instead of recoiling from the same dangers that had killed his kin, he shifted closer to them. 'I saw him suffer in front of me. Unfortunately he didn't make it. I thought when he is dead I need to become him now, and when I joined the gang I received all the love'. Gavin figuratively stepped into the mythologised character of his brother, becoming a Mongrel, and later joining the 28s. 'No danger came through my mind. I witnessed danger. So I was used to it, and thought: why must I be scared of it? I knew we all must die', said Gavin. He was a 13-year-old whose heritage had instilled in him a fatalistic sense of what can be expected from life in an informal settlement. Gun blasts, police sirens and funerals were all regular occurrences, breeding a pattern of 'terminal thinking' (Garbarino, 2000) that has been observed in youth traumatised by such environments. Unable to envision the next month or year, Gavin lived day-to-day. That is just what a gangster does.

Not to say that Gavin did not have relationships with people that intimated a different type of behaviour for him. He did. Two friends from his adolescence, especially, represented what his life might have been. 'They both finished matric and got good jobs today. They were positive', said Gavin. 'Like their mother and father, they were always there for them. The one had an older brother who finished matric and made it, and he looked to him as a role model'. Comparable behavioural repertoires were lacking in Gavin's household. Thus, while Gavin gravitated towards gang fighting, his friends took an alternate route:

> I remember once we were in a fight at school and he told me he can fight, but he didn't want to jeopardise his education. So he resolved the conflict positively. He was more dedicated [to school]. But me and my other friends were more dedicated to the streets. I didn't get how he could walk away like that, in front of everybody. Nah, not me man. I would have been all-in.

Nobody at that point had taught Gavin that education might be more useful than reputation. But he learned first-hand the immediate and very tangible benefits that participating in street culture brings. Over the years, drug sales and gang hits had helped Gavin's family get by in their scanty shack. Staying in school and working hard on homework assignments and quizzes, on the contrary, could only be cashed in for grades and the promise of a job someday – maybe – if he was among the fortunate few who could find steady work.

Gavin's ambitions were limited growing up. In addition to wanting to be a gangster, he aspired to be a footballer. 'When I was in primary school, I was always telling my teachers I will either be in prison or a football player', Gavin stated. 'I will be a gangster, or a football player, one of the two'. Celebrated Coloured footballer Benedict 'Benni' McCarthy, especially, made an impression on him. McCarthy was born in 1977 in Hanover Park and played professionally for many years in Europe, suiting up for a number of top clubs that included: Ajax, Porto, Blackburn Rovers and West Ham United. Actually, McCarthy was often referenced with pride elsewhere in interviews as an example of a Coloured man who had made it from the Flats to find international success:

> When I was a kid, my big dream was always to go to Europe like
> Benni, or the Brazilians. I like them, man. Because they all did
> make it out of the ghetto. And the other side when it comes to
> gangsters, you know that's another side that's a side of my brother
> and them... how they live with money, cars, and everything.

The football field and the street field are cast in contrast to each other, with
Gavin's attention caught between trying to be like Benni and trying to be like
his brother. The former is a stand-in for the potential to play by the rules, while
the latter symbolises the spoils of unlawful interests. It was not much of a
competition though. The gangster easily beat out the footballer. When his
prospects of becoming a soccer star started to look progressively distant, Gavin
fixed his gaze on gangs. As a Mongrel, he would find immediate social approval, a
feeling of purpose and a source of income. In other words, he found a way of
making sense of his world and excelling in it. Although he was not famous like
Benni, the ghetto fame Gavin achieved made him a local hero and allowed him to
manage his marginalisation and keep dreaming big.

6.2 Deeper into the Game

'When he died, there was nobody else. It was just the old school gangsters around
and they saw me as the chosen one', said Gavin. Carrying on his brother's
gangster legacy seemed to him almost prophetic. 'My mindset changed. From
there, being a gangster, there was no light, or no way out. I was very young at the
time. I started believing I was a boss or a leader, as young as I [was]'. It was at this
point that Gavin's detachment from his family and his community gave way
totally and he sought a closer connection to the gang, via a process that was part
paternal and part parasitic:

> There was one older gangster in particular, after he came out of
> prison he showed me a lot of love. He was a Mongrel and a 26.
> The day they shot my brother this guy took me away from the
> scene. Because I didn't want to leave. He told me I'm a man and
> not to cry. I went with him. He [also] told me not to worry and that
> [death] must happen in this game. He made me believe I'm a man.
> Then my brother's gang started investing in me more to become a
> gangster.

Gang members are primed over the course of their lives to accept and expect
terror, injury and even death. The elder Mongrels represented to Gavin street-
capitalised behavioural ideals that valorised stoicism, showing him a way of
coping with loss in the long-term. Such fearlessness is a necessary strategy for
managing the rampant trauma that afflicts communities like his. Taking this into
account, Gavin's words from the preface are prescient. 'You need to be hard like

this place to survive here. So that [others] can't make a carpet of you. So that they can't walk over you', he stated then. Social skills are not a qualifier for prosperity in the *kampie* because kindness is viewed as a weakness and sympathy as something that should be suppressed. By comparison, embracing toughness allows a person to stand tall in spite of persistent hardship.

Going back to the preface again, remember Gavin described 'how the little kids grow up in the ghetto', their parents directing at them a vocabulary of argumentation and abuse, in an inherited intergenerational 'pain' that they in turn bequeath to their offspring. Knowingly or not, mothers and fathers are desensitising their sons and daughters to better endure the humiliations of the hostile environment they will grow up in. Distress flows from parent to child, repeating when those children had children of their own. Of course, any boy or girl progressing through a childhood of slings and arrows is better prepared to one day graduate to guns. Today, the *kampie* is filled with kids who are not yet in a gang, but who have already been in the streets for years, bearing witness both to the petty insults of informal living and to the shots people take at overcoming them. Gavin's life history substantiates how the street field connects social habitat and social habit via habitus, sowing the seeds of street culture in Ottery's hardened soil and creating the generative conditions for a small boy to grow into a stone-cold killer.

When he was officially in the gang, Gavin's induction into street culture intensified, with the older Mongrels taking him under their wing to show him how to amass street capital. 'They told me everything. How to walk, talk, [and] what to do in prison. How you need to handle things. How to be gangster', said Gavin. 'The history of the Mongrels is all about blood... And that's how we lived, because that's how we were taught and raised'. The gang's mythology is an example of how collective agency and structure interact in the long-term to bring about identifiable and durable social groupings that live through the collective practices of the gang. The imagery of the Mongrel – a dog of no definable breed or owner – bears a likeness to the type of defiant individualism often identified with street culture (Sánchez-Jankowski, 1991):

> You know that word 'Mongrel'... it means to like fight for survival. It's like a dog. If you look at a dog on the street it fights for survival. It will do anything just to survive... You know there's dogs that doesn't have owners. What must they do? They must survive. They must survive on their own. For me, I used to look at dogs. I'm like, wow, that dog doesn't have owners but look at him, [he's] grown. How did he get that big? He did survive. He did hustle hard for food to eat. He did get his food. So I said to myself: you know I'm a dog, which means I need to hustle hard, to go and get my money. I need to go and get anything what I need.

It is easy to see why Gavin would identify with the Mongrel, an unloved stray mutt, who growls and grows most fearsome when it is most fearful. True to its name, the Mongrel gang finds pride in this lack of identity and purpose and honour in fighting – unaided and forgotten – through punishing austerity. Gavin fully adopted the street hustler persona by drawing on the symbolic power of the street dog. 'If you look around how a dog lives, he got no heart. He don't give a shit. That make me believe I'm a dog. I need to live cruel', he said. The very characteristics of his marginalisation became a basis for strength. To be forlorn signified freedom and independence; contending with adversity became synonymous with tenacity, street-smarts and personhood; violent cruelty was identified with dignity and the ability to stare down the hostile gaze of a society set against him. If need be, a Mongrel would be heartless, having no fear of or regard for others, or even for what the personal consequences of such heartlessness would be:

> You know, to kill somebody is like – wow, man! – I don't know how to explain to you that. You must have a heart. You must have guts to kill somebody – broad daylight, or in front of people... You know it's either you going to die after this, or you go to jail. So what do you do? You already know it. I'm going to die. I don't care if I'm going to die, I'm just going to do it. But the other people, you know, are going to think twice before they are going to do it while you already just did it.

Becoming a Mongrel and a murderer was Gavin's best chance to get what he could, while he could. Little regard was given to potential repercussions. If that meant taking a life in broad daylight, so be it. It was a necessary evil, essential for building a reputation for being unflinching and uncompromising.

However, once you have created an expectation, you must see it through all the way. As Gavin explained, earning a reputation for violence is just the first battle in the long war to sustain one's street credibility. 'You need to work to earn reputation. You need to work hard. Then to keep this thing you need to fight for it, because people are going to come to take your title', he warned. 'So you need to fight. No matter if you must kill, or what you must do, just to keep your title. Even though you [are] on top, it doesn't mean you can relax now'. Everyday violence is the metric against which gang reputations are measured. To attain and keep the title of top dog one has to keep killing. Eventually, constant killing comes to define street-oriented individuals, as it is dispositioned deeper and deeper with each shooting, stabbing and assault. Collectively, every act of violence spawns another in a self-sustaining cycle of threat and retaliation that spreads outwards as conflictual, continual and cannibalistic social contagion. Gavin's brother was a killer. When he was murdered, the young pup also became a Mongrel. Then Gavin began to kill as well. This led to threats and retaliations against him, which were repaid in kind. On it went – an eye for an eye – until he got penned up in Pollsmoor for murder, wasting 10 years of his life before he would start to wipe the slate clean.

6.3 Changing Life Course

Once in prison, Gavin was initiated into the 28s, further following the footsteps of his mentor. 'I joined the 28s because of my brother. I just wanted to be like him. He was a

28', said Gavin. 'I knew when I went to prison that it is part of the life, a part of the game. When you join the gang you're already in prison. You're prepared. [Even] the language gangsters use is a prison language'. Street culture is prison culture, and vice versa. 'The culture of violence [in South African prisons] is, ironically, a failed attempt to restore the order of things that has been toppled by the perversity of prison life, to erase some of the intolerable ambiguities... that confront men behind bars' (2004, n.p.), writes Steinberg. In other words, it is a way of coping with hostile conditions. 'You see it as a way to survive. If you [are] not a prison gangster, your life will be hell: you will be used, raped... So I joined the 28s', said Gavin. Prison violence mirrors and reinforces gang-related violence outside, further entrenching an ideal in which brutality is to be expected, endured and celebrated. For gang members, a rap sheet symbolises a positive cultural asset and a source of prestige. That is why some Coloured youngsters seek out a prison record as a way of securing street cred (Samara, 2011).

So, on one hand, Gavin's experiences in detention support research indicating how the South African system normalises gangsterism. But, on the other hand, they are also the case study of how imprisonment can spark scepticism about gang life; for example, going to jail might play on people's panic about being separated from family and community (Berger, Abu-Raiya, Heineberg, & Zimbardo, 2017; Moloney, Mackenzie, Hunt, & Joe-Laidler, 2009). The prevalence and power of the number makes disengagement in prison dangerous. However, research from Cape Town has demonstrated that first doubts about gang membership can develop there (Dziewanski, 2020b). Extracurricular programmes are one positive socialising influence that shows inmates that there is life outside of gangs. We already know that the direction of Gavin's own narrative began to alter after attending high school classes in Pollsmoor. Although he still stayed a 28 to keep safe, the prison's schooling programme offered an opportunity to think about a subject other than gangs:

> I attended classes and all these things and started joining the rehabilitation classes and I was told there is life after prison... They told me I'd be good in the corporate world. But I didn't know the meaning. I only knew the underworld. I never knew what everyone was on about because I wasn't used to that world.

The distinction created between what Gavin termed the 'underworld' and the 'corporate world' circumscribed the two social fields he was attempting to decipher. He would over time come to see his education as an opportunity to shift from one field to the next.

School offered him a chance to accumulate institutionalised cultural capital 'in the form of academic qualifications' (Bourdieu, 1986, p. 247). Gavin worked hard to get his high school accreditation. 'I initially failed all my tests, and started doubting myself. But [my teacher] told me I can still make it. He said I must spend time with my books, and I did that', said Gavin. But the classroom was not simply a venue where he learned to read and write. It was also a keyhole into the values of legitimate living, as well as somewhere to cultivate and grow new pro-social practices:

> All my free time was in my books... In my assignments and essays I was getting nice marks. I was learning to study and concentrate, and to like behave. Then I got more assistance, because I wanted to pass.

He did pass, finally, applying himself to understanding class dynamics, as much as he did to studying for his classes:

> I attended all my classes just to equip and develop myself... I kept building myself in classes to learn more about school. But also about what things are in that world where there is money, the world where there is not any gangsterism.

He is still building himself like that today – by degrees – deliberately learning about foreign social spaces and successively trying to break out of poverty. Gavin frequently speaks about penetrating 'the corporate world' or 'the city', going to 'where there is money... where there is not any gangsterism'. It is there that he believes he can access the promises of the lifestyle he wants. Gavin hopes against hope that with the right contacts and the proper cultural capital he will one day get there.

In the meantime, he makes do with what he has, tirelessly stitching together available opportunities, and looking to what is present around him to help make sense of the future. When he was a boy, Gavin's vision for himself was represented by his brother the Mongrel gangster and Benni McCarthy the football player. Today, Tupac Shakur is a special source of inspiration. The dead rap star represents a two-sided repertoire that has actually been a constant presence in Gavin's life, in one form or another. Initially, Tupac helped push Gavin into gangs. 'You wanted to live the same as the rappers... I grew up listening to Tupac. I can relate to his music because I witness these things every day and what I'm going through', he said. 'I was still a little boy back then...watching that 'Hit 'Em Up' shit. The first time I saw that music video, my older brother said: this is Tupac'. 'Hit 'Em Up' is a ferocious diss track in which Tupac calls out and threatens his enemies with a disruptive anger that is reminiscent of the violence found in street culture.

Gavin had previously believed Tupac was just a cartoon character, after watching the animated video for the song 'Do For Love'. On display here is the toxic nature of subcultural imagery leaching into a social environment even before its effects can be consciously absorbed by a young boy. At that point Gavin could not even understand Tupac's lyrics, since he spoke only Afrikaans. Yet, the music's deeper experiential significance still exerted considerable sway over him. 'I just see the big boys, they always moving Pac-style... And I'm just a little motherfucker, moving with my brother and them', he said. In this way, Tupac's mythical persona connected to real-life gang repertoires embodied by Gavin's brother and the other Mongrels. 'In our minds, our dreams were to go to prison because we knew when you come out you going to be a mirror to someone else like Tupac. Everyone is going to look to him', stated Gavin.

While the most obvious interpretation of Tupac's connection to a gang member like Gavin is of the gangster rapper broadcasting hypermasculine discontent and disorder, the attuned ear registers a more subtle message. For marginalised people living in Cape Town, Tupac represents a powerful repertoire that they turn to for strength and esteem in ways that both reinforce and resist street culture (Dziewanski, 2020d). 'Listening along to his songs, males and females alike find a shared refrain in survival and pride, echoing their personal defiance against racism, violence, and poverty in Tupac's own voice' (2020), writes Dziewanski of the rap legend's ubiquitous influence in Cape Town. Gang members connect to the defiant aggression often projected through Tupac's music. But to others, Tupac serves as a cultural resource they look to for motivation to get out of or stay out of gangs. At first, Gavin connected to Tupac as the street soldier. Later, it was Tupac the ghetto prophet who proved more salient.

As Gavin's relationship with gangs shifted, so too did his perceptions of gangster rap. 'Tupac was a super-big inspiration to me, when I was in prison... [The warders] allow me to come into my cell with a Tupac poster and a bible', stated Gavin. That he juxtaposed rap and religion is significant. These are two of the few social resources available to individuals trying to disengage from gangs. Hip-hop offers a rich narrative for constructing personal impressions of self (Perry, 2004), just like religion does. Within hip-hop debates, Tupac is frequently referred to as a 'ghetto saint' (Dyson, 2006, p. 267), whose canonisation is seemingly confirmed on an album released months after his death. Cover art depicting Tupac nailed, Christ-like to a cross fed the urban legend surrounding him – not just as a rapper but also as a messianic figure. Speculation that he did not die and was preparing for a 'second coming' (Pinn & Easterling, 2009, p. 32) adds to the radical devotion expressed by fans.

While the power of gangsterism at the end of the day receded from Gavin's worldview, rap and religion remained important means of self-orientation; for instance, he stated, 'I'm Tupac ... I'm the chosen one, bra. That nigga help me out of hell. God used him to inspire me'. Gavin even tattooed himself with 'Life Goes On'[3] as a reminder that 'life had to go on in prison' even though he was serving 10 years for murder. Then, with one eye on his hero and one eye on God, Gavin decided to leave gangs for a career in hip-hop, attempting to find hits in the stacks of notebooks he filled with lyrics while incarcerated; he wants to set an example, he said, 'like Pac [did], for another kid like me, that is coming from the gutter'. One song he wrote, entitled 'Inspired Growing', captures the profound

---

[3] A popular track from the Tupac album *All Eyez on Me*.

rupture between hardships and hopes of somebody trying to make it out of 'the gutter': 'I hustle while I pray/just hoping every day/that my life will get better/ that my aims will get bigger/to shoot for future/I have to pull the trigger'. Rap music helped Gavin imagine a different vision for what his world could be. But fantasies of better days are merely the bare-bones beginnings of action. They must be fleshed out, shaped and given body and life. If imagination can be turned to action, and if those actions are reprised recurrently, new habits may eventually become second nature. Only then will new dispositions emerge, as one's life is slowly directed towards a different course. It is exactly this process that Gavin is painstakingly trying to undertake as he attempts to once and for all leave the streets behind.

6.4 Getting into Gangs Is Easy…

Gavin's journey challenges the Capetonian adage that 'getting into gangs is easy, but getting out is impossible'; so do the other narratives chronicled in this book. The statement is obviously hyperbolic – thankfully so. Nevertheless, it draws attention to the steep and stony course that gang members must brave when departing gangs. Gavin's charisma, smarts and perseverance make him better equipped than most to surmount the impediments in front of him. Using the very same indefatigable temperament that drove him to success with the Mongrels, Gavin is now hustling to scrounge together opportunities for studio time and exposure as a rapper, while at the same time trying to find housing, funding, training and employment. He was able to secure free room and board at a local rehabilitation centre for almost three years. Later, he received funding for multiple trainings and participated in a six-month leadership programme that even took him to Uganda. He also managed to use me as a contact to get a job at a café in Cape Town. Yet, for a long time, he was still struggling on the fringes of society, unable to totally break free from the Mongrels or the 28s.

Gavin went back to Pollsmoor on a number of instances since his initial murder sentence. The first time, in 2015, after a night of drinking, he opened the door to a police cruiser to abet a friend in escaping arrest. In doing so, he violated his parole and was arrested himself. The self-destructive episode occurred after he had been cheated out of a month's commission earned through a sales position that he held briefly. Desperate and despondent, he acted out impetuously, feeling he had invested time, labour and intention into a professional endeavour that yielded zero returns. 'Maybe I am just born to be a gangster', he concluded following that escapade. It is a refrain that I have heard from him often over the years, usually repeated after some major setback – failed attempts to find work, being targeted by enemies, getting arrested by police, etc. Every such incident is just confirmation of his suspicions that there is really nothing for him besides gangsterism. Gavin knows there is at all times a home waiting for him in the

Mongrels and in number, as well as rank, reputation and a modicum of material reward. Normal life, by comparison, has been stingy and unreceptive.

In addition to Gavin's stints in prison, he was shot at numerous times and almost killed, attempts on his life that he attributes to popular perceptions that he was 'weak' for distancing himself from the streets. Gavin's past affiliation with the Mongrels is also a prevailing threat. 'I still don't walk past the enemy [territory]. I don't want to commit suicide', he stated. On trips to see family or friends around the Cape Flats, he must 'always find out who is fighting there' to determine which parts of each community are safe enough to visit. Such spatial immobility plays itself out in several ways, most apparently impeding connections to relatives and peers, but also constraining professional possibilities. During a discussion about obtaining employment, I naively suggested that he seek work in Retreat, a working-class suburb a few kilometres from Ottery. I did so without realising that much of the area is controlled by the Junky Funky Kids, a gang with long-standing animosities against the Mongrels. 'You want the Funkies to put a bullet in my head? I can only go where there's Mongrels and 28s – done. Those [other] motherfuckers won't look at me as a changed man. They only see [a] gangster', Gavin retorted, admonishing my inability to comprehend just how hampered his life still was by his former gang involvement. Here is the world telling Gavin once more that he can never be more than a gangster.

The same message is unambivalently written all over the faces of people he passes in the city and even marked all over his own body. When Gavin takes off his shirt, his inked torso and arms read like a memoir of 15 years spent in gangs, something that does not play well when navigating the cultural contours of Cape Town:

> I have to wear long sleeves for jobs; and not just for jobs, when I enter decent areas… I always protect myself. If you don't know me, it would be easier for us to communicate. But as soon as they see my tattoos they become judgmental.

Long sleeves are protection against the judgement, condescension and apprehension he often encounters. To bring this point home, Gavin described the treatment he received from waiting staff while with an international student group at a restaurant in the posh beachside neighbourhood of Camps Bay. 'I was sweating. That day was so hot. But I couldn't take off my top [because of my tattoos]', he recalled. 'These staff at the place kept looking like: why am I here? Only when the white people [from the group I was with] arrived was it a bit ok'. As a Mongrel, micro-aggressions like this would be the least of his worries. Aggression was a game he had perfected, taking on any and all challengers. Now he covers and contorts himself to fit the requirements of others.

Gavin fashions strategies to try to transcend Cape Town's exclusionary symbolic order. Playing into the public's fixation on gangs is one such strategy. In this regard, his persona as a hip-hop artist leans heavily on the types of street stories that are the conventions of gangster rap. In addition, he has largely drawn on his gang repertoire by: playing a hardcore gangbanger in a theatre production about the dangers of joining gangs, acting as a gang member in a television series, speaking to media and academics about his experiences in gangs, participating in a photography exhibition focussing on gang tattoos and giving presentations at Cape Town high schools about his involvement in street life. As a researcher you get a sense of how gang stereotypes can be traded for personal benefit when consulting with the great many interviewees who have previously sold their stories to the stream of scholars, filmmakers and journalists looking to document them. In performing gangsterism like this, Gavin is just stepping into what limited sociocultural space is afforded him. The fault lies with photographers, journalists, researchers and readers – with society at large – not with Gavin. Most still have little utility for poor Coloured men outside of their ability to confirm the classic parody of the *skollie*; Gavin uses this to his advantage, flipping it on its head, taking on the guise of a dodgy gang member in an attempt to shake off his own history of gangsterism.

Try as he might to gain entry into dominant Capetonian society, however, it is difficult to escape the fact that much of the city is still restricted to him. Signs specifying that 'right of admission is reserved' are omnipresent in Cape Town. These are an heirloom of apartheid and now serve as a barely coded instrument at policing of class and colour in mainstream shops, eateries and businesses (Fick, 2014). Caught on the outside looking in, Gavin thinks that proximity to whiteness is one sure way to open doors for himself. 'Me and you must do more to explore Cape Town in the city… We'll go clubbing in the city, at the white clubs', he encouraged me at one point, suggesting that I have the power to facilitate the right of admission where he does not. Our experiences together have only confirmed to me how real his suspicions are. A notable example comes to mind during a weekend visit to a popular bar frequently packed with North American and European travellers. I wandered into the place with no problem, while the bouncer rebuffed Gavin at the door. We had both paid admission. None of that counted though. Once I motioned to the security guard that we were together Gavin was allowed in. Discrimination of this sort is almost prosaic in the Mother City. People of colour experience racism daily, even being barred access to Cape Town's beaches (Dalton, 2018) and restaurants (Legg, 2015a). Citizens and security guards alike are vigilant of Blacks and Coloureds who appear to be from the townships, monitoring their movements for confirmation of a criminality that thrives in the anxious imaginations of the upper and middle classes.

'I walk down the street I'm a gangster… They [the other people in Cape Town] will just see a robber, stealer, drug dealer, killer. That's what they see', Gavin stated bluntly. The apartheid-era *skollie* stereotype is still oppressively present in explaining how Coloured people are perceived today. 'They see trouble. For me, it's hard to break through… But a guy can have gold teeth and baggy pants and he's just some guy trying to take care of himself'. When seen in a particular light, Gavin may in fact be 'all street'. This is on balance the impression he has of himself. 'I'm too gangster for this place... These clothes, they just looks gangster', he said, when asked why he was denied at the door at the club we went to. That retort is one part ego-talk and one part real-talk. It is true that worn-in sneakers, baggy denim and oversized flannel did not scream affluence. But Gavin could also have been an average man looking to have a drink and a dance on a Sunday afternoon. It is telling that the security guard's intuitive appraisal of him was as *persona non grata*. The exact motivation for this cannot be known. What is obvious, though, is that the embodied and objectified markers of race and class – less melanin, more money – grant access to privilege in Cape Town. Society's doors remain shut for somebody who looks like Gavin. So seeking proximity to a white foreigner is a sociocultural resource that can be leveraged to his advantage in the social field of mainstream society. Gavin is learning to sustain himself in the city, just as he had sustained himself in the streets, by taking a place near the purveyors of privilege. This is why he got into the Mongrels when he was a teen. This is also how he got into the club that day with me.

6.5 Making Street Life History

It must be noted that, in seeking admittance to mainstream spots in Cape Town, Gavin is not merely attempting to pass as a 'coconut' (Lindegaard, Miller, & Reynald, 2013, p. 982), a derogatory term used to describe an individual that is Coloured on the outside and white on the inside. That label is overly simplistic and inaccurate. He does not want pale skin or straight hair. What he wants is equal opportunity. It is unfair to expect members of a disempowered group to refrain from pursuing the social capital and cultural capital of the dominant one, implying that they are somehow acting inauthentically or pandering to power. Their overtures are based on a fundamental desire to experience life more abundantly and more freely, or at the very least to walk into a bar or shop without fear of being stopped by security staff.

Gavin has a fine appreciation for the relationships between race, culture, affluence and aspiration in Cape Town. Exchanges about a leadership course in which he participated in late 2016 and early 2017 were especially revealing in this regard:

> I try hard to understand your white culture man 'cause I was born and raised with Black and Coloured culture... Just to speak English is not enough because here [in Cape Town] there like is two different languages... I've never been surrounded by white people like this before in my life, bra. So I just learn out of them. You know, [mainstream] Cape Town is all white. That's why I just want to understand white people as an artist [and an] emcee... So that's actually the advantage in the things that I learn out of them.

Again, Gavin's focus on 'white culture' clearly has nothing to do with racial envy. It is about amassing cultural capital that can be useful to him in getting ahead in mainstream social spaces. 'I am learning to be white, bro. Who would have thought that I would be eating with a knife and fork?', he asked facetiously. This rhetorical question is a commentary on the type of manners required when dining among the well-to-do. In it are both an indication of aspiration towards mainstream culture and an acknowledgement of the street culture that had shaped Gavin's life up until then. On another occasion, as we were eating at a pub in Muizenberg, he again alluded to the use of a knife, saying, 'this used to be my best friend [in street culture]. And now? I eat with it. I use it to cut my food'. Whether using it to stab somebody or stab his steak, the changing symbolism of the blade is like cultural capital itself – a tool – its application and effectiveness changing depending on the context it is being used in. To use it the right way, in the right place, requires a cultural adroitness that Gavin is still trying to get a handle on. With further practice, he hopes that he will one day have a ready seat at a table he had thus far been excluded from.

The parts of Cape Town that Gavin aspires to have their own language, behaviour and miscellaneous traditions, as any cultural field does. His initial experiences with these unfamiliar social spaces have thus far been dislocating. 'This white life is hard to adapt to, bro. The lifestyle and stuff... I'm learning, but they're too corporate. So the ghetto must first fade away. I still don't fit in, bro', he said. Later Gavin was more specific in describing the differences between that social field and the street field:

> Their lifestyle is not like the [Cape Flats] style. It's not like the ghetto life. The way that they speak. The way they talk. They do things politely – respectfully, you know. They not aggressive. They not full of anger or talk with pain. They talk more with emotions. And I wasn't used to voices of emotions, you know. Every time when they like talk to me, I'm like: wow, this is with emotions [and] I don't understand emotions... My voice was always full of pain. I was always hard, you know. And I'm like: wow, do I make this people scared, or what do I do?

Too much time invested in becoming a gangster has yielded a 'negative value' (Bourdieu, 1986, p. 244) for the significant street capital Gavin has acquired over his life. That which signifies success on the streets is stigmatised in society. In spite of his desire to belong to the group, Gavin is still being betrayed by the hard Cape *Kaaps* he speaks, his tendency to become heated and boastful and other lingering street practices. All of these things indicate his outsiderness. Realising this, Gavin used the participants in his leadership programme as a reference point for his own behaviours, just as he had emulated his brother and the older Mongrels and 28s beforehand. 'I would just ask others... to see how best to act. And then just watch and learn to copy what I am seeing in front of me', he explained. 'So it takes some time. But now the people are more comfortable with me, and I can understand better too how to talk and act around them'.

He later went through a similar cultural baptism when starting work at a Green Point café that caters to consumers of upmarket coffee culture. Again Gavin found that the street-based dispositions he had perfected earlier in his life obstructed him when he swapped social settings:

> I can see how people move, and I can move like them. But when it comes to thinking, it's very hard to think like these guys… I always ask over and over the same questions. I'll ask one day and then the next day again… Like: what is *Jalapeño* or what is *habanero* [sauce]? I have both in my hand, but I don't know which one is which. Like if I had *tik* and *unga*, I will know this one is *tik* and this one is *unga*. But with the sauces, I have to bring you [the customer] both and just let you choose… and that's how it moves. It's like knowing what's in front of you, but not knowing what it means. So, to adapt is hard.

The comparison is so obvious that it requires no commentary. What is interesting, and needs mention, is how Gavin has evolved as an employee from the time of his initial interview. That introductory meeting was arranged with a manager whom I had befriended after a few years of using the café as a makeshift office, leveraging my own social capital to explain Gavin's situation and to vouch for the integrity of his character. The manager agreed to speak to Gavin despite his criminal record. I was not present for the meeting itself, but it appeared to be jarring for Gavin. He emerged frustrated, asking: 'why did you bring me to this fake place? This place isn't gangster like the Cape Flats, man. It's fake shit'. In denigrating the café, he was attempting to attack and disarm the obvious disconnectedness he felt from a world where cultural acumen is measured by one's refined knowledge of different condiments; it is poles apart from the realms he was used to, where being able to price, sell and market *tik* and *unga* takes precedence. Imagine if our roles were swapped, with me loitering on a street corner in Ottery hawking amphetamines and opiates. While I, no doubt, would have been deathly inept as a drug dealer, Gavin got the job and quickly thrived in it. As he became familiar with his new social space, he also came to embrace it, even finding some motivation in it. 'What drives me the most, is the environment of [the café]. Just to be there. The money is shit. [But] no matter how shit the work is. At least I'm in the environment', he said, after a few months at his post. It seems that what is real and fake is just a matter of perspective and time. Certainly, the café culture he criticised initially is just as much a social construction as is street culture. Both are defined by unique practices, skills and knowledge, which equally seem incomprehensible and irrational to interlopers. Gavin originally recoiled at the thought of working in an uppity downtown establishment, pouring macchiatos and serving up eggs Florentine to Green Point's cool crowd. Now that he has started to infiltrate the city, however, he has also begun to buy into its cultural marketplace.

He is working strategically to better his social position. Though he does not earn much as a busboy, Gavin remarked that he makes enough to support himself. With the little money that he has, he buys himself stuff that he 'can see' and 'touch': a little television, some DVDs or some clothes. It is enough to keep motivated and demonstrate some material uplift of his circumstance. The longer this routine prevailed, the more his personality started to change as well. Where Gavin was once prone to foolhardy and nasty outbursts, he has now grown more thoughtful, measured and disciplined. The Mongrels sense his change too. 'They see exactly that I'm not a threat and not a benefit [to the gang]', declared Gavin. 'I'm like just a normal person, that just moves to work; or is walking up and down with people; or just staying there by my mother [and father], with them. I'm like more in the normal way of living'. As with others whose gang-leaving experiences have been described above, the steady application of the repertoires of normal life is used to prove to former brothers he is serious about embracing his reformation. In Gavin's specific situation, he is showing that he has relinquished the street capital he used to rely on, by earning legitimately as a workingman:

> In the early stages [of disengagement], they would *Sabela* [at me], and all that. Or say that: this happened to my brother, or some other guy; then they come and they expect me to do what I had to do... to retaliate quickly to deal with it. But I would try to leave it. You knew me then, it was hard. A lot of stuff was happening – shootings, and the stabbings, and fights, and stuff. It was tough to avoid it all... But then, you know, they were like we've tried everything in the book. But this guy [Gavin] is just like still normal. He's not the same anymore. They don't even worry anymore. They don't try to come and test me anymore.

Over time, the Mongrels reluctantly accepted that Gavin's allegiance had shifted, after some time leaving him be. They carried on with their business and he with his, waking for work each morning and coming back each night to rest, trying as best he could to stay away from the gang and out of trouble.

Although the Mongrels rarely test him anymore, provocations are still plenty. For instance, a few months after starting his café job, he was robbed of his phone. It was a significant loss that amounted to the better part of a month's wages. Yet, Gavin took it in stride, hoping that avoiding conflict would pay off in the long run:

> You do get tested. For example, somebody can threaten you, or somebody can rob you. Like [when] I got robbed. For me, I thought: I can retaliate. But I was like: fuck it, I'm not going back to that life again. Because this sort of thing can trigger me back to violence... And if I now go get my homies to retaliate on this guy, then when they need me to fight I'll have to help them back. That's how the game goes, and that's how you get back into the game.

He chose to be conciliatory instead of being contentious, accepting the lost phone as the cost of gaining another few months out of the game. This type of survival strategy is typical for ex-gangsters in Cape Town; stay away from confrontation when you can, avoid making it worse when you cannot, and all the while eke out a life for yourself in the small ways afforded to you.

While it is possible to keep interpersonal conflict to a minimum, structural violence is unremitting. 'Not having money tests you. I just live in this shack still, and it's easy to sell drugs. I've done it all my life, like. Instead, now I'm struggling', Gavin confided. 'Like you ask if I'm afraid to go back to jail – I'm moving in the right direction, but anything can happen when you live like this'. Privation and precariousness go hand in hand. Until Gavin's circumstances change, recidivism remains a risk. He might give a stickup man leeway by choosing not to retaliate after a robbery, but finding enough food, adequate shelter, decent clothes, some entertainment and life's other basic elements is non-negotiable. Going without these necessities is possible only for so long, before wondering: do I not deserve more? And then getting what you think you deserve by any means necessary.

Still Gavin persists, hoping that transitioning further from gangs will create more opportunities to participate in off-street forms of living. A training course in film and media, a leadership course at a church group and a job at a café in Green Point are all sites of daily struggle to acquire and practice those tastes, thoughts and expressions that might be exchanged for some advantage later:

> I hope to learn even more, you know what I mean. In like the next five, ten, or twenty years, to take what I'm learning and actually become like a boss at work. You know, you can be in a gang, but that doesn't make you a gangster. You need, like, to do gangster [stuff] to be a gangster... In the normal life, or in the decent life, it's the same, but it's different. In the normal life, you like need to be settled, be like any other man, and get married, get children, and work – just like live that normal life... You might start as a cleaner, but now maybe you become a boss. In a way, you have to build yourself up.

Gavin is referring to a form of 'learning' that has less to do with academic credentials or professional qualifications than mapping the patterns of speech, dress and action that can be used to chart a course through what is still a strange social space. 'I'm just trying to learn that new world, like I said: different thinking and everything. So, I'm working for nothing', he stated. 'But I'm working for the future. I'm like investing. I can take whatever experience I can take, learning what's normal here'. Like everybody else chronicled in this study, Gavin is trying to master the art of normal living, by investing time in a vocation and a religion – eventually family – to slowly attain the cultural capital that can keep him off the streets. The struggle is straining though. Anybody coming out of gangs in Cape Town moves forward under the heaviest of burdens, carrying everywhere considerable stress, judgement and criminalisation, slowly stalking towards a cityscape that is distant and quite possibly out of reach. Yet, there is little else that Gavin can do. It is either turn back or go forward. By choosing to carry on, he is holding fast to a brighter tomorrow and a better version of himself.

'I don't think anymore so much like the streets, and move like the streets is moving. I move differently. Not like with the aggressive moves, or hustling [by selling drugs]. I speak differently', Gavin declared. 'Whatever I learned in work, I apply it at home. To be less aggressive, to be civil, to be reasonable, to be understanding, to know things better and to see things differently'. A few years spent outside of gangs has already shown him that an array of storylines are available. Previously, Gavin's life narrative was wholly dictated by gangs. 'You know, because if you're on the streets, you only see it one way – the gangster way', he stated. Today, Gavin has a broader outlook on life:

> Gavin: I never had a choice to live [outside of gangs]. I never had a choice to not go into crime. Now I can see the meaning of choosing between right and wrong.
>
> Dariusz: But you did have a choice.
>
> Gavin: To have a choice, it's like you have to see two opportunities. But if you don't think that this other life is possible, then there's really only one choice. If somebody shows you that you have more choices, then you're seeing for the first time... Before, I never saw it. Now I can see, if I do this, it will go like that. If I choose another way, then it'll go like that.

As an outsider to Gavin's moral universe, I am reminded of a number of valuable lessons here: life is complicated; options are imperfect; perspective is relative; and people make mistakes that hurt others and themselves. The problem with my thinking at the time of our conversation was that it implied there is a right choice and a wrong choice in any situation. When, in fact, some of the time there might just be a least bad choice, among even worse ones. Real choices require perspective and prospects. Gavin had neither. By enlisting with the Mongrels, he took a stab at material and social success – for that sense of self that all people look for, in their own ways – because he knew just gangs at that time and saw no other options.

6.6 Towards an Uncertain Future

Gavin presents a case study of an intrepid cultural character intent on finding his way around a society whose manners, motives and ambitions are foreign to him. In the *kampie*, there is a collective anticipation that he will go 'hard'; because countervailing arguments are scarce, or unachievable, street repertoires become a hermeneutic frame for seeing his world. One person adopts the repertoire of gangsterism, has success, earns street capital and provides an example for another. If such a trend continues, the currency of violence gains value, and aggressive exchanges become more common. After a while, violent behaviour is the norm. It is anticipated and expected. But if other ways are proved possible, then substitute models for socialisation can be developed. When Gavin was presented with options and was provided with some opportunities to pursue those options, differential definitions for what is normal began to emerge. Testing new possibilities, and finding some success, turned them into reality. Keeping alive, staying out of the Mongrels, avoiding prison, getting a bursary, completing some training, finding a job and buying a television and some DVDs are all corroborations of a credible future narrative that sees Gavin finally leaving street life behind for good.

Let us be careful though not to overplay his redemption story. While he is trying to push forward, social structures are pushing back, keeping him wedged awkwardly between life as he desires it to be and life as it is:

> In one day, I live in these two different worlds – the city and *kampie*. That's the most hardest part of my life, to face these different worlds in one day. It's so fucked up. I know that this [*kampie*] is my life, but [in the city] that's where I'm working and want to be. Now I'm in the middle of two worlds. I'm still coming back at the end of the day... then I have to go back to my shack, and these people all go to big buildings. It makes you think: what a fucked up world this is. I mean, just look at these two worlds... Now I'm asking myself: where do I really stand, and where do I belong?

In absolute terms, Gavin's situation is improving. Yet, in relative terms, he has very little. Spending money and basic shelter are all that is on offer to him right now. If this is what he can expect from the straight and narrow, is it not reasonable to think that Gavin might go back to the Mongrels at some point? It should be easy to understand why he might. Dark-skinned, covered in tattoos, sporting sagging jeans and a faux-gold 'Cape Flats smile'[4] he is frequently dismissed as a *skollie* anyway. We pass by young men like Gavin every day, feeling alarm and judgement, associating 'them' with the violence they might due to 'us', conveniently overlooking atrocities being committed every day against them too. The violence most people in the City Bowl and suburbs fear is fiction, while that encountered in *kampies* and townships across Cape Town is a practical reality.

All of Cape Town's active industries, lively markets, film production, creative design, superlative tourism, natural wonder, fine wine and world-class dining benefit a minority of people, who then have the audacity to ask: why do the rest not just put their heads down and work hard? What's with all this violence? Why can't these people just behave? These are questions that easily slip off the tongue while clinking Pinotage at the Test Kitchen. They are the result of one of the most

---

[4]The Cape Flats smile, or passion gap, is a dental modification in which people deliberately remove the upper front teeth for fashion and status. It is popular by gang members, but not exclusively so.

insidious effects of inequality – how it obscures the suffering of others. Most city dwellers do not stop to consider the ways they are connected to gang violence. For one, poverty on the periphery is the cheap labour supply that drives a high standard of living for those with wealth. This is the polished flipside of the so-called gang problem. What makes the city such an 'affordable' destination for foreigners like myself is the same thing that makes untold thousands of young Capetonians turn to gangs for income and empowerment. Policing in the city is also focused on fortifying the restaurants and shops of the downtown core, while conflict in township communities is merely controlled and contained (Samara, 2011). Without protection from police and courts, more kids join gangs. Others still, who are kept out of the city's beaches and restaurants because of racism, likely find gangs more welcoming. To let this continue is itself to do violence; not only by disregarding the senseless murders of boys and girls, but also by allowing structural violence to kill them slowly through alienation, exclusion and marginalisation. And if one is to condemn Gavin for seeking out street culture in such circumstances, one must also condemn the systems that sustain street culture and the role of wider society in perpetrating these systems through its wilful ignorance. Let us not compound our sins of omission by also ignoring the trials confronting the young men and women trying to rise above gangsterism. They need understanding and support. Without it, even reluctant gang members are more likely to stay in the streets and continue the killing that so many in Cape Town decry.

Gavin was once devoted to the rituals and ornaments of the Mongrels and 28s, believing they could deliver him from hellish circumstances. At best he found a kind of purgatory, boasting and blustering to gain temporary authority over his streets, his neighbours and his own life. However, he soon came to discover that gangs are a dead end and that any promise of 'owning the streets' is but a pipe dream. Gavin did not design the settlement he lives in or the houses and tenements around it; nor did he lay out the avenues and alleyways that criss-cross the Cape Flats. Gang members like Gavin merely populate the streets for a moment, before being overpowered by someone gunning for their spot and their standing; so they live for today because tomorrow you never know. Gavin has barely survived his own story, cheating death to find a life that is, in many ways, as uncertain and precarious as what he had been through earlier. Along the way he has bartered a roguish persona for social and professional benefit, doing so with the belief that society may someday acknowledge that he is more than just a gangster.

What keeps Gavin going is the belief that he can gain sufficient social and cultural capital and find the right opportunity to leave his encampment forever. While plenty of people look to the family man for inspiration, he doggedly keeps an eye fixed on professional goals. Acquiring steady employment is a stride towards a normal life. If needed, Gavin the workingman seeks support in spirituality. His efforts to find and collect new social and cultural resources have been incredibly deliberate, representing an agent-driven pursuit that is typically forgotten when talking about those struggling in street culture. Getting one person out of gangs is not the same as dismantling the system that sustains gangsterism. But Gavin and others in this study show that it is possible to resist the overwhelming durability that is usually attributed to the street field. When one person's experiences are extrapolated to a community, we can begin to form a sense of how gang violence might become less normal, assuming such personal successes can be extended into and multiplied among the collective. If policy-makers, community mobilisers, and researchers can facilitate a scaling up of the disengagment process, maybe there is a chance that gang-related violence in Cape Town will abate.

Chapter 7

Beyond the Street

Cape Town's gangs germinated amid apartheid, flourished and proliferated as a result of South Africa's lopsided transition into democracy, and are still being nourished today by the unfulfilled promises of the neo-apartheid Rainbow Nation. Their growing ferocity is evidence that the social contract between the South African state and South African society is fraying. Persistent poverty, service imbalances, racial discrimination, spatial alienation and other forms of structural oppression all tell a familiar origin story, one that has been recited many times in similarly unequal and unfair urban spaces across Africa. Gangs, bands of street kids, self-defence groups, political militias and terrorist organisations all over the continent brandish violent street culture as a weapon to fight back against marginality. Youngsters everywhere try to do what they can with what has been done to them; where opportunities are in short supply, participation in an armed group – be it a gang, clique or posse – presents itself as a palatable option for defending oneself and pursuing life's objectives.

Explanation is not justification. But we cannot overlook the ways in which gangs hold a looking glass to our societies, for better or worse, telling us something about our relationship with our fellow human beings. What we caught sight of in Cape Town is not pretty. In its downtown and suburbs, people do not expect their personal safety to be encroached upon, and they need not walk around believing that the people around them are an imminent threat. Those neighbourhoods are places of relative safety, where sidewalks are spacious and clean, where crime is generally suppressed by police or by private security, and where nobody picks fights over little things because they already have plenty. Contrast this with township settings, where life is imbued with real danger – murder stats do not lie – making residents take defensive postures and pre-emptively pursue aggressive actions. Some choose to join gangs. In Hanover Park, Manenberg, Mitchells Plain, Ottery and other Cape Flats communities, gangs are oppositional and aspirational forms of collective organisation, used to hit back at the ever-creeping risks to the lives and livelihoods of the city's most cash-strapped populations.

Gang members are able to dominate others to get ahead. Every violent incident they commit is embedded in a street repertoire that becomes a

Gang Entry and Exit in Cape Town, 147–156
Copyright © 2021 Dariusz Dziewanski
Published under exclusive licence by Emerald Publishing Limited
doi:10.1108/978-1-83909-730-020210007

simulacrum for success and power. Each time a shooting or stabbing is committed, it is more likely to be seen and imitated – by one person, and then by one more, and so on – as individualised street habits spill over into street habitus. The source of street cultural opposition might be oppression, but its self-destructive nature means that it serves no good as a force for real resistance. Internecine gang wars kill and maim innocent bystanders and wreak havoc on society and the economy in the communities they halfheartedly claim to protect. Gangsterism is not about making claims for a more just society; physical force is used to segregate among the already segregated in clashes that serve to reproduce the misery and weariness of combatants and bystanders alike.

Be that as it may, gangs are a refuge of last resort. Of the more than 100 gang members I have interviewed over the years, the vast majority would prefer neither to be subjected to violence nor to commit it, either because they genuinely came to appreciate it as wrong or because it brought trouble from foes, from authorities and from family; an ocean and a continent away, in the United States, Kennedy reaffirms my findings in his own, saying:

> It is important to recognize that, in such an environment, all involved may show a high propensity toward violence, and thus play a part in maintaining a dynamic that sustains the violence, *without necessarily actually supporting the norms that undergird such behaviour* [emphasis in original]. If faced with a situation in which one must react to a slight with violence or become victimized oneself, many will choose violence, even while not wishing to or believing that the world should be governed so. (2012, p. 459)

However, opting out of the violence can be torturous, as enemies, peers and even the community are often willing to take advantage of anybody that does.

For individuals and groups caught in cycles of gangsterism, sometimes it seems like there is no way out. However, this book showed how gang members are able to break from the streets, accumulating non-gang cultural capital by taking on repertoires that revolved around loving, working and praying. Gavin's early predilections towards troublemaking did not mean he was pre-destined to die an outlaw. Neither were Mikey, Ryan, William, Taahir, Emmanuel, Marcus, Ruan, Prince, Patrick, Jayden, Jerome, Joanna, Declan, Byron, Emerson or Ashwin; nor were the many whose stories contributed to the research but who were not referenced explicitly. Everyone who shifted away from street culture strived instead for a life that was less hectic, less bellicose, less ruthless and less risky, slowly finding succour in repertoires related to home, work, and spirituality. Disengagement from gangs happened interactionally, incrementally, determinedly and continually, in a process that was more lived than learned, as study participants replaced well-worn ganging practices with fresh pro-social pursuits. That they did so amid continuing poverty, injustice, criminalisation, stigma and threat is all the more note-worthy. Their stories are an important indicator for those men and women looking to likewise progress away from gangs. Politicians, activists, community workers and researchers would do well to take note too, so that they might be better able to assist as more and more gang members disengage from gangs in Cape Town in the years to come.

7.1 Lessons from the Streets

All across the African continent, gangs and gang-like groups are engaged in pitched battles against structural violence in their own nations. Studies on gangs in sub-Saharan Africa are few relative to North America, Latin America and Europe. The chapter in this book on African armed groups was an attempt to synthesise available literature on the subject. More comparative gang studies of this variety could help generate cross-national, cross-historical and cross-cultural research that parses out the similarities and differences of collective crime and violence on the continent. Critical comparisons, especially, can help steer present-day anti-gang strategies in Africa away from efforts to isolate and police gangs as an anti-social problem, as current orthodoxy does. South Africa's go-to gang prevention strategy relies heavily on trying to control and criminalise gangs. It was on full display in 2019–2020, when 1,300 military personnel were deployed to help police fight violence and drugs in Cape Town's 10 deadliest communities. Putting boots on the ground was an opportunity to bust some heads and crack down on pariahs, reprobates and miscreants – the so-called bad guys. But when the army packed up and left there was no discernible impact. Gangs are just as present – and just as violent – as they were before the cavalry rode in. Indeed, that was hardly the first time the South African military was called upon to wage war on crime, drugs and violence in Cape Town. It happened in 2017 and 2015 as well. There was also little effect on gang presence or levels of criminal violence then. Few lessons were learned apparently, since the same mistakes are being repeated again. One wonders how many more times the military will be called upon before this strategy can finally be scrapped for a more plausible one.

If there is something to take away from this study for future gang prevention efforts, it is that gangs cannot be beaten into submission. Violence simply begets more violence. Police violence, gang violence and structural violence each ravage townships, reigning down blows on trampled populations just trying to find some refuge and a respite from the terror. If the country's strategy to tackle gangs were only ineffective that would be bad enough. But it is also counterproductive. That 84–95% of prisoners in South Africa's jails are likely to go back there (Vandala & Bendall, 2019) indicates that corruptive forces override any restorative or deterring effects of the prison system. Then there are the grotesque conditions of South African prisons. Overcrowding (Republic of South Africa, 2017) and torture (Langa, 2014) are not uncommon. Meant to rehabilitate, they often do the opposite, perpetuating the destructive and unhealthy behaviours that led to incarceration in the first place (Langa, 2007). The dehumanising way that the South African criminal justice system has treated offenders is pivotal to the genesis and growth of the country's prison gangs (Steinberg, 2004b). Large numbers of inmates align with the 26s, 27s and 28s for security reasons, which normalises violent gang culture when ex-prisoners eventually return to the townships (Samara, 2011).

Yet there are those who continue to counter-argue that Cape Town's war on gangs is being lost because it is not being fought hard, enough, that lax laws need to be toughened and more police officers must be marshalled so that more gangsters can be rounded up and tossed into prison. Even if this were an effective way forward – it is not – arresting and jailing any meaningful proportion of the city's gang population would probably bankrupt the South African state. At the very least it would blow up its correctional services budget. Bear in mind that there are an estimated 100,000 gang members in the Western Cape, and only around 7,000 people are detained in Pollsmoor Prison at any one time. In other words, Cape Town's gangsters could fill a total of 13 more Pollsmoors by themselves – the equivalent of almost two-thirds of the total number of inmates in the entire country (Republic of South Africa, 2019). At an annual cost of about 133,000 rands per prisoner (Makou, Skosana, & Hopkins, 2018; Parliamentary Monitoring Group, 2017), this misguided carceral project would take up 90% of the funds allotted to imprisoning people nationally.[1] On top of this there would also be the additional costs of building more prisons, paying and equipping cops, constructing courts, training lawyers and judges, etc. Can South Africa afford to attempt this costly criminological experiment? For anybody not convinced that the answer is no, consider that all the immense intelligence capabilities, policing firepower and punitive infrastructure of the world's biggest economy have proved unconvincing in preventing crime in America (Pranis & Greene, 2007). What hope then does this middle-income country, with its high rates of social inequality and its huge public spending shortages, have in pursuing the same course?

There is a place for law enforcement in efforts to prevent gang violence in Cape Town. But only if better criminal justice is pursued as part of holistic prevention. Police and judges alone cannot keep communities safe because the criminal justice system does not address the social determinants of gangs – disorganisation, disempowerment, disrepair, despair, etc. An inability to adequately acknowledge this shortcoming in current anti-gang efforts is nothing short of a negligent obstinacy that insists on seeing a gang tattoo before seeing the human being behind it. It is naturally easier when there is no confusion about who is a deviant and who is not. However, the story of gangs in the city of Cape Town is one without villains and heroes in the classical sense, just secondary characters – normal people – hell-bent on rehearsing and reprising the enmity of a world created to their disadvantage. Gang members' lives cannot be discussed as good or bad, or be rendered in black and white. They are grey and opaque, laid out in hues that are not easily discernible far afield from the everyday conflicts taking place in Capetonian streets, courtrooms and prisons. Outsider perspectives on

---

[1]Actual expenditure on incarceration was 14.4 billion rands in the fiscal year 2018/2019, compared to just 1.8 billion on rehabilitation, 1 billion on reintegration and 2.2 billion on health care in prison (Republic of South Africa, 2019).

gangs tend to over-simplify street life in a manner that does not give proper account to the fluidity, contingency and contextuality of gang identity (Fraser & Atkinson, 2014). That is the best case. At worst, arm's-length analysis presents people as vectors of violence, reinforcing stereotypes about deviance and crime, providing cover for self-righteous anti-gang crusaders, even as hundreds more bodies wash by like flotsam each year.

Whatever the origins of someone's propensity to violence, how we respond to him or her on an individual, social or institutional level will be impactful. Depending on the response, that impact will be either to prop up the processes that contribute to violence or to lessen them. To check the flood of violence in Cape Town, much more must be done to overcome the city's great many social failures. Supporting anybody trying to get out of gangs is a place to start. The little evidence that exists in South Africa on disengagement programming suggests that the best initiatives target multiple areas of members' lives simultaneously by offering psychosocial, educational and economic support (Cooper & Ward, 2012b). Future projects to assist gang exit should also draw on what has been evaluated as effective in other gang-affected environments,[2] adjusting international interventions to the particularities of the local context. In terms of regulating the harmful, dispositional behaviours that underpin violent action, cognitive behavioural therapy has shown promise as a possible programming option (Park, 2017). This approach teaches concrete methods of better relating to one's environment that can soothe cantankerous and anti-social behaviours (Blattman, Jamison, & Sheridan, 2017). There are also intervention models that can address the repertoires of revenge associated with retaliatory killings by supporting mediation and conflict resolution among gangs before disputes topple over into wars (Safarloo, 2015).

Moreover, this book finds that some life raft also has to be thrown to those navigating the turbulent waters of transition, while they struggle to find solid ground in normal life through work, family and spirituality. Expediting connections to forms of social and cultural capital that are found outside of the gang can smooth the way out of gangs. To this end, counsellors, community workers, parole officers, parents and friends assisting gang members trying to leave can benefit from a better understanding of the types of networks, processes and practices associated with normal living. Projects that support the uptake of non-street repertoires might be more likely to find success where other initiatives have failed. Workplace repertoires are central to staying afloat financially. Without steady work, ex-members might drift into the murk of infrequent informal labour, while others will be pulled back into the depths of gang life. Religion and relatives are also key. Respondents depended intensely on informal modes of support throughout their role transitions, meaning that

---

[2]Research elsewhere indicates that effective disengagement interventions should be long-term, supportive of positive relationships, driven by theory, appropriately timed, socio-culturally relevant and multi-dimensional in their approach (Nation et al., 2003). There are a number of proven disengagement initiatives that can serve as examples (see: Arbreton & McClanahan, 2002; Densley & Jones, 2016; National Research Council, 2005; Spergel, 1986).

family, friends, community and church should also be able to help intervene during disengagement; studies of disengagement (Decker, Pyrooz, & Moule, 2014) and desistance (Veysey, Martinez, & Christian, 2012) in high-income countries also demonstrate the importance of support from informal mechanisms in withdrawing from gangs. Given the scarcity of programming infrastructure and funding in Cape Town's township areas, aiding community-based structures would give gang members the best chance to transition to roles that are connected to family, non-gang peers and community. Such local interventions must be adequately resourced by the state, and its partners, in a way that facilitates local successes that can be scaled up. Moreover, any retributive form of justice that cuts people off from participating in society, finding work and seeing their family is only likely to undermine objectives towards social rehabilitation and reintegration.

It will also be important to remember that fighting gangs requires that disengagement initiatives be complemented by efforts to tackle the drivers of gang formation and participation. Some gang scholars have suggested that if individual gang members could participate in more non-gang activities, the gang itself would be weakened (Spergel, 1995). However, evaluations of gang disengagement programmes generally conclude that individual gang members will be assisted in quitting, but others will replace those who left because the social and economic conditions that maintain gangs remain unaltered (Howell, 1998). This is not to say that disengagement interventions have no utility. They are life-changing for the people participating in them. Still, the objectives of disengagement programming absolutely need to be undertaken as a part of larger efforts at collectivised prevention efforts. Respondents in the study struggled with structural issues related to unemployment, powerlessness, discrimination and lack of state support during their gang exits. Without a more equitable distribution of social openings, cultural possibilities and economic opportunities, personal transitions like those reviewed above will be limited, and the presence of gangs in Cape Town will continue unabated.

Right now people's idea of 'making it' is about just making it out of the hood. What needs to happen is to make the hood history altogether through a systematic integration of Cape Town, uniting as citizens people of different races, those in different locations and those of different classes. At a minimum, actions should be taken that favour broad economic redistribution. Fair, compassionate and effective criminal justice is another necessary underpinning of any endeavour to fight gangs and violence. Desegregation is also a key area of intervention. Numerous researchers have suggested the same. For instance, Standing concluded that:

> Elevating crime as the most important criterion in motivating and evaluating government policy in high crime areas such as the Cape Flats threatens to distract from a fundamental point, namely that social policies, such as housing, transport, security, employment, access to good health care and recreational facilities, should be pursued as basic human rights, not as means to win the war against crime. (2006, pp. 290–291)

Real progress, robust development and lasting security are social character-istics that are grown endogenously. In this sense, they are not the result of a police strategy or military intervention, but of a social system that makes streets secure to walk freely no matter what neighbourhood you live in.

Most people in any community will not join gangs, while some get in and manage to get out again, others stay in forever or die before they can get out. Increasing the number that avoid or get out relative to the other groups is the name of the game. Gang prevention is a contest of probabilities. Grinding out a win means losing fewer to the streets every year, by making an eight-year-old from Ottery, Hanover Park, or Manenberg believe that society has a place for him or her as a carpenter, nurse, lawyer, doctor, banker or CEO, and then helping make those beliefs into reality. If that kid can make it, then others will see that they can make it too. They might also attempt to set their own example for somebody else. More will follow. After a while the probabilities of the game may change, tilting social life away from the streets, and towards work, family, spirituality and the assorted ancillary options for finding fulfil-ment outside of gangs. But if Capetonians insist on abandoning each other, if politicians mismanage the economy and if academics underwrite philosophies of punishment aimed at going to war with gangs, then all hope is lost. Violent struggle for survival will remain a permanent condition of the Cape Flats, and the most 'crazy' and most ruthless will continue to have their heyday.

7.2 Thinking Practically about Gangs in Cape Town

Street gangs are everywhere in Cape Town, beating at its very heart in the City Bowl and coursing through its main arteries on the Cape Flats. No longer confined to their nerve centre in Pollsmoor Prison, the bloodlines of the number have now spread into township neighbourhoods as well. Smaller cliques and crews round off the list of the more than 100 street cultural groups fighting it out for identity, influence and income around the city. Established and up-and-coming gangs alike are capitalising on shortfalls in governance, development and security that leave large portions of Cape Town's population without the prospects of employment, little in the way of social benefits and lacking adequate policing and public services. Many hard-pressed men and women are turning to street culture because it can be used to accumulate social authority and financial assets. Gangsterism is for them a way of facing down society's challenges. If one considers this, gangs cease to be the product of some warped or psychotic per-sonality, or a sociological challenge best dragged before a judge and detained. That is critical as a starting point for understanding why Gavin would choose to follow his brother into the grave by joining the Mongrels and 28s; or why Ruan cursed out a magistrate instead of taking a more lenient jail term; or how Ryan came to believe it would be *lustig* to become a 28 General; or why Joanna and Ashwin would lapse into violence after each being out of gangs for a decade already.

Theirs are just some of the 24 life histories of former gang members collected for this book. Together they tell a tale of Cape gangs that was spun locally, not one copied and pasted from western experiences. Adding more localised, more personalised and more empathetic qualitative gang research of this type can perhaps overcome the failures in imagination that still persist among policy-makers who refuse to acknowledge the humanity and dignity of society's most vilified members. If one hopes to convince a gangster that society wants him or her to reform, we cannot after all treat that individual as a degenerate that is not worthy of our time. In restating that gang members are social actors, and not just reprobates and criminals, there is also an opportunity to restore the autonomy of people battling back against malaise, passivity and resignation. Every exit chronicled above strikes a blow against the belief that 'wandering into the gang and remaining an entrenched member can be seen as an unavoidable consequence of the social and economic contradictions of life' (Standing, 2006, p. 135). The way out of gangs in Cape Town is difficult and dangerous, for sure; still, there is a way out. That this is the case reasserts agency into street cultural writings that to this point have largely presented gangs as an iron cage – solid and permanent.

This project falls within more critical sociological traditions that have adapted Bourdieusian social theory into criminology (see: Fraser, 2013; Sandberg & Pedersen, 2011; Shammas, 2018; Shammas & Sandberg, 2016). But it breaks from this tradition in its call to greater sensitivity to the dialectic relationship between agency and structure in gang research, dovetailing recent work from Cape Town that considers how street culture can be creatively applied by street virtuosos (Dziewanski, 2020a), gang girls (Dziewanski, 2020c) and hip-hop fans (Dziewanski, 2020d). Research also speaks to scholarship highlighting the 'practical dimensions' of Bourdieusian thought (see: Harker, 1984; King, 2000), which argues against structurally produced social realities by replacing determinism with dialectic. Importantly, the findings of this book support work showing how society is shaped partly as a result of agentic innovation (King, 1995) within dispositions of habitus that influence social interactions but do not determine them (King, 1999).

Giving a more prominent place to disengagement narratives in gang research braces the forces of personal transformation against the influences of social reproduction, reiterating that marginal communities are more than just 'fields of forces'; they are also 'fields of struggle' (Bourdieu & Wacquant, 1992, p. 101). This is what Bourdieu intended from the start. In taking such an intellectual turn one must accept: that social structure does not work as some monolithic and synchronous system, and that people's agency is asserted *interactively,* not *reactively.* When visualising the world like this there is no longer the individual and the society, or the subject and the object, there are only individuals struggling against other individuals. Street habitus, in specific, is simply the sustained interaction of gang members struggling against what affiliates, enemies, police and politicians do to meet their personal and collective interests over time. Thus, agency is untethered from its structural constraints, to provide greater scope for street cultural actors – for all social actors really – to oppose the social conditions that oppress them, even in settings marked by persistent dangers and disparities. The struggle in the streets is real, and the competition over cultural, symbolic and economic capital is fierce – cruel even. But gang members are neither aggressive automatons, nor mere objects of perpetration and victimisation. They are the subjects of their own stories.

Shifting the locus of control in social practice towards personal autonomy might even be world-building. Since the individual is society's most basic unit, reimagining a city of 4 million starts with changing just one life; as Bourdieu stated:

> Actions of subversion... have the functions and in any case the effect of showing in practice that it is possible to transgress the limits imposed, in particular the most inflexible ones, which are set in people's minds... The symbolic transgression of a social frontier has a liberatory effect in its own right because it enacts the unthinkable. (2000, p. 236)

Acts that subvert society's expectations, norms and institutions probe the conditions under which structures of race, space and economy can be destabilised, so that they might ultimately be challenged and changed. Especially those gang members like Gavin who attempt to leave gang life behind and go beyond the boundaries of the divided city, are not simply reimagining their own lives, but also the reimagining of Cape Town as a more equitable and more inclusive society. Gavin's incursions into mainstream Capetonian society, however small they may seem, scratch at the surface of the city as he would want it to be, according to an alternate vision of what and who is allowed to be normal.

This is certainly not to put the onus on any one individual for pushing down immense structural obstacles that have been built up over generations. It is still up to policy-makers, community workers, police, researchers and everybody else working for social justice to adequately support people and communities working towards better life options, so as to shape the emergence of social spaces that are more prosperous and secure. To date, we have not been able to achieve this laudable goal. Despite the not-insignificant knowledge available about the individual, community and social risk factors driving gang membership and violent offending, we are somehow still yet to design an effective solution to gangs. Part of the fault for this is no doubt due to the insufficiency of our efforts in this regard. Disengagement efforts around the world generally get little funding and occur at a scale that is tiny relative to the magnitude of issues they are attempting to address. But a large part of the blame also goes to the way that 'the problem of gangs' is approached – thinking of gangs as a blight on communities, rather than as admitting that they are communities themselves.

Debates around the conceptual problematisation of gangs are not merely academic. There is a relationship between the character of theoretical understanding and the forms of policy and programming it subsequently sponsors. If we can better learn from how street cultures come about, then the poisonous power of violence can serve as a type of antivenin. Helping someone from the streets, and into society, is the first stage of stripping down the culture of criminal violence entombed in street habitus. Each victorious transition into normal life is a validated attestation of possibilities for anybody else to also start a family, get a job and be accepted by a spiritual community; or they might demonstrate that there are other possibilities out there. Ashwin became a community activist, Ruan is working with prisoners, Gavin got a job in the city, Ryan gave up the number for a Bible and Declan proved that peace was possible despite festering animus. Their successful disengagements are individual brush strokes that help make up the 'big picture' of how township life in Cape Town is composed, criss-crossing, layering and bleeding into millions of other lives, which taken together are forever framing – and reframing – how social life there is conceived. If supported with sufficient resources and at a sufficient scope and scale, Cape Flats communities can become more secure. At some point, visions of normal life will become more dominant than those offered by crime bosses. But people living in gang-affected communities cannot continue to struggle alone. Unless the contours of the fragmented city can be redrawn to more meaningfully include marginalised spaces in contemporary depictions of what Cape Town is, all the efforts at disengagement will come to naught.

Coming up to 30 years after apartheid, most Capetonians are not much better off than they were in 1994; from the optimism of newborn liberty came the following oath:

> Let there be justice for all. Let there be peace for all. Let there be work, bread, water, and salt for all. Let each know that for each the body, the mind and the soul have been freed to fulfil themselves. (Mandela, 1994)

The public mood is decidedly more uneasy today than when Nelson Mandela was inaugurated as the country's first Black president. People are frustrated. Grand promises and pretty oratory are no longer satisfactory. Cape Town is still a poor-rich, black-white city suspended between neo-liberalism and neo-apartheid, offering leisure and free enterprise to the few, and discrimination, deprivation, segregation and anguish to the rest. Full citizenship for all requires total partnership in the fortunes and future of their society. So the prospects for Africa's deadliest urban centre can only be as bleak or as bright as the prospective lives of those struggling to get by in its poorest neighbourhoods – not as discounted South Africans, but as complete citizens and equals. Either all Capetonians commit themselves to the construction of a cohesive, just and sustainable society, or life in the picturesque city by the sea will remain to be as rocky and rough as the sheer cliffs it is pushed up against.

References

Adhikari, M. (1992). The sons of Ham: Slavery and the making of coloured identity. *South African Historical Journal, 27*(1), 95–112.

Adhikari, M. (2005). Contending approaches to coloured identity and the history of the coloured people of South Africa. *History Compass, 3*(1).

Adisa, J. (1994). Adisa, Jinmi. In E. E. Osaghae, I. Touré, N. 'G. Kouamé, & I. O. Albert (Eds.), *Urban violence in Africa: Pilot studies (South Africa, Côte-d'Ivoire, Nigeria)* (pp. 139–175). Ibadan: Institut Français de Recherche en Afrique.

Ajibade, B. (2006). Anti-bullet charms, lie-detectors and street justice: The Nigerian youth and the ambiguities of self-remaking. In *Paper presented at the International Conference. Youth and the Global South: Dakar, Senegal, 13 –15* October.

Akers, R. (1998). *Social learning and social structure: A general theory of crime and deviance.* New Brunswick, NJ and London: Routledge.

Akinwale, A. A., & Aderinto, A. A. (2011). Crisis of governance and urban violence in Nigeria. *African Journal of Criminology and Justice Studies, 5*(1/2), 49–77.

Aliyu, A., & Amadu, L. (2017). Urbanization, cities, and health: The challenges to Nigeria – a review. *Annals of African Medicine, 16*(4), 149–158. doi:10.4103/aam. aam_1_17

Anderson, E. (1998). The social ecology of youth violence. *Crime and Justice, 24,* 65–104.

Anderson, E. (2000). *Code of the street: Decency, violence, and the moral life of the inner city.* New York, NY: W. W. Norton & Company.

Aptekar, L., & Stoecklin, D. (2013). *Street children and homeless youth: A cross-cultural perspective.* Dordrecht: Springer Science & Business Media.

Arbreton, A., & McClanahan, W. (2002). *Targeted outreach: Boys and Girls clubs of America approach to gang prevention and intervention.* Philadelphia, PA: Public/ Private Ventures.

Ball, R., & Curry, G. D. (1995). The logic of definition in criminology: Purposes and methods for defining gangs. *Criminology, 33*(2), 225–245.

Barker, J. D. (2013). Negative cultural capital and homeless young people. *Journal of Youth Studies, 16*(3), 358–374.

Barnes, B. (2000). *Understanding agency: Social theory and responsible action.* London, Thousand Oaks, CA, and New Delhi: SAGE.

Berger, R., Abu-Raiya, H., Heineberg, Y., & Zimbardo, P. (2017). The process of desistance among core ex-gang members. *American Journal of Orthopsychiatry, 87*(4), 487–502. doi:10.1037/ort0000196

Bjerk, D. (2008). *How much can we trust causal interpretations of fixed-effects estimators in the context of criminality?.* SSRN Scholarly Paper ID 1144201. Rochester, NY: Social Science Research Network. Retrieved from https://papers.ssrn.com/abstract= 1144201

Bjorgo, T. (2008). Processes of disengagement from violent groups of the extreme right. In T. Bjorgo & J. Horgan (Eds.), *Leaving terrorism behind: Individual and collective disengagement* (pp. 30–48). Oxon: Routledge.

Blair, D. (2006). Children of the streets feel wrath of Mugabe. *The Telegraph*, May 15. Retrieved from https://www.telegraph.co.uk/news/worldnews/africaandindianocean/zimbabwe/1518542/Children-of-the-streets-feel-wrath-of-Mugabe.html

Blattman, C., Jamison, J., & Sheridan, M. (2017). Reducing crime and violence: Experimental evidence from cognitive behavioral therapy in Liberia. *American Economic Review, 107*(4), 1165–1206.

Bolden, C. (2013). Tales from the hood: An emic perspective on gang joining and gang desistance. *Criminal Justice Review, 38*(4), 473–490.

Bottero, W. (2009). Relationality and social interaction. *British Journal of Sociology, 60*(2), 399–420.

Bourdieu, P. (1977). *Outline of a theory of practice*. Cambridge: Cambridge University Press.

Bourdieu, P. (1985). The social space and the genesis of groups. *Theory and Society, 14*(6), 723–744.

Bourdieu, P. (1986). The forms of capital. In J. Richardson (Ed.), *Handbook of theory and research for the sociology of education* (pp. 241–258). New York, NY: Greenwood Press.

Bourdieu, P. (1988). Vive la crise!: For heterodoxy in social science. *Theory and Society, 17*(5), 773–787.

Bourdieu, P. (1989). Social space and symbolic power. *Sociological Theory, 7*(1), 14–25.

Bourdieu, P. (1990). *The logic of practice*. Standford, CA: Stanford University Press.

Bourdieu, P. (1993). *The field of cultural production: Essays on art and literature*. New York, NY: Columbia University Press.

Bourdieu, P. (2000). *Pascalian meditations*. Standford, CA: Stanford University Press.

Bourdieu, P. (2005). The political field, the social science field, and the journalistic field. In R. Benson & E. Neveu (Eds.), *Bourdieu and the journalistic field* (pp. 29–47). Cambridge: Polity Press.

Bourdieu, P., & Wacquant, L. (1992). *An invitation to reflexive sociology*. Chicago, IL: University of Chicago Press.

Bourdillon, M. (1991). *Poor, harassed but very much alive: An account of street people and their organisation*. Harare: Mambo Press.

Bourdillon, M. (1994). Street children in Harare. Africa: Journal of the International African Institute, *64*(4), 516–532. doi:10.2307/1161371

Bourdillon, M. (2016). Thinking about street children and orphans in Africa: Beyond survival. In A. Invernizzi, M. Liebel, B. Milne, & R. Budde (Eds.), *'Children out of place' and human rights: In memory of Judith Ennew* (pp. 51–62). Berlin: Springer.

Bourgois, P. (1996). In search of masculinity: Violence, respect and sexuality among Puerto Rican crack dealers in East Harlem. *British Journal of Criminology, 36*(3), 412–427. doi:10.1093/oxfordjournals.bjc.a014103

Bourgois, P. (2002). *In search of respect: Selling crack in El Barrio*. New York, NY: Cambridge University Press.

Bourgois, P. (2011a). The continuum of violence in war and peace: Post-cold war lessons from El Salvador. In N. Scheper-Hughes & P. Bourgois (Eds.),

Violence in war and peace: An anthology (pp. 425–434). Madlen, MA: Blackwell Publishing.

Bourgois, P. (2011b). US inner-city apartheid: The contours of structural and interpersonal violence. In N. Scheper-Hughes & P. Bourgois (Eds.), *Violence in war and peace: An anthology* (pp. 301–307). Madlen, MA: Blackwell Publishing.

Bowers Du Toit, N. (2014). Gangsterism on the cape flats: A challenge to 'engage the powers'. *HTS Teologiese Studies/Theological Studies, 70*(3), 7.

Branson, L., Clare, H., Joy, P., & Needham, S. (2015). Post-school education: Broadening alternative pathways from school to work. In A. De Lannoy, S. Swartz, L. Lake, & C. Smith (Eds.), *South African child gauge 2015* (pp. 42–50). Cape Town: UCT and Children's Institute.

Bray, R., Gooskens, I., Kahn, L., Moses, S., & Seekings, J. (2010). *Growing up in the New South Africa: Childhood and adolescence in post-apartheid Cape Town.* Cape Town: HRSC Press.

Brenneman, R. (2011). *Homies and Hermanos: God and Gangs in Central America.* New York, NY: Oxford University Press.

Brotherton, D., & Barrios, L. (2011). *Banished to the homeland: Dominican deportees and their stories of exile* New York, NY: Columbia University Press.

Brotherton, D. (2015). *Youth street gangs: A critical appraisal.* London, New York: Routledge.

Burawoy, M., & Von Holdt, K. (2012). *Conversations with Bourdieu: The Johannesburg moment.* Johannesburg: Wits University Press.

Bushway, S., Piquero, A., Broidy, L., Cauffman, E., & Paul, M. (2001). An empirical framework for studying desistance as a process. *Criminology, 39*(2), 491–516.

Campany, R. F. (2012). Religious repertoires and contestation: A case study based on Buddhist miracle tales. *History of Religions, 52*(2), 99–141.

Campbell, H., & Hansen, T. (2012). Getting out of the game: Desistance from drug trafficking. *The International Journal on Drug Policy, 23*(6), 481–487. doi:10.1016/j.drugpo.2012.04.002

Cape Times. (2019, September 18). Total shutdown protest to affect major arterial roads in Cape Town on September 25. Retrieved from https://www.iol.co.za/capetimes/news/total-shutdown-protest-to-affect-major-arterial-roads-in-cape-town-on-september-25-33184263

Carson, D., & Esbensen, F.-A. (2016). Motivations for leaving gangs in the USA: A qualitative comparison of leaving processes across gang definitions. In C. Maxson & F.-A. Esbensen (Eds.), *Gang transitions and transformations in an international context* (pp. 139–155). New York, NY: Springer.

Casey, C. (2012). Hypocrite, spatial (in)justice and youthful 'policing' in northern Nigeria. In B. Bret, P. Gervais-Lambony, C. Hancock, & F. Landy (Eds.), *Justice et injustices spatiales. Sciences Humaines et Sociales* (pp. 201–218). Nanterre: Presses universitaires de Paris Nanterre. Retrieved from http://books.openedition.org/pupo/436

Casey, C. (2013). Mediating justice: Youths, media, and 'affective justice' in the politics of Northern Nigeria. In W. Adebanwi & E. Obadare (Eds.), *Democracy and prebendalism in Nigeria: Critical interpretations* (pp. 201–225). New York, NY: Palgrave Macmillan.

Cassidy, L. (2012). Salford 7/district six. The use of participatory mapping and material artefacts in cultural memory projects. In L. Roberts (Ed.),

Mapping cultures: Place, practice, performance (pp. 181–200). Hampshire: Palgrave Macmillan.

CCSPJP. (2020). Boletín ranking 2019 de Las 50 Ciudades más violentas Del mundo. *Seguridad, Justicia y Paz* (Blog), June 1. Retrieved from http://www. seguridadjusticiaypaz.org.mx/sala-de-prensa/1590-boletin-ranking-2019-de-las-50-ciudades-mas-violentas-del-mundo

Chouliaraki, L., & Fairclough, N. (1999). Language and power in Bourdieu: On Hasan's 'the disempowerment game. *Linguistics and Education, 10*(4), 399–409.

Christie, S. (2016). *Under Nelson Mandela Boulevard: Life among the stowaways.* Johannesburg and Cape Town: Jonathan Ball Publishers.

City of Cape Town. (2018). *State of Cape Town 2018.* Cape Town: City of Cape Town.

Civilian Secretariat for Police. (2016). *2016 white paper on safety and security.* Pretoria: Government Publisher.

Colley, H., James, D., Diment, K., & Tedder, M. (2003). Learning as becoming in vocational education and training: Class, gender and the role of vocational habitus. *Journal of Vocational Education and Training, 55*(4), 471–498.

Collyer, F., Willis, K., Franklin, M., Harley, K., & Short, S. (2015). Healthcare choice: Bourdieu's capital, habitus and field. *Current Sociology, 63*(5), 685–699. doi:10.1177/0011392115590082

Cooper, A. (2009). Gevaarlike transitions': Negotiating hegemonic masculinity and rites of passage amongst coloured boys awaiting trial on the cape flats. *Psychology in Society,* 37, 1–17.

Cooper, A., & Ward, C. (2012a). Gangs and child safety. In A. Van Niekerk, S. Suffla, & S. Mohamed (Eds.), *Crime, violence and injury in South Africa: 21st century solutions for child safety* (pp. 148–161). Cape Town: MRC.

Cooper, A., & Ward, C. (2012b). Intervening with youths in gangs. In C. Ward, A. Dawes, & A. van der Merwe (Eds.), *Youth violence: Sources and solutions in South Africa* (pp. 241–274). Cape Town: UCT Press.

Courson, E. (2009). Movement for the emancipation of the Niger delta (MEND): Political marginalization, repression and petro-insurgency in the Niger delta. Discussion Paper 47, The Nordic Africa Institute, Uppsala.

Crankshaw, O. (2012). Deindustrialization, professionalization and racial inequality in Cape Town. *Urban Affairs Review, 48*(6), 836–862.

Cunnen, C. (2012). Postcolonial perspectives for criminology. In M. Bosworth & C. Hoyle (Eds.), *What is criminology?* (pp. 249–262). New York, NY: OUP Oxford.

Currid-Halkett, E. (2017). *The sum of small things: A theory of the aspirational class.* Princeton, NJ: Princeton University Press.

Curry, G. D. (2011). Gangs, crime, and terrorism. In B. Forst, J. R. Greene, & J. P. Lynch (Eds.), *Criminologists on terrorism and homeland security* (pp. 97–112). New York, NY: Cambridge University Press.

Dalton, J. (2018). Angry clashes at South Africa beach after security guards 'told black people to leave'. *The Independent* (Blog), December 30. Retrieved from https://www.independent.co.uk/news/world/africa/racism-protest-rape-clifton-4th-beach-cape-town-south-africa-security-guards-sheep-slaughter-a8704036.html

Daniels, D., & Adams, Q. (2010). Breaking with township gangsterism: The struggle for place and voice. *African Studies Quarterly, 11*(4), 45–57.

de Benitez, S. T. (2007). *State of the world's street children.* London: CSC.

De Boeck, F. (2011, May). Inhabiting ocular ground: Kinshasa's future in the light of Congo's spectral urban politics. Retrieved from http://evols.library.manoa.hawaii.edu/handle/10524/31843

De Boeck, F. (2012). City on the move: How urban dwellers in central Africa manage the Siren's call for migration. In K. Graw & J. S. Schielke (Eds.), *The global horizon: Expectations of migration in Africa and the Middle East* (pp. 59–86). Leuven: Leuven University Press.

De Boeck, F. (2018). Children, youth and generational change in the democratic republic of Congo. Presented at the Expert Group Meeting on The Role of Families and Family Policy in Supprting Youth Transition, Doha, Qatar, 11–12 December.

De Boeck, F., & Baloji, S. (2016). *Suturing the city: Living together in Congo's urban worlds.* London: Autograph ABP.

Decker, S. (2012). The impact of organizational features on gang activities and relationships. In M. Klein, H.-J. Kerner, C. Maxson, & E. Weitekamp (Eds.), *The Eurogang paradox: Street gangs and youth groups in the U.S. and Europe* (pp. 21–39). Berlin: Springer Science & Business Media.

Decker, S., & Lauritsen, J. (2002). Leaving the gang. In R. Huff (Ed.), *Gangs in America III* (pp. 51–67). Thousand Oaks, CA: SAGE.

Decker, S., & Pyrooz, D. (2015). Street gangs, terrorists, drug smugglers, and organized crime: What's the difference?. In S. Decker & D. Pyrooz (Eds.), *The handbook of gangs* (pp. 294–308). Hoboken, NJ: John Wiley & Sons.

Decker, S., Pyrooz, D., & Moule, R. (2014). Disengagement from gangs as role transitions. *Journal of Research on Adolescence, 24*(2), 268–283.

Densley, J., & Jones, D. S. (2016). Pulling levers on gang violence in London and St. Paul. In C. Maxson & F.-A. Esbensen (Eds.), *Gang transitions and transformations in an international context* (pp. 291–305). Cham: Springer International Publishing. doi:10.1007/978-3-319-29602-9_16

Deuchar, R. (2018). *Gangs and spirituality: Global perspectives.* Cham: Springer.

Dixon, B., & Johns, L.-M. (2001). Gangs, Pagad and the state: Vigilantism and revenge violence in the Western Cape. *Violence and transition series*, Vol. 2. Johannesburg: CSVR.

Dolley, C. (2019). *The enforcers: Inside Cape Town's deadly nightclub battles.* Johannesburg: Jonathan Ball.

Dube, L. (1997). Street children versus 'officialdom': The search for a solution to the phenomenon of street children in Harare, Zimbabwe. *Journal of Psychology in Africa, 1,* 31–46.

Durrheim, K. (2005). Socio-spatial practice and racial representations in a changing South Africa. *South African Journal of Psychology, 35*(3), 444–459.

Dyson, M. E. (2006). *Holler if you hear me.* New York, NY: Basic Books.

Dziewanski, D. (2019). In a cape town crackdown on guns and gangs, South Africans fear becoming collateral damage. *Globe and Mail*, October 10. Retrieved from https://www.theglobeandmail.com/world/article-in-a-cape-town-crackdown-on-guns-and-gangs-south-africans-fear/

Dziewanski, D. (2020a). Commanding the 'art of killing': How virtuosic performances of street culture disrupt gang rules. *British Journal of Criminology, 60*(5), 1368–1386. doi:10.1093/bjc/azaa028

Dziewanski, D. (2020b). Leaving gangs in cape town: Disengagement as role exit. *Journal of Contemporary Ethnography, 49*, 507–535.

Dziewanski, D. (2020c, April). Femme fatales: Girl gangsters and violent street culture in Cape Town. *Feminist Criminology*. Retrieved from https://journals.sagepub.com/eprint/VVZDT5RFEFUEKCTRIN5A/full

Dziewanski, D. (2020d, May). From East Harlem to Cape Town: Tupac Shakur's legacy as a globalised oppositional repertoire. *Ethnography*. doi:10.1177/1466138120923372

Ebaugh, H. R. F. (2013). *Becoming an ex: The process of role exit*. Chicago, IL and London: University of Chicago Press.

Elfversson, E., & Höglund, K. (2019). Violence in the city that belongs to no one: Urban distinctiveness and interconnected insecurities in Nairobi (Kenya). *Conflict, Security and Development, 19*(4), 347–370.

Evens, T. M. S. (1999). Bourdieu and the logic of practice: Is all giving Indian-giving or is 'generalized materialism' not enough?. *Sociological Theory, 17*(1), 3–31.

Eyewitness News. (2020, March 27). Cele: Lockdown of SA a success. Retrieved from https://ewn.co.za/2020/03/27/cele-lockdown-of-sa-a-success

Fagan, J. (1989). Social organization of drug use and drug dealing among urban gangs. *Criminology, 27*(4), 633–670.

Farmer, P., Bruce, N., Stulac, S., & Keshavjee, S. (2006). Structural violence and clinical medicine. *PLoS Medicine, 3*(10), e449.

Farrington, K. (2014). *Maximum security*. London: Arcturus Publishing.

Feavel, K., & Pyrooz, D. (2014). Desistance from gangs. In G. Bruinsma & D. Weisburd (Eds.), *Encyclopedia of criminology and criminal justice* (pp. 978–988). New York, NY: Springer New York. doi:10.1007/978-1-4614-5690-2_126

Fick, A. (2014). Right of admission reserved. *ENCA*, October 6. Retrieved from http://www.enca.com/opinion/right-admission-reserved

Flores, E. O. (2014). *God's gangs: Barrio ministry, masculinity, and gang recovery*. New York, NY: NYU Press.

Flores, E. O., & Hondagneu-Sotelo, P. (2013). The public talk of negotiating Chicano masculinities: The public talk of negotiating Chicano masculinities. *Social Problems, 60*(4), 476–490. doi:10.1525/sp.2013.60.4.476

Fourchard, L. (2006). Lagos and the invention of Juvenile delinquency in Nigeria, 1920-60. *The Journal of African History, 47*(1), 115–137.

Fourchard, L. (2010). The making of the Juvenile delinquent in Nigeria and South Africa, 1930–1970. *History Compass, 8*(2), 129–142. doi:10.1111/j.1478-0542.2009.00669.x

Fourchard, L. (2011). *Partisan politics, vigilantism and security in South Africa*. Retrieved from https://www.politics.ox.ac.uk/materials/centres/oxpo/working-papers/wp_10-11/OXPO_10-11e_Fourchard.pdf

Fraser, A. (2015). *Urban legends: Gang identity in the post-industrial city*. Oxford: Oxford University Press.

Fraser, A. (2017). *Gangs & Crime: Critical alternatives*. London: SAGE.

Fraser, A. (2013). Street habitus: Gangs, territorialism and social change in Glasgow. *Journal of Youth Studies, 16*(8), 970–985.

Fraser, A., & Atkinson, C. (2014). Making up gangs: Looping, labelling and the new politics of intelligence-led policing. *Youth Justice, 14*(2), 154–170.

Garbarino, J. (2000). *Lost boys: Why our sons turn violent and how we can save them.* New York, NY: Anchor Books.

Garot, R. (2010). *Who you claim: Performing gang identity in school and on the streets.* New York, NY: NYU Press.

Gartman, D. (1991). Culture as class symbolization or mass reification? A critique of Bourdieu's distinction. *American Journal of Sociology, 97*(2), 421–447.

Gastrow, P. (1998). *Organised crime in South Africa: An assessment of its nature and origins.* Monograph 28. Pretoria: ISS.

Gastrow, P., Mosse, M., & Bagenda, P. (2003). *Penetrating state and business organised crime in southern Africa.* Pretoria: ISS.

Gaulier, A., & Martin, D.-C. (2017). *Cape Town harmonies: Memory, humour and resilience.* Cape Town: African Minds.

Geenen, K. (2009). 'Sleep occupies NO space': The use of public space by street gangs in Kinshasa. *Africa, 79*(3), 347–368. doi:10.3366/E0001972009000850

Geneva Declaration Secretariat. (2008). *Global Burden of armed violence 2008* Cambridge: Cambridge University Press.

Giordano, P., Stephen, C., & Rudolph, J. (2002). Gender, crime, and desistance: Toward a theory of cognitive transformation. *American Journal of Sociology, 107*(4), 990–1064.

Giroux, H. A. (2001). *Theory and resistance in education: Towards a pedagogy for the opposition.* Westport, CT: Greenwood Publishing Group.

Glaser, D. (1964). *The effectiveness of a prison and parole system.* Indianapolis, IN: Bobbs-Merrill Company.

Glaser, C. (2000). *Bo-Tsotsi: The youth gangs of Soweto, 1935–1976.* Johannesburg: James Currey.

Global Initiative Against Transnational Organized Crime. (2020a). Civil society observatory of illicit economies in Eastern and Southern Africa. *Risk Bulletin Issue, 11*(August–September), 1–29.

Global Initiative Against Transnational Organized Crime. (2020b). Hard livings: Who killed Rashied Staggie? Assassination theories abound as uneasy peace follows gang boss's murder. *Daily Maverick* (Blog), April 5. Retrieved from https://www.dailymaverick.co.za/article/2020-04-05-who-killed-rashied-staggie-assassination-theories-abound-as-uneasy-peace-follows-gang-bosss-murder/

Godfrey, B., & Richardson, J. (2004). Loss, collective memory and transcripted oral histories. *International Journal of Social Research Methodology, 7*(2), 143–155.

Goga, K. (2014a). Taking stock of the last 20 years: Responses to organised crime in a democratic South Africa. *South African Crime Quarterly, 48*, 63–73.

Goga, K. (2014b). *The drug trade and governance in Cape Town.* ISS Paper 263. Pretoria: ISS. Retrieved from https://issafrica.s3.amazonaws.com/site/uploads/Paper263.pdf

Gomment, T. I., & Esomchi, O. S. (2017). Nigeria: Breeding future terrorists. A study of Almajiri of Northern Nigeria and Islamist Militia. *Conflict Studies Quarterly,* (18) (January), 80–92.

Gordon, R., Lahey, B., Kawai, E., Loeber, R., Stouthamer-Loeber, M., & Farrington, D. P. (2004). Antisocial behavior and youth gang membership: Selection and socialization. *Criminology, 42*(1), 55–88.

Goredema, C. (2014). *Mapping crime networks in Southern Africa: A new approach.* Policy Brief 58. Pretoria: ISS.

Gore, C., & Pratten, D. (2003). The politics of plunder: The rhetorics of order and disorder in Southern Nigeria. *African Affairs, 102*(407), 211–240.

Gould, C. (2014). *Why is crime and violence so high in South Africa?*. Africa Check, September 17, 2014. Retrieved from http://africacheck.org/2014/09/17/comment-why-is-crime-and-violence-so-high-in-south-africa-2/

Gustafsson, M. (2011). *The when and how of leaving school: The policy implications of new evidence on secondary schooling in South Africa.* Stellenbosch Working Paper Series 09/2011.

Hacking, I. (2004). Between Michel Foucault and Erving Goffman: Between discourse in the abstract and face-to-face interaction. *Economy and Society, 33*(3), 277–302.

Haferburg, C. (2003). *Ambiguous restructurings of post-apartheid Cape Town: The spatial form of socio-political change.* Münster: LIT Verlag Münster.

Hagedorn, J. (1994). Homeboys, dope fiends, legits, and new jacks. *Criminology, 32*(2), 197–219. doi:10.1111/j.1745-9125.1994.tb01152.x

Hagedorn, J. (2008). *A world of gangs: Armed young men and gangsta culture.* Minneapolis, MN: University of Minnesota Press.

Hagedorn, J., & Macon, P., (1988). *People and folks: Gangs, crime, and the underclass in a rustbelt city.* Chicago, IL: Lake View Press.

Hannerz, U. (1969). *Soulside: Inquiries into ghetto culture and community.* Chicago, IL: University of Chicago Press. Retrieved from http://www.press.uchicago.edu/ucp/books/book/chicago/S/bo3644525.html

Harding, D. (2007). Cultural context, sexual behavior, and romantic relationships in disadvantaged neighborhoods. *American Sociological Review, 72*(3), 341–364.

Harding, D. (2010). *Living the drama: Community, conflict, and culture among inner-city boys.* Chicago, IL: University of Chicago Press.

Harding, S. (2014). *The street casino: Survival in violent street gangs.* Bristol: Policy Press.

Harding, S., & Palasinski, M. (2016). Preface. In S. Harding & M. Palasinski (Eds.), *Global perspectives on youth gang behavior, violence, and weapons use* (pp. xvii–xxv). Hershey, PA: IGI Global.

Harker, R. (1984). On reproduction, habitus and education. *British Journal of Sociology of Education, 5*(2), 117–127.

Harnischfeger, J. (2003). The Bakassi boys: Fighting crime in Nigeria. *The Journal of Modern African Studies, 41*(1), 23–49. doi:10.1017/S0022278X02004135

Haysom, S. (2019). *Hiding in plain sight: Heroin's stealthy takeover of South Africa.* Policy Brief 07. Pretoria: ENACT.

Haysom, S. (2020). From the maskani to the mayor: The political economy of heroin markets in East and Southern Africa. Research Paper. Pretoria: ENACT.

Haysom, S., Gastrow, P., & Shaw, M. (2018). The heroin coast: A political economy along the eastern African seaboard. Research Paper. Pretoria: ENACT.

Hazen, J., & Rodgers, D. (2014). Introduction: Gangs in a global comparative perspective. In J. Hazen & D. Rodgers (Eds.), *Global gangs: Street violence across the world* (pp. 1–28). Minneapolis, MN: University of Minnesota Press.

Heap, S. (2009). Their days are spent in gambling and loafing, pimping for prostitutes, and picking pockets: Male juvenile delinquents on Lagos Island, 1920s–1960s. *Journal of Family History, 35*, 48–70, October. Doi:10.1177/0363199009348306.

Hendriks, M., Ponsaers, P., & Shomba Kinyamba, S. (2013). Street children in Kinshasa: Striking a balance between perpetrator and victim through agency. *Etnografia e Ricerca Qualitativa, 1,* 82–96.

Higginson, A., & Benier, K. (2015). Gangs in African, Asian, and Australian settings. In S. Decker & D. Pyrooz (Eds.), *The handbook of gangs* (pp. 538–557). Hoboken, NJ: John Wiley & Sons.

Horgan, J. (2009). *Walking away from terrorism: Accounts of disengagement from radical and extremist movements.* New York, NY: Routledge.

Howell, J. (1998). Promising programs for youth gang violence prevention and intervention. In R. Loeber & D. Farrington (Eds.), *Serious and violent juvenile offenders: Risk factors and successful interventions* (pp. 284–312). Thousand Oaks, CA: SAGE Publications, Inc.

Hübschle, A. (2010). *Organised crime in Southern Africa: First annual review.* Pretoria: ISS. Retrieved from https://issafrica.org/research/books-and-other-publications/organised-crime-in-southern-africa-first-annual-review

Human Rights Watch. (2014). *Operation Likofi police killings and enforced disappearances in Kinshasa, Democratic Republic of Congo.* New York, NY: Human Rights Watch.

Hunt, G., Moloney, M., Joe-Laidler, K., & McKenzie, K. (2011). Young mother (in the) hood: Gang girls' negotiation of new identities. *Journal of Youth Studies, 14*(1), 1–19.

Ibrahim, M. (2006). *An empirical survey of children and youth in organised armed violence in Nigeria: Egbesu boys, OPC and Bakassi boys as a case study.* Abuja: Centre for Democracy and Development.

IDRC. (2016). *Urban violence and exclusion in the Democratic Republic of Congo.* Safe and inclusive cities research results. Ottawa, ON: IDRC.

Ilan, J. (2012). Street social capital in the liquid city. *Ethnography, 14*(1), 3–24.

Ilan, J. (2015). *Understanding street culture: Poverty, crime, youth and cool.* London: Macmillan International Higher Education.

INCB. (2008). *International narcotics control board: Report 2008.* Vienna: INCB.

INCB. (2014). *International narcotics control board: Report 2014.* Vienna: INCB.

ISS. (2019). ISS crime statistics wizard. *ISS Crime Hub* (Blog). Retrieved from https://issafrica.org/crimehub/facts-and-figures/crime-statistics-wizard

Jaki, J. (2016, February 10). South Africa: Post-apartheid district six slow to rise again. Retrieved from http://allafrica.com/stories/201602110240.html

Jensen, S. (2006). Capetonian back streets: Territorializing young men. *Ethnography, 7*(3), 275–301.

Jensen, S. (2008). *Gangs, politics and dignity in Cape Town.* Oxford: James Currey.

Jensen, S. (2010). The security and development nexus in Cape Town: War on gangs, counterinsurgency and citizenship. *Security Dialogue, 41*(1), 77–97.

Jensen, S. (n.d.). *The rise and fall of New York: Understanding gangs on the Cape Flats.* Forthcoming.

Jimerson, J., & Oware, M. (2006). Telling the code of the street: An ethnomethodological ethnography. *Journal of Contemporary Ethnography, 35*(1), 24–50. doi:10.1177/0891241605280417

Johnson, A., & Densley, J. (2018). Rio's new social order: How religion signals disengagement from prison gangs. *Qualitative Sociology, 41*(2), 243–262. doi: 10.1007/s11133-018-9379-x

Kagwanja, P. M. (2003). Facing mount Kenya or facing Mecca? The Mungiki, ethnic violence and the politics of the Moi succession in Kenya, 1987–2002. *African Affairs, 102*(406), 25–49.

Kagwanja, P. M. (2006). 'Power to Uhuru': Youth identity and generational politics in Kenya's 2002 elections. *African Affairs, 105*(418), 51–75.

Kahola-Tabu, O. (2014). Ordinary violence towards street children (Shegue) in Lubumbashi (D.R.C.). In J. Bouju & M. de Bruijn (Eds.), *Ordinary violence and social change in Africa* (pp. 130–142). Leiden: Brill.

Kakwagh, V., & Ikwuba, A. (2010). Youth unemployment in Nigeria: Causes and related issues. *Canadian Social Science, 6*(4), 231–237. doi:10.3968/j.css.1923669 720100604.025

Kanneworff, A. B. (2008). "These dread-locked gangsters." The Mungiki as dramatic actors in Kenya's public Arena: From protest to political participation?. In J. Abbink & A. van Dokkum (Eds.), *Dilemmas of development: Conflicts of Interest and their resolutions in modernizing Africa* (pp. 115–130). Boston, MA: African Studies Centre.

Katz, S. R. (1997). Presumed guilty: How schools criminalize Latino youth. *Social Justice, 24*(4), 77–95.

Kennedy, D. (2012). *Deterrence and crime prevention: Reconsidering the prospect of sanction.* New York, NY: Routledge.

Khoisan, Z. (2001). *Jakaranda time: An investigator's view of South Africa's truth and reconciliation commission.* Cape Town: Garib Communications.

Kilonzo, S. (2012). The trajectories of survival of the Mungiki youth in Nairobi. In M. Bourdillon & A. Sangaré (Eds.), *Negotiating the livelihoods of children and youth in Africa's urban spaces* (pp. 229–248). Dakar: CODESRIA.

King, A. (1995). Outline of a practical theory of football violence. *Sociology, 29*(4), 635–651.

King, A. (1999). Football hooliganism and the practical paradigm. *Sociology of Sport Journal, 16*(3), 269–273.

King, A. (2000). Thinking with Bourdieu against Bourdieu: A 'practical' critique of the Habitus. *Sociological Theory, 18*(3), 417–433.

King, A. (2001). Violent pasts: Collective memory and football hooliganism. *The Sociological Review, 49*(4), 568–585.

Kinnes, I. (2000, June). *From urban street gangs to criminal empires: The changing face of gangs in the Western Cape.* Monograph 48. Pretoria: ISS. Retrieved from https://issafrica.s3.amazonaws.com/site/uploads/Mono48.pdf

Kirschner, A. (2009). Youth terror or terrorized youth? Youth violence in Nigeria: Redefining spaces of politics and belonging. In M. Vardalos (Ed.), *Engaging terror: A Critical and interdisciplinary approach* (pp. 369–386). Boca Raton, FL: BrownWalker Press.

Klein, M., & Maxson, C. (2006). *Street gang patterns and policies.* New York, NY: Oxford University Press. Retrieved from http://ebookcentral.proquest.com/lib/soas-ebooks/detail.action?docID=281238

Kloot, B. (2009). Exploring the value of Bourdieu's framework in the context of institutional change. *Studies in Higher Education, 34*(4), 469–481.

KNCHR. (2008). *"The cry of blood": Report on extra-judicial killings and disappearances.* Nairobi: KNCHR.

Kolind, T., Friis Søgaard, T., Hunt, G., & Thylstrup, B. (2017). Transitional narratives of identity among ethnic minority youth gangs in Denmark: From collectivism to individualism. *Journal of Scandinavian Studies in Criminology and Crime Prevention, 18*(1), 3–19.

Konecki, K. (2006). Reproduction of organizational culture – what does organizational culture recreate?. *Problems and Perspectives in Management, 4*(January), 26–41.

Kuperus, T. (1999). *State, civil society and apartheid in South Africa: An examination of Dutch reformed church-state relations.* London: Palgrave Macmillan.

Kwaghga, B. (2014). Criminal gangs in urban areas: A threat to democratic governance in Nigeria. In H. Agbajor, E. E. Asamaigo, & A. Anigala (Eds.), *Counselling for functional and sustainable education: A 21st century approach.* Nigeria: Science and Education Development Institute.

Kynoch, G. (1998). From Ninevite to Comtsotsi: Township gangs, divided communities and urban violence in twentieth century South Africa. African Studies Seminar, Paper presented 18 May. University of the Witwatersrand, Institute for Advanced Social Research, Johannesburg.

Kynoch, G. (2008). Urban violence in colonial Africa: A case for South African exceptionalism. *Journal of Southern African Studies, 34*(3), 629–645.

Lamb, G. (2020). How to turn the tide against South Africa's crime wave. *The Conversation* (Blog), February 21. Retrieved from http://theconversation.com/how-to-turn-the-tide-against-south-africas-crime-wave-131839

Lambrechts, D. (2012). The impact of organised crime on state social control: Organised criminal groups and local governance on the Cape Flats, Cape Town, South Africa. *Journal of Southern African Studies, 38*(4), 787–807.

Lamont, M., & Lareau, A. (1988). Cultural capital: Allusions, gaps and glissandos in recent theoretical developments. *Sociological Theory, 6*(2), 153–168.

Langa, M. (2007). Working with juvenile offenders: An evaluation of trauma group intervention. *African Safety Promotion, 5*(2), 63–82.

Langa, M. (2014). *Analysis of existing data on torture in South Africa.* Johannesburg: CSVR.

Laub, J., & Sampson, R. (2001). Understanding desistance from crime. *Crime and Justice, 28*, 1–69.

LeBas, A. (2013). Violence and urban order in Nairobi, Kenya and Lagos, Nigeria. *Studies in Comparative International Development, 48*(3), 240–262. doi:10.1007/s12116-013-9134-y

Legg, K. (2015a). Elite Cape Town restaurant denies racism. *IOL News* (Blog), January 5. Retrieved from https://www.iol.co.za/news/south-africa/western-cape/elite-cape-town-restaurant-denies-racism-1801645

Legg, K. (2015b). PICS: Army moves into Manenberg. *IOL News*, May 21. Retrieved from http://www.iol.co.za/news/crime-courts/pics-army-moves-into-manenberg-1861462

Lindegaard, M. R. (2017). *Surviving gangs, violence and racism in Cape Town: Ghetto Chameleons.* Oxford: Routledge.

Lindegaard, M. R., & Gear, S. (2014). Violence makes safe in South African prisons: Prison gangs, violent acts, and victimization among inmates. *Focaal, 2014*(68), 35–54.

Lindegaard, M. R., & Jacques, S. (2014). Agency as a cause of crime. *Deviant Behavior*, *35*(2), 85–100.

Lindegaard, M. R., Miller, J., & Reynald, D. (2013). Transitory mobility, cultural heterogeneity, and victimization risk among young men of color: Insights from an ethnographic study in Cape Town, South Africa. *Criminology*, *51*(4), 967–1008.

Lindegaard, M. R., & Zimmermann, F. (2017). Flexible cultural repertoires: Young men avoiding offending and victimization in township areas of Cape Town. *Ethnography*, *18*(2), 193–220.

Lindwa, B. (2019). Gang violence is putting pressure on the Western Cape health budget. *The South African* (Blog), July 30. Retrieved from https://www.thesouthafrican.com/news/gang-violence-is-putting-pressure-on-the-western-cape-health-budget/

Lovell, T. (2000). Thinking feminism with and against Bourdieu. *Feminist Theory*, *1*(1), 11–32.

Mabin, A. (1992). Comprehensive segregation: The origins of the group areas act and its planning apparatuses. *Journal of Southern African Studies*, *18*(2), 405–429.

Makou, G., Ina, S., & Hopkins, R. (2018). FACTSHEET: The state of South African prisons. Africa Check, July 18, 2018. Retrieved from https://africacheck.org/factsheets/factsheet-the-state-of-south-africas-prisons/

Mammon, N. (2016). Inclusive cities: The pursuit of urban social and spatial freedoms for all. In G. Karuri-Sebina (Ed.), *The state of South African cities report 2106* (pp. 125–159). Johannesburg: SACN.

Mandela, N. (1994). Inaugural speech. Pretoria, May 10.

Marima, R., Jordan, J., & Kenna, C. (1995). Conversations with street children in Harare, Zimbabwe. *Zambezia*, *22*(1), 1–24.

Maruna, S. (2007). *Making good: How ex-convicts reform and rebuild their lives.* Washington, DC: American Psychological Association.

Maruna, S., & Roy, K. (2007). Amputation or reconstruction? Notes on the concept of 'knifing off' and desistance from crime. *Journal of Contemporary Criminal Justice*, *23*(1), 104–124.

Maruna, S., Wilson, L., & Curran, K. (2006). Why god is often found behind bars: Prison conversions and the crisis of self-narrative. *Research in Human Development*, *3*(2–3), 161–184. doi:10.1080/15427609.2006.9683367

Mattes, R. (2019). Democracy in Africa: Demand, supply, and the 'dissatisfied democrat'. Afrobarometer Policy Paper No. 54. Cape Town: Afrobarometer.

Matusitz, J., & Repass, M. (2009). Gangs in Nigeria: An updated examination. *Crime, Law and Social Change*, *52*(5), 495–511. doi:10.1007/s10611-009-9208-y

Melde, C., & Esbensen, F.-A. (2013). Gangs and violence: Disentangling the impact of gang membership on the level and nature of offending. *Journal of Quantitative Criminology*, *29*(2), 143–166.

Moffitt, T. E. (1993). Adolescence-limited and life-course-persistent antisocial behavior: A developmental taxonomy. *Psychological Review*, *100*(4), 674–701.

Moloney, M., Mackenzie, K., Hunt, G., & Joe-Laidler, K. (2009). The path and promise of fatherhood for gang members. *The British Journal of Criminology*, *49*(3), 305–325.

Moore, J. (1994). The chola life course: Chicana heroin users and the barrio gang. *International Journal of the Addictions*, *29*(9), 1115–1126.

Morselli, C. (2008). *Inside criminal networks.* New York, NY: Springer Science & Business Media.

Mudhovozi, P., & Chireshe, R. (2012). Socio-demographic factors influencing career decision-making among undergraduate psychology students in South Africa. *Journal of Social Sciences, 31*(2), 167–176.

Mugove, K. (2017). Behaviours of street children that attract the attention of law enforcement agencies. *International Journal of Scientific and Research Publications, 7*(1).

Mugove, K., & Lincoln, H. (2015). Problems experienced by adolescent street children in Harare. *International Journal of Scientific and Research Publications, 5*(10). Retrieved from http://www.ijsrp.org/research-paper-1015.php?rp=P464667

Mulinge, M., & Lesetedi, G. (1998). Interrogating our past: Colonialism and corruption in sub-Saharan Africa. *African Journal of Political Science/Revue Africaine de Science Politique, 3*(2), 15–28.

Mullins, C. (2013). *Holding your square*. London and New York, NY: Routledge.

National Research Council. (2005). *Firearms and violence: A critical review.* Washington, DC: National Academies Press.

Nation, M., Crusto, C., Abraham, W., Kumpfer, K., Seybolt, D., Morrissey-Kane, E., & Davino, K. (2003). What works in prevention. Principles of effective prevention programs. *The American Psychologist, 58*(6–7), 449–456.

New York City Youth Board. (1960). *Reaching the fighting gang*. New York, NY: The Board.

Nombembe, P. (2020). Zane Kilian charged alongside alleged members of Terrible West Siders gang. *TimesLIVE* (Blog), October 27. Retrieved from https://www.timeslive.co.za/news/south-africa/2020-10-27-zane-kilian-charged-alongside-alleged-members-of-terrible-west-siders-gang/

Numbi, N. L. W. (2013). *Sortir de la rue: Les trajectoires des jeunes de Lubumbashi en RDC*. Louvain-la-Neuve: Academia.

Nyathi, A. (2018). Gang violence combatting efforts cost city of CT over R60mn. *Eye Witness News* (Blog), June 18. Retrieved from https://ewn.co.za/2018/07/18/gang-violence-combatting-efforts-cost-city-of-ct-over-r60-million

Ojermark, A. (2007). *Presenting life histories: A literature review and annotated bibliography*. CPRC Working Paper 101. Manchester: CPRC.

OJJDP. (1998). Youth gangs and violence. *Juvenile Justice Bulletin*, August. Retrieved from https://www.ojjdp.gov/jjbulletin/9808/youth.html

Okolo, P., & Ejime, P.A. (2018). Governance failure and terrorism in Nigeria. *EBSU Journal of Social Sciences and Humanities, 8*(1), 65–78.

Olaniyan, A., & Asuelime, L. (2014). Boko Haram insurgency and the widening of cleavages in Nigeria. *African Security, 7*(2), 91–109. doi:10.1080/19392206.2014.909246

Owen, M., & Greeff, A. P. (2015). Factors attracting and discouraging adolescent boys in high-prevalence communities from becoming involved in gangs. *Journal of Forensic Psychology Practice, 15*(1), 1–32. doi:10.1080/15228932.2015.977137

O'Regan, C., & Pikoli, V. (2014). *Report of the commission of inquiry into allegations of police inefficiency and a breakdown in relations between SAPS and the community of Khayelitsha*. Cape Town: Khayelitsha Commission.

Park, A. (2017). Practicing choices, preventing crime. *J-PAL Policy Bulletin*, June.

Parliamentary Monitoring Group. (2017, June 23). Question to the Minister of Justice and correctional services – NW1615. Retrieved from https://pmg.org.za/committee-question/5880/

Paterson, C. (2009). *Prohibition and resistance: A socio-political exploration of the changing dynamics of the Southern African cannabis trade, c. 1850–the present.* Master's thesis, Rhodes University, Grahamstown.

Pattillo-McCoy, M. (2000). *Black picket fences: Privilege and peril among the black middle class.* Chicago, IL and London: University of Chicago Press.

Perry, I. (2004). *Prophets of the hood: Politics and poetics in Hip Hop.* Durham, NC: Duke University Press.

Peterson, T. (2019). Gang wars Part 3 | one month, 883 gunshots – Hanover Park's gunfire in numbers. *News24* (Blog), July 9. Retrieved from https://www.news24.com/ SouthAfrica/News/gang-wars-part-3-one-month-883-gunshots-hanover-parks-gunfire-in-numbers-20190709

Peterson, D., Taylor, T., & Esbensen, F.-A. (2004). Gang membership and violent victimization. *Justice Quarterly, 21*, 793–816.

Petrus, T. (2015). Enemies of the 'state': Vigilantism and the street gang as symbols of resistance in South Africa. *Aggression and Violent Behavior, 22*(May), 26–32. doi: 10.1016/j.avb.2015.02.006

Petrus, T. (2017). 'Die Klipgooiers': Gangsterism and the influence of the stone-throwing subculture in a gang-affected community in the eastern cape, South Africa. *Acta Criminologica: African Journal of Criminology & Victimology, 30*(5), 38–50.

Petrus, T., & Kinnes, I. (2019). New social bandits? A comparative analysis of gangsterism in the Western and Eastern Cape provinces of South Africa. *Criminology and Criminal Justice, 19*(2), 179–196. doi:10.1177/1748895817750436

Pieterse, E. (2009). *Post-apartheid geographies in South Africa: Why are urban divides so persistent?.* Leuven: Leuven University.

Pinnock, D. (1997). *Gangs, rituals and rites of passage.* Cape Town: African Sun Press with the Institute of Criminology, University of Cape Town.

Pinnock, D. (2016). *Gang Town.* Cape Town: Tafelberg.

Pinnock, D. (n.d.). What, really, was district six?. Unpublished Paper.

Pinn, A., & Easterling, P. (2009). Followers of Black Jesus on alert: Thoughts on the story of Tupac Shakur's life/death/life. *Black Theology, 7*(1), 31–44.

Pitt, C. (2018). Anti-gang unit makes 119 arrests, including 'high-flying gangsters' – Cele. *News24* (Blog), November 29. Retrieved from https://www.news24.com/ SouthAfrica/News/anti-gang-unit-makes-119-arrests-including-high-flying-gangsters-cele-20181129

Plüddemann, A., Parry, C., Louw, A., & Burton, P. (2002). Background and methodology of the 3-motrol arrestee study. In T. Leggett (Ed.), *Drugs and crime in South Africa: A study of three cities.* Monograph 69. Pretoria: ISS.

Pranis, K., & Greene, J. (2007). *Gang wars: The failure of enforcement tactics and the need for effective public safety strategies.* Washington, DC: Justice Policy Institute.

Pratten, D. (2008). The politics of protection: Perspectives on vigilantism in Nigeria. *Africa, 78*(1), 1–15. doi:10.3366/E0001972008000028

Putnam, R., Leonardi, R., & Nanetti, R. (1994). *Making democracy work: Civic traditions in modern Italy.* Princeton, NJ: Princeton University Press.

Pyrooz, D. (2014). From your first cigarette to your last dyin 'day': The patterning of gang membership in the life-course. *Journal of Quantitative Criminology, 30*(2), 349–372.

Pyrooz, D., & Decker, S. H. (2011a). Leaving the gang: Logging off and moving on. Paper commissioned by Google Ideas. Retrieved from https://www.cfr.org/report/save-supporting-document-leaving-gang

Pyrooz, D., & Decker, S. (2011b). Motives and methods for leaving the gang: Understanding the process of gang desistance. *Journal of Criminal Justice*, *39*(5), 417–425.

Pyrooz, D., Decker, S., & Webb, V. (2014). The ties that bind: Desistance from gangs. *Crime & Delinquency*, *60*(4), 491–516.

Raedeke, A., Green, J., Hodge, S. S., & Valdivia, C. (2009). Farmers, the practice of farming and the future of agroforestry: An application of Bourdieu's concepts of field and habitus. *Rural Sociology*, *68*(1), 64–86.

Rasmussen, J. (2014). 'We are the true blood of the Mau Mau': The Mungiki movement in Kenya. In J. Hazen & D. Rodgers (Eds.), *Global gangs: Street violence across the world* (pp. 213–236). Minneapolis, MN: University of Minnesota Press.

Rasmussen, J. (2020). Gangs and vigilantism. In N. Cheeseman, K. Kanyinga, & G. Lynch (Eds.), *The oxford handbook of Kenyan politics* (pp. 435–451). Oxford: Oxford University Press.

Republic of South Africa. (1998). Prevention of organized crime act. Government Gazette, 402 (19553).

Republic of South Africa. (2017). *Department of correctional services, vote no. 18, Annual Report 2016/2017 financial year*. RP 23/2017. Pretoria: Department of Correctional Services.

Republic of South Africa. (2019). *Department of correctional services Annual report 2018/2019*. Pretoria: Department of Correctional Services.

Rodgers, D. (2003). Dying for it: Gangs, violence and social change in Urban Nicaragua. Crisis States Programme Working Papers Series No. 35.

Rodgers, D., & Jensen, S. (2008). Revolutionaries, Barbarians or war machines? Gangs in Nicaragua and South Africa. *Socialist Register*, *45*, 220–238.

Rodgers, D., & Jensen, S. (2015). The problem with templates: Learning from organic gang-related violence reduction. *International Journal of Security & Development*, *4*(1), 1–16.

Roks, R. (2017). Crip or die? Gang disengagement in The Netherlands. *Journal of Contemporary Ethnography*, *47*(5), 695–716.

Roloff, N. (2014). *Gang typologies of the Western Cape*. The Safety Lab.

Rurevo, R., & Bourdillon, M. (2003). Girls: The less visible street children of Zimbabwe. *Children, Youth, and Environments*, *13*(1), 150–166.

Ruteere, M. (2008). *Dilemmas of crime, human rights and the politics of Mungiki violence in Kenya*. Nairobi: Kenya Human Rights Institute.

SACN. (2019). *State of urban safety in South African cities report 2018/19*. A report of the urban safety reference group. Johannesburg: South African Cities Network.

Safarloo, A. (2015). Trauma centers partner with cure violence partners to stop retaliatory violence. *Cure Violence* (Blog), June 1. Retrieved from http://cureviolence.org/post/trauma-centers-partner-with-cure-violence-partners-to-stop-retaliatory-violence/

Salaam, A. O. (2011a). Street life involvement and substance use among 'Yandaba' in Kano, Nigeria. *African Journal of Drug and Alcohol Studies*, *10*(2), 119–129. doi: 10.4314/ajdas.v10i2

Salaam, A. O. (2011b). Yandaba on the streets of Kano: Social conditions and criminality. *Vulnerable Children and Youth Studies, 6*(1), 68–77.

Salaam, A. O. (2011c). Motivations for gang membership in Lagos, Nigeria: Challenge and resilience. *Journal of Adolescent Research, 26*(6), 701–726. doi: 10.1177/0743558411402333

Salaam, A. O., & Brown, J. (2012). Lagos 'area boys', substance usage and potential risk factors. *International Journal of Mental Health and Addiction, 10*(1), 83–96.

Salo, E. (2004). *Respectable mothers, tough men and good daughters: Producing persons in Manenberg township South Africa*. PhD dissertation, Emory University, Atlanta, GA.

Salo, E. (2005). Mans is Ma Soe: Ganging practices in Manenberg, South Africa and the ideologies of masculinity, gender and generational relations. Gordon's Bay, Western Cape. Retrieved from http://www.csvr.org.za/images/cjc/mans_is_ma_soe.pdf

Samara, T. R. (2011). *Cape Town after apartheid*. Minneapolis, MN: University of Minnesota Press.

Sampson, R., & Laub, J. (2005). A life-course view of the development of crime. *The Annals of the American Academy of Political and Social Science, 602*(1), 12–45.

Sánchez-Jankowski, M. (1991). *Islands in the street: Gangs and American Urban society*. Oakland, CA: University of California Press.

Sanday, P. R. (2007). *Fraternity gang rape: Sex, brotherhood, and privilege on campus*. New York, NY: NYU Press.

Sandberg, S. (2008). Street capital: Ethnicity and violence on the streets of Oslo. *Theoretical Criminology, 12*(2), 153–171.

Sandberg, S., & Fleetwood, J. (2017). Street talk and Bourdieusian criminology: Bringing narrative to field theory. *Criminology and Criminal Justice, 17*(4), 365–381.

Sandberg, S., & Pedersen, W. (2011). *Street capital: Black cannabis dealers in a white welfare state*. Bristol: Policy Press.

SAPS. (2018). *Annual crime report 2017/2018: Addendum to the SAPS Annual report*. Pretoria: SAPS.

Schäfer, D. (2016). MEC Debbie Schäfer launches three-year project to employ youth. Retrieved from http://www.gov.za/speeches/wced-plans-place-nearly-10-000-interns-western-cape-schools-26-jun-2016-0000

Schatzki, T. (1997). Practices and actions a Wittgensteinian critique of Bourdieu and Giddens. *Philosophy of the Social Sciences, 27*(3), 283–308.

Scheper-Hughes, N. (1993). *Death without weeping: The violence of everyday life in Brazil* (Revised ed.). Berkeley, CA: University of California Press.

Scheper-Hughes, N., & Bourgois, P. (2011). Introduction: Making sense of violence. In N. Scheper-Hughes & P. Bourgois (Eds.), *Violence in war and peace: An anthology* (pp. 1–31). Madlen, MA: Blackwell Publishing.

Schroeder, R., & Frana, J. (2009). Spirituality and religion, emotional coping, and criminal desistance: A qualitative study of men undergoing change. *Sociological Spectrum, 29*(6), 718–741.

Sefali, P. (2014). *Young, high and dangerous: Youth gangs and violence in Khayelitsha*. At the coalface: Essays in safety and violence 1. Cape Town: UCT and SaVI.

Shammas, V. (2018). Bourdieu's five lessons for criminology. *Law and Critique, 29*(2), 201–219.

Shammas, V., & Sandberg, S. (2016). Habitus, capital, and conflict: Bringing Bourdieusian field theory to criminology. *Criminology and Criminal Justice*, *16*(2), 195–213.

Shaw, M. (1998). *Organised crime in post-apartheid South Africa*. Occasional Paper No 28. Pretoria: ISS.

Shaw, M. (2001). Regional Traffick: Towards an understanding of West African criminal networks in Southern Africa. *African Security Review*, *10*(4), 74–94.

Shaw, M. (2002). West African criminal networks in South and Southern Africa. *African Affairs*, *101*(404), 291–316.

Shaw, M. (2016). A tale of two cities: Mafia control, the night time entertainment economy and drug retail markets in Johannesburg and Cape Town, 1985–2015. *Police Practice and Research*, *17*(4), 353–363. doi:10.1080/15614263.2016.1175181

Shaw, M. (2017). *Hitmen for hire: Exposing South Africa's underworld*. Johannesburg: Jonathan Ball Publishers.

Shaw, C., & McKay, H. (1942). *Juvenile delinquency and urban areas: A study of rates of delinquents in relation to differential characteristics of local communities in American cities*. Chicago, IL: University of Chicago Press.

Sherif, M., & Sherif, C. (1964). *Reference groups; exploration into conformity and deviation of adolescents* (1st ed.). New York, NY: Harper & Row.

Smith, D. J. (2007). Violent vigilantism and the state in Nigeria: The case of the Bakassi boys. In E. Bay & D. Donham (Eds.), *States of violence: Politics, youth, and memory in contemporary Africa* (pp. 127–147). Charlottesville, VA: University of Virginia Press.

Spergel, I. (1986). The violent gang problem in Chicago: A local community approach. *Social Service Review*, *60*(1), 94–131.

Spergel, I. (1990). Youth gangs: Continuity and change. *Crime and Justice*, *12*, 171–275.

Spergel, I. (1995). *The youth gang problem: A community approach*. New York, NY: Oxford University Press.

Standing, A. (2003). *The social contradictions of organised crime on the Cape flats*. ISS Paper 74. Pretoria: ISS.

Standing, A. (2005). *The threat of gangs and anti-gangs policy*. ISS Paper 116. Pretoria: ISS.

Standing, A. (2006). *Organised crime: A study from the Cape Flats*. Pretoria: ISS. https://www.issafrica.org/publications/books/organised-crime-a-study-from-the-cape-flats

Statistics South Africa. (2015). *General household survey 2105*. Pretoria: Statistics South Africa.

Steinberg, J. (2004a). *Nongoloza's children: Western Cape prison gangs during and after apartheid*. Braamfontein: Centre for the Study of Violence and Reconciliation.

Steinberg, J. (2004b). *The number: One man's search for identity in the Cape underworld and prison gangs*. Johannesburg: Jonathan Ball Publishers.

Steinberg, J. (2005). *A mixed reception: Mozambican and Congolese refugees in South Africa*. ISS Monograph No. 117. Pretoria: ISS.

Suttles, G. (1968). *The social order of the slum: Ethnicity and territory in the inner city*. Chicago, IL: University of Chicago Press.

Sweeten, G., Pyrooz, D., & Piquero, A. (2013). Disengaging from gangs and desistance from crime. *Justice Quarterly, 30*(3), 469–500.

Swidler, A. (1986). Culture in action: Symbols and strategies. *American Sociological Review, 51*(2), 273–286.

Szreter, S., & Woolcock, M. (2004). Health by association? Social capital, social theory, and the political economy of public health. *International Journal of Epidemiology, 33*(4), 650–667.

The Economist. (2000). *Hopeless Africa*. May 11. Retrieved from https://www.economist.com/leaders/2000/05/11/hopeless-africa

The Economist. (2011). The sun shines bright. December 3 Retrieved from https://www.economist.com/briefing/2011/12/03/the-sun-shines-bright

Thornberry, T., Huizinga, D., & Loeber, R. (2004). The causes and correlates studies: Findings and policy implications. *Juvenile Justice, 9*(1), 3–19.

Thornberry, T., Krohn, M., Lizotte, A., Smith, C., & Tobin, K. (2003). *Gangs and delinquency in developmental perspective.* Cambridge: Cambridge University Press. Retrieved from https://books.google.com/books/about/Gangs_and_Delinquency_in_Developmental_P.html?id=d7YJl0ygziIC

Thrasher, F. M. (1927). *The gang: A study of 1,313 gangs in Chicago.* Chicago, IL: University of Chicago Press.

Umar, B. A. (2007). Urban gangs ('Yan Daba) and security in Kano state: A review of trends and challenges. In A. U. Adamu (Ed.), *Chieftaincy and security in Nigeria: Past, present, and future* (pp. 326–338). Kano: Research & Documentation Directorate, Office of the Executive Governor.

Utas, M. (2014). 'Playing the game': Gang-Militia logics in war-torn Sierra Leone. In J. M. Hazen & D. Rodgers (Eds.), *Global gangs: Street violence across the world* (pp. 171–192). Minneapolis, MN: University of Minnesota Press.

Van Damme, E. (2018). Gangs in the DRC and El Salvador: Towards a third generation of gang violence interventions?. *Trends in Organized Crime, 21*(4), 343–369. doi:10.1007/s12117-017-9316-5

Vandala, N. G., & Bendall, M. (2019). The transformative effect of correctional education: A global perspective. *Cogent Social Sciences, 5*(1), 1677122.

Veysey, B., Martinez, D., & Christian, J. (2012). 'Getting out': A summary of qualitative research on desistance across the life course. In C. L. Gibson & M. D. Krohn (Eds.), *Handbook of life-course criminology: Emerging trends and directions for future research* (pp. 233–260). New York, NY: Springer Science & Business Media.

Vigil, J. D. (1988). *Barrio gangs: Street life and identity in Southern California.* Austin, TX: University of Texas Press.

Vigil, J. D. (2003). Urban violence and street gangs. *Annual Review of Anthropology, 32*(1), 225–242.

Wacquant, L. (1987). Symbolic violence and the making of the French agriculturalist: An enquiry into Pierre Bourdieu's sociology. *The Australian and New Zealand Journal of Sociology, 23*(1), 65–88.

Wamue, G. N. (2001). Revisiting our indigenous shrines through Mungiki. *African Affairs, 100*(400), 453–467.

Ward, C., & Bakhuis, K. (2010). Intervening in children's involvement in gangs: Views of Cape Town's young people. *Children & Society, 24*(1), 50–62.

Western, J. (1997). *Outcast Cape Town.* Berkeley, CA: University of California Press.

Wolf, E. (1990). Distinguished lecture: Facing power - old insights, new questions. *American Anthropologist, 92*(3), 586–596.

Wolters, S. (2011). *Elections in the democratic Republic of Congo*. Briefing. Pretoria: ISS.

Wright, H. (2014). *The child in society*. Los Angeles, CA, London, New Delhi, Singapore, and Washington, DC: SAGE.

Yablonsky, L. (1959). The delinquent gang as a near-group. *Social Problems, 7*(2), 108–117.

Yablonsky, L. (1970). *The violent gang*. Baltimore, MD: Penguin.

Ya'u, Y. Z. (2000). Youth, economic crisis and identity transformation: The case of the Yandaba in Kano. In A. Jega (Ed.), *Identity transformation and identity politics under structural adjustment in Nigeria* (pp. 161–180). Uppsala: Nordic Africa Institute.

Index

Acting Street., 62–70
  aggression, 54–55
  crazy, 67, 70
  fearlessness, 129–130
  kapadien, 63
African Gangs, 19, 21, 35–37
  Central Africa, 29–31
  East Africa, 26–29
  Southern Africa, 24–26
  West Africa, 31–35
Agency, 7, 44, 77, 130, 154
Anderson, 61–62, 74
Apartheid, 8, 10–11, 13, 70, 137, 156
  District Six, 9
  Group Areas Act, 9
  swart gevaar, 16–17
Area boys, 33–35

Bakassi Boys, 32–33
Bashege, 30–31
Beachboys, 26–27
Black Sowetan gangsters. *See also*
    Tsotsis, 19–20
Boko Haram, 32–33
Bourdieusian sociological theory, 77
  constructivist structuralism, 73–74
  cultural capital, 6, 39
  habitus, 6–7, 72
  social capital, 39
  social field, 6–7, 41–42, 121
  social practice, 6–7, 64
  social reproduction, 7–8, 72, 154–155
  social transformation, 72
  symbolic capital, 45
  symbolic violence, 43–44
Bourgois, 11–12, 96

Cape Town, 1, 11, 39, 44, 138
  Americans, 1–2, 56

Cape Flats, 1–2, 4, 11, 16–17
City Bowl, 1, 6
cliques, 20–21
crews, 20–21
Ghetto Kids, 2, 45
Hard Livings, 1–2, 96
informal settlement, 47, 127, 130,
    137–138, 143–144
Laughing Boys, 2, 4, 43, 86
Mongrels, 2, 45, 47–48, 130, 135,
    139
prison gangs, 14–15, 47
street gangs, 1–2
Stoepa Boys, 60–61
suburbs, 13, 41–42
Vatos, 20–21
Victoria and Alfred Waterfront
    (V&A Waterfront), 43
Vuras, 20–21
Central Africa, gangs in, 29–31
Colonialism in Africa, 22–23
Coloured people, 8
  communities, 1–2
  history, 8
  identity, 8
Critical criminology, 36–37
Cultural capital, 6, 39
  negative cultural capital, 66
Cultural repertoire, 19–20, 82–83,
    116

Delinquency, 23–24, 37
Democratic Republic of Congo
    (DRC), 29
Desistance, 107
Disengagement, 78, 80–81, 107, 113,
    122
  barriers, 72–73, 75
  de-identification, 80

de-embeddedness, 80
maturation, 77–78
Domestic repertoire, 93–94
  breadwinning, 92
  children, 4
  marriage, 81–82
Dressing street, 55–62
  brand names, 10–11, 60
  sneakers, 45, 108, 112
  street style, 19–20, 109–110, 112
Drugs in Cape Town, 16, 149
  heroine, 26–27, 31, 68, 140
  Mandrax, 10–11, 24, 68
  marijuana, 10–11, 24
  methamphetamine, 31, 68, 96–97,
    140
Drug trafficking in Southern Africa,
  31

East Africa, gangs in, 26–29
Eswatini, 24

Fraser, 21, 25–26, 72–73

Gang(s). *See also* African Gangs, 1–3,
    19–20
  definition, 1–2
  membership, 4–5, 44
  nicknames, 5, 120–121
  prevention, 16–18, 50, 120–121,
    149–150
  tattoo, 54, 60, 150–151
  typologies in Cape Town, 21
Gangsterism, 4, 6–7, 9–10, 19–20,
    49–50, 65–66, 94–95, 147
  definition, 2–3, 6–7
  risk factors, 78
Gang violence, 4, 19, 144–145
  benefits, 22, 151–152
  cycles of, 148–149
  drivers, 78, 152
  murder statistics in Cape Town, 1,
    12
  offending, 116
  victimisation, 3, 11–12

Hacking, 57

Kaapse Klopse, 50–51
Kenya, 21, 27–28, 37
Kikuyu, 27
Kuluna, 29–31, 36

Looping effect, 57

Movement for the Emancipation of the
    Niger Delta (MEND),
    32–33
Mungiki, 27–28, 36

Nelson Mandela Bay gangs, 19
Neo-apartheid, 12
  discrimination, 156
  inequality, 21
  segregation, 12, 40
  unemployment, 5–6
Normal life, 7–8, 82–83
  normality, 82–83
  repertoires, of normal life. *See also*
    Domestic repertoire;
    Professional repertoire;
    Religious repertoire, 82–83,
    140–141
Nigeria, 21, 31, 33, 36–37
  Kano, 33–35
  Lagos, 33–35

Organised crime, 9–10, 24, 29

Passion gap, 144
People Against Gangsterism and
    Drugs (PAGAD), 33
Policing, 16, 26, 137, 150
  hard policing, 15, 18
Political militias, 23–24, 147
Port Elizabeth gangs. *See also* Nelson
    Mandela Bay gangs, 19
Prison gangs, 1–2, 16–17
  Franse, 50–51
  Ndotas, 50–52, 65, 93, 125, 131–132
  number, the, 5, 26–27, 51–53,
    155–156

Sabela, 46, 48–51, 63, 93, 104–105, 131–132
Professional repertoire, 82–83
  barriers to finding work, 99
  employment, 5, 41–42

Qualitative research, 17
  ethnography, 36–37
  life history, xiv–xv, 130

Religious repertoire, 89, 110
  church clothes, 107–108
  churchgoing, 108
  kerk broer, 88–89, 108
  man of God, 89
  religion, 107
  scripture, 104–105, 113
  spirituality, 123

Sandberg, 41–42, 72–73
Skollie, 16–17
Social disorganisation, 150–151
  Cape Town, 18
  theory, 37
South African National Defence
      Forces (SANDF), 16
  Operation Lockdown, 16
South African Police Service, 33
  Anti-Gang Unit, 16
South African Prevention of Organised
      Crime Act (POCA), 13–15
Southern Africa, gangs in, 24–26
Speaking Street, 49–55
  Kaaps, 48–49, 53, 93
  Sabela, 46, 48–51, 63, 93, 104–105, 131–132
Street-based youth, 25–26
Street children, 25–26
Street culture, 6–7, 75, 77, 109

Bourdieusian criminology, 7–8
  global street culture, 6–7, 44–45
  locking-in effect, 7
  practical dimensions of street
        practice, 73–75
  street-based dispositions, 96, 140
  street capital, 44, 49, 94, 118
  street habitus, 70–73
  street repertoire, 45–46
  street talk, 49, 122
  street virtuosos, 74–75, 95, 154
Structure, 13–14, 19, 40–41, 90, 107, 130
Structural violence, 12

Tanzania, 26–27, 36
Terrorism, 32–33
Tsotsis, 19–20
Tupac Shakur, 34–35, 133
  globalised oppositional repertoire, 34–35
  'Hit 'Em Up', 133–134

United States gang policy, 13–14, 19
  Racketeer Influenced and Corrupt
        Organizations Act (RICO
        Act), 13–14
  war on gangs, 15, 27–28

Vigilantism. *See also* Self-defence
        groups; Self-protection
        groups, 19, 33, 147

West Africa, gangs in, 31–35

Yandaba, 34–35

Zimbabwe, 24–26, 36

www.ingramcontent.com/pod-product-compliance
Lightning Source LLC
Chambersburg PA
CBHW070333270326
41926CB00017B/3858